Handbook to
Life in America

Volume VIII
Postwar America
1950 to 1969

Handbook to
Life in America

Volume VIII
Postwar America
1950 to 1969

Rodney P. Carlisle
GENERAL EDITOR

Facts On File
An imprint of Infobase Publishing

Handbook to Life in America: Postwar America, 1950 to 1969

Facts On File, Inc.
An Imprint of Infobase Publishing
132 West 31st Street
New York, NY 10001

Library of Congress Cataloging-in-Publication Data

Handbooks to life in America / Rodney P. Carlisle, general editor.
    v. cm.
  Includes bibliographical references and index.
  Contents: v. 1. The colonial and revolutionary era, beginnings to 1783—v. 2. The early national period and expansion, 1783 to 1859—v. 3. The Civil War and Reconstruction, 1860 to 1876—v. 4. The Gilded Age, 1870 to 1900—v. 5. Age of reform, 1890 to 1920—v. 6. The roaring twenties, 1920 to 1929—v. 7. The Great Depression and World War II, 1929 to 1949—v. 8. Postwar America, 1950 to 1969—v. 9. Contemporary America, 1970 to present.
  ISBN 978-0-8160-7785-4 (set : hc : alk. paper)—ISBN 978-0-8160-7174-6 (v. 1 : hc : alk. paper)—ISBN 978-0-8160-7175-3 (v. 2 : hc : alk. paper)—ISBN 978-0-8160-7176-0 (v. 3 : hc : alk. paper)—ISBN 978-0-8160-7177-7 (v. 4 : hc : alk. paper)—ISBN 978-0-8160-7178-4 (v. 5 : hc : alk. paper)—ISBN 978-0-8160-7179-1 (v. 6 : hc : alk. paper)—ISBN 978-0-8160-7180-7 (v. 7 : hc : alk. paper)—ISBN 978-0-8160-7181-4 (v. 8 : hc : alk. paper)—ISBN 978-0-8160-7182-1 (v. 9 : hc : alk. paper) 1. United States—Civilization—Juvenile literature. 2. United States—History—Juvenile literature. 3. National characteristics, American—Juvenile literature. I. Carlisle, Rodney P.
  E169.1.H2644 2008
  973—dc22
                                    2008012630

Contents

Volume VIII

Postwar America
1950 to 1969

Preface

". . . the greatest tragedy of this period . . . was not the strident clamor of the bad people, but the appalling silence of the good people."
— Martin Luther King, Jr.

THE FLAVOR OF daily life in previous eras is usually only vaguely conveyed by examining the documents of state and the politics of the era. What people ate, how they spent their time, what entertainment they enjoyed, and how they related to one another in family, church, and employment, constituted the actual life of people, rather than the distant affairs of state. While governance, diplomacy, war, and to an extent, the intellectual life of every era tends to be well-documented, the way people lived is sometimes difficult to tease out from the surviving paper records and literary productions of the past.

For this reason in recent decades, cultural and social historians have turned to other types of physical documentation, such as illustrations, surviving artifacts, tools, furnishings, utensils, and structures. Statistical information can shed light on other aspects of life. Through examination of these and other kinds of evidence, a wholly different set of questions can be asked and tentatively answered.

This series of handbooks looks at the questions of daily life from the perspective of social and cultural history, going well beyond the affairs of government to examine the fabric and texture of what people in the American past experienced in their homes and their families, in their workplaces and schools. Their places of worship, the ways they moved from place to place, the nature of law and order and military service all varied from period to period. As science and technology advanced, the American contributions to those fields became greater and contributed to a different feel of life. Some of this story may be familiar, as historians have for generations commented on the disparity between rural and city life, on the impact of technologies such as the cotton gin, the railroad and the steamboat, and on life on the advancing frontier. However in recent decades, historians have turned to different sources. In an approach called Nearby History, academic historians have increasingly worked with the hosts of professionals who operate local historical societies, keepers of historic homes, and custodians of local records to pull together a deeper understanding of local life. Housed in thousands of small and large museums and preserved homes across America, rich collections of furniture, utensils, farm implements, tools, and other artifacts tell a very different story than that found in the letters and journals of legislators, governors, presidents, and statesmen.

FRESH DISCOVERIES

Another approach to the fabric of daily life first flourished in Europe, through which historians plowed through local customs and tax records, birth and death records, marriage records, and other numerical data, learning a great deal about the actual fabric of daily life through a statistical approach. Aided by computer methods of storing and studying such data, historians have developed fresh discoveries about such basic questions as health, diet, life-expectancy, family patterns, and gender values in past eras. Combined with a fresh look at the relationship between men and women, and at the values of masculinity and femininity in past eras, recent social history has provided a whole new window on the past.

By dividing American history into nine periods, we have sought to provide views of this newly enriched understanding of the actual daily life of ordinary people. Some of the patterns developed in early eras persisted into later eras. And of course, many physical traces of the past remain, in the form of buildings, seaports, roads and canals, artifacts, divisions of real estate, and later structures such as railroads, airports, dams, and superhighways. For these reasons, our own physical environment is made up of overlapping layers inherited from the past, sometimes deeply buried, and at other times lightly papered over with the trappings of the present. Knowing more about the many layers from different periods of American history makes every trip through an American city or suburb or rural place a much richer experience, as the visitor sees not only the present, but the accumulated heritage of the past, silently providing echoes of history.

Thus in our modern era, as we move among the shadowy remnants of a distant past, we may be unconsciously receiving silent messages that tell us: this building is what a home should look like; this stone wall constitutes the definition of a piece of farmland; this street is where a town begins and ends. The sources of our present lie not only in the actions of politicians, generals, princes, and potentates, but also in the patterns of life, child-rearing, education, religion, work, and play lived out by ordinary people.

VOLUME VIII: POSTWAR AMERICA

The two decades from 1950 to 1969 saw the burgeoning of the Cold War between the United States and its allies on the one side and the Union of Soviet Socialist Republics and its satellite nations on the other side. Overseas, Americans fought in Korea (1950–53) and increasingly in Vietnam, from 1964 on through the period. A massive arms race with the Soviet Union led to the development of intercontinental ballistic missiles and thermonuclear weapons, neither ever deployed in combat in the 20th century. In fact, the stand-off in terrible weapons of mass destruction was widely credited with keeping the two nations and their allies at peace, with the only conflicts fought in the "proxy" wars in Korea and Vietnam, and in low-level insurgencies and civil wars in Africa and Latin America. The two decades were a period of increasing prosperity, further technological change, and a society marked by widespread upheavals that left the country profoundly changed.

A Supreme Court decision, *Brown v. Topeka*, in 1954 brought an end to the court's support for the doctrine of "separate but equal" that had been used to justify racial segregation in schools and in other public facilities since 1896. However, since state and federal legislation had not outlawed such practices, to overthrow racial segregation required that court cases be fought, one by one, to ensure integration in such facilities. The result was the "Civil Rights revolution" through the decade 1954–64, in which advocates of racial justice, both black and white, risked arrest or violence by violating local rules, laws, and customs that enforced racial segregation. Finally, in 1964 and 1965, federal legislation outlawed segregation in public facilities, prohibited racial discrimination in employment and housing, and ensured the right to vote. Over the next decade, the forces of the federal government could be brought to bear to work toward more equal treatment.

As part of the backlash against racial integration, many white communities, both in the South and the North, sought to establish private schools that would be open to white pupils only. Christian academies flourished, but at the same time, racial segregation by neighborhood and community meant that many public schools, while technically open to all races, were in point of fact nearly all-white or all-black in student population. To overcome this segregation by housing pattern, some districts initiated school busing programs to move black students to formerly all-white schools, such as a program initiated in Milwaukee in 1958. As other communities followed suit, and as courts sometimes ordered integration through school-busing programs, these efforts became extremely controversial in the late 1960s and early 1970s.

The generation of activists who had fought for the gains in racial equality soon turned to other causes, and the mid and late 1960s saw the rise of unrest on college campuses over governance of the institutions and over the military draft. The younger generation of Baby Boomers born after World War II first began to come into adulthood in the 1960s, and unlike their parents, this generation was quick to challenge those in authority, whether in government, education, or business.

Meanwhile, the fruits of technological progress continued to reshape the way Americans lived. Television, that before World War II had been a technical novelty, soon became a new mass medium, replacing radio as the main form of home entertainment by the late 1960s. Although bulky in form and primitive by the standards of a later generation, the black-and-white television sets of the 1960s brought the lively products of popular culture into millions of homes. Commentators noted the political and social effects of the new medium, as it changed the nature of political elections, brought sympathy to the underdogs in the racial clashes of the Civil Rights decade, and made it increasingly difficult for the military to conduct warfare by the traditional ruthless means in Vietnam. Both in its program content and in its advertising, television tended to further homogenize American culture.

The development of an effective oral contraceptive, Enovid, first approved by the Food and Drug Administration in 1960, and widely marketed in 1961, led to a decreased birth rate. Its introduction marked the end of the Baby Boom, but its impact on mores and relationships was also profound. For one thing, by reducing the risk of pregnancy and child-bearing as a consequence of sex, oral contraceptives removed one barrier to pre-marital sex. Furthermore, since taking oral contraceptives was a decision made by a woman and not by a man, the development went far toward empowering women in their relationships with men.

Other technical developments of the era had still other kinds of social impact. Highway transportation proliferated with the construction of the Interstate Highway System, beginning in the 1950s. Not only linking major cities, but also providing a criss-crossing set of excellent highways, the roads themselves had social consequences, further uniting the country and reducing the isolation of small communities.

The defense and aerospace industries flourished, with expansion of centers of manufacture in southern California, Washington, Texas, and Alabama building on expansion that had begun during World War II. Tens of thousands of employees worked on weapons system components and weapons-delivery systems. The arms race between the Soviets and the United States became converted under president John F. Kennedy into a "space race" in a 1961 speech in which he asked the nation to commit to landing a man on the moon by the end of the decade. From 1961 through 1969, the Gemini and Apollo programs employed tens of thousands. As the economy boomed through the two decades, the service sector flourished, including governmental, clerical, administrative, and retail jobs.

Eating habits changed with the products available in grocery stores, with the introduction of frozen ready-made meals, or TV dinners, in 1954. The microwave oven, introduced by Raytheon in 1954, gradually contributed to changed eating habits at home, while franchised inexpensive restaurants, led by Colonel Sanders Kentucky Fried Chicken (1952) and McDonalds (1955), brought fast-food technology to millions of customers. In a parallel development, convenience stores proliferated, and the Southland Corporation opened its 100th 7-Eleven in 1952. These marketing developments were made possible by dozens of technological developments in food preparation, food handling, refrigeration, and transportation, combined by imaginative entrepreneurs into completely new ways of doing business.

Highways and automobiles transformed the suburbs in these decades, with vast new housing developments. At first driven by federally-supported home mortgages and veterans' benefits, low-cost, mass-produced housing was pioneered by William Levitt and his firm Levitt and Sons. By 1951, he had built over 17,000 homes in his original development in New York State and planned others in Pennsylvania and New Jersey. His methods of mass-producing homes were emulated by other developers, and almost overnight, old suburbs grew with imitation Cape Cod and one-story "rancher" homes, and completely new communities like Levittown flourished. In the same period, the split-level home became popular, with an entry foyer that led to short flights of stairs down to common living areas and up to bedrooms. The new building methods and the new transportation systems allowed the new suburbs to far outdistance their predecessors in size and social impact.

The cult of domesticity, revived in the postwar era, relegated women to the role of housewives and mothers, and an idealized version of that lifestyle was portrayed in the popular culture of films, television shows, and literature. Partly stimulated by the civil rights movement of the 1950s and early 1960s, the National Organization for Women (NOW) was formed in 1966. The organization not only sought equal employment opportunities for women, but also sought to challenge more deeply held stereotypes.

The two decades of the 1950s and 1960s represented a time of social contrast and change. On the one hand, the desire for stability and security brought on by the crises of the 1930s and 1940s led to a culture of conformity, expanding home ownership, and a widespread admiration for and emulation of a middle-class lifestyle in which the husband commuted to a job outside the home, while the wife stayed home and raised a small family. At the same time, the Civil Rights revolution, women's rights organizations, and the beginnings of other anti-establishment movements such as environmentalism and advocacy of disarmament, demonstrated that the bland appearance of the popular culture was deceptive. The social ferment of the era that surged behind the facade of complacency reflected changing values, producing social reforms and yielding long-term consequences.

RODNEY CARLISLE
GENERAL EDITOR

Chapter 1

Introduction

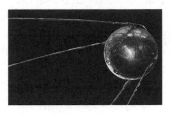

"And so, my fellow Americans, ask not what your country can do for you; ask what you can do for your country."
—President John F. Kennedy

AT THE CONCLUSION of World War II the mood of the United States was one of optimism and triumph. The country's attitude reflected a belief that an age of wealth and peace was at hand. Democratic values appeared to have been not only validated but redeemed. In addition there was not the feeling of malaise and disappointment that followed World War I, although there persisted among many people an initial fear that following demobilization there would be an accompanying end to wartime prosperity. Would peace augur a return to 1930s unemployment levels, Depression era deprivation, and an end to New Deal reforms and aspirations? After President Roosevelt's death in 1945, his successor Harry Truman (1884–1972) continued New Deal Democratic policies in the shape of his Fair Deal administration, but in the face of Republican congressional opposition his plans had only mixed success.

America had emerged after 1945 with its homeland and industries untouched, rationing was minimal and temporary, and other wartime inconveniences were short-lived. Much of Europe and Asia were devastated from the impact of years of destruction, upheaval, and war, but America was prosperous and vibrant, culturally, socially, and economically. The future suggested a further extension of what was clearly an American Century, where American strength, ideas, and successes became a beacon for others to follow. However, this confidence was soon shattered after 1945 by the emergence of a Cold War, and a seemingly inevitable struggle against the Soviet Union and Communism that at times threatened world peace and security, as well as America's ascendancy as the dominant postwar power.

COLD WAR

An increasingly acrimonious Cold War shattered the World War II coalition with the Soviet Union, and became, during the years 1950 to 1969, the most difficult and perplexing issue to face the United States. Many political, military, and economic efforts were placed at the disposal of a succession of governments, both Democratic and Republican, to address the problems surrounding the threat of Communist totalitarianism around the world.

The Marxist-Leninist model furnished a major contrast to the United States' political, social, and economic worldview. The Soviet Union, following the devastating sacrifices stemming from the Nazi invasion, was intent on preserving their autocratic state, and Stalin's international paranoia was as great as his domestic suspicions. Furthermore this attitude was preserved intact and passed to his successors after his death in 1953. Beginning with the Truman presidency, it was determined that Communism would be resisted and whenever possible pushed back from its existing European and Asian occupations. The fall of China to Communism in 1949 increased the urgency of this resistance.

The goal of American diplomacy during these years would be the containment of Communism, beginning in the Middle East and Mediterranean in the form of the Truman Doctrine aimed at protecting Turkey and Greece. In addition, the $17 billion Marshall Aid Plan that lasted from 1948 until 1953 invigorated and rebuilt European economies in an effort to restore stability. This was especially important for war-torn Germany, which was split into Allied Zones of occupation, including the former capital, Berlin, which was surrounded by the Russian sector and easily blockaded as it was in 1948. This Soviet blockade for some marked the formal beginnings of a more substantial Cold War agenda.

The Marshall Plan helped stimulate American trade as well as European industry. Furthermore the idea of collective security became a pillar of the postwar world when the United States and 11 other countries in 1949 organized the North Atlantic Treaty Organization to resist attacks on any of its members. This format provided the outline for other security organizations that would take shape in both Asia and the Middle East during the 1950s with various levels of success. All had a similar aim to resist the spread of Communism.

The most serious manifestation in these early years of the Cold War turning hot came in June 1950 when the North Korean Communists, backed by Stalin and the Soviet Union, as well as Mao's Red China, crossed the 38th parallel, the dividing line between Korean occupation zones established after the defeat of Japan. The North Koreans advanced, taking Seoul, the South Korean capital, and initially pushed the Allied forces into a southern pocket.

General Douglas MacArthur (1880–1964) commanded the United States and Allied resistance, which was backed by a United Nations resolution (the Soviet Union was absent from the Security Council and couldn't veto the measure) that labeled the North Koreans as the aggressors. After heavy fighting, threats of nuclear bombing, and Chinese intervention, the Communists were eventually pushed back north of the 38th parallel and truce talks commenced. A cease-fire ended the conflict in July 1953 during the early months of the Eisenhower presidency. The war also produced political casualties, most prominently General MacArthur, whose imperial style challenged presidential authority, leading to the general's dismissal in April 1951. For Truman the war and his handling of the conflict reduced his popularity substantially, making way for the return of Republican leadership in 1952 after a period of 20 years. The Republican ascendancy came in the form of the highly popular World War II Allied Commander of Europe and now President Dwight D. Eisenhower (1890–1969).

General Douglas MacArthur (right) viewing the front lines north of Suwon, Korea, in January 1951, just a few months before his dismissal.

The Eisenhower presidency continued with even more strident Cold War containment policies geared to a strategy of massive retaliation, which resulted in America's arsenal expanding with ever more numerous and powerful hydrogen bombs. This threat did not stop Communist encroachments, but it perhaps can be credited in halting a degree of Communist expansion, most notably China's attempt to seize Taiwan. However, after 1949 the Soviet Union also possessed atomic weapons, and this bred a new level of insecurity and caution in terms of policy reactions. This could be seen in administration restraint in using nuclear weapons against the Chinese in Korea, or in Indochina in 1954, following the French defeat by the Vietnamese. Restraint was also shown in American opposition to the combined British, French, and Israeli attacks on Egypt in 1956 following the nationalization of the Suez Canal by President Nasser, and most notably during the Hungarian uprising of 1956, which resulted in America doing little to support the Hungarian revolt against Soviet occupation and control.

The arrival of John F. Kennedy (1917–63) to the presidency brought another committed anti-Communist to the White House. However, the failure of the Cuban Bay of Pigs invasion, which was backed by the Central Intelligence Agency (CIA), in his first months in office made him reluctant to pursue a hard Cold

Reconnaissance photos taken by spy planes played a central role in the 1962 Cuban missile crisis. These Strategic Air Command personnel are shown examining photos during the crisis.

War agenda. The loss of Cuba to Communist domination 90 miles off America's shore, as well as Laos's move toward Communist control in 1960, challenged the Kennedy administration. In addition the building of the Berlin Wall in the face of only mild protests had further emboldened Soviet leader Nikita Khrushchev (1894–1971) and the Communist leadership to try the administration's nerve.

This test of wills led to the most serious issue of the entire Cold War: the 1962 Cuban Missile Crisis. The Soviets had secretly moved offensive missiles to Cuba and when discovered, President Kennedy declared that Cuba faced quarantine and the U.S. Navy would intercept any Soviet ships supplying the island. For days the world stood on the brink of nuclear war, but in the end the Soviet Union relented and withdrew their missiles in exchange for similar American compromises in Turkey. Kennedy risked all and emerged as the decisive leader of the West. The crisis perhaps helped encourage other negotiations as seen in the Nuclear Test Ban Treaty of 1963 signed by the United States, the Soviet Union, and Great Britain that eliminated nuclear tests in the atmosphere.

VIETNAM

Indochina, and specifically Vietnam, emerged for Kennedy, and later the Johnson and Nixon administrations, as the most persistent and complex Cold War issue during the 1960s. The 1954 defeat of the French in Vietnam made the country vulnerable to Communist revolution. In light of this situation President Eisenhower withdrew support for the proposed 1956 elections to unite the country as called for by the 1954 Geneva Convention. Instead America backed a two-state solution that led to the creation of the Republic of South Vietnam led by Ngo Dinh Diem, and a separate People's Republic of North Vietnam headed by Ho Chi Minh. The justification for this action was explained by a domino theory that argued that if Vietnam fell to the Communists, all of Indochina would soon follow. Kennedy also accepted this analysis and increased America's involvement in South Vietnam in the form of military advisers and aid. This came at a time when North Vietnamese interference in the south through its Viet Cong surrogates was increasing. The situation steadily worsened, leading Kennedy to support a 1963 coup d'état of South Vietnam that also included the assassination of Diem.

Kennedy's assassination in November 1963 turned resistance to Communist aggression in South Vietnam over to the new president, Lyndon B. Johnson (1908–73). Following North Vietnamese attacks on two American destroyers in the Gulf of Tonkin in August 1964, Johnson received congressional backing to pursue the war more vigorously. Johnson's re-election in 1964 (although Johnson was presented as a peace candidate when contrasted with his Republican opponent, Barry Goldwater) allowed him to raise the military stakes in Vietnam. Steadily American troops and involvement increased from 25,000 troops in 1965 to 500,000 in 1968. With increased fighting came increased

President John F. Kennedy poses for photographers at the White House on March 13, 1961, during a meeting with West Berlin Mayor Willy Brandt.

American losses, as well as the bombardment of both north and south Vietnam. The war became a major political dividing line and the apparent lack of military success, given the sacrifices, made it seem a war without end. Vietnam sealed the fate of the Johnson presidency and tarnished his Great Society domestic ambitions.

The presidential election of 1968 was shaped by the Vietnam War's unpopularity. The August Democratic nominating convention in Chicago was disrupted by violent protests. The previous March saw President Johnson withdraw from contention as a candidate, and in April, Martin Luther King, Jr. was assassinated. In June, Senator Robert Kennedy, seeking the candidacy as an antiwar candidate, was also assassinated. Ultimately the Democrats nominated Vice President Hubert Humphrey as their candidate, and he was opposed by the Republican nominee, Richard M. Nixon (1913–94). Nixon campaigned for a "Peace with Honor" and a "Vietnamization" of the conflict, which rested on building the fighting effectiveness of South Vietnam's army.

Nixon achieved a narrow victory and launched the Paris peace negotiations at the same time as he pursued the war, including his contested 1970 Cambodian incursion aimed at disrupting North Vietnamese supply lines. Protests and unrest grew, but in 1973, following Nixon's 1972 re-election, a cease-fire was agreed and America steadily withdrew its troops. The cease-fire proved an illusion and South Vietnam fell to the Communists in 1975 after the loss of 58,000 American lives, as well as the immense suffering of the Vietnamese. The war deeply divided the nation and left a legacy of pessimism and a need for quick and decisive victories in future conflicts.

SPACE RACE

The origins of the Space Race began during the Cold War and lasted from the launch in October 1957 of the beach ball sized satellite, Sputnik, until 1975. At the height of the Cold War space became another frontier for rivalry between the United States and the Soviet Union, and mastery of aeronautical science and technology was the goal of both nations. This competition involved not only a search for firsts in the area of exploration, but also was a key propaganda tool for each ideological system.

The space race involved the materials that controlled the future in the form of missile technology and satellite communications, and satellites offered sophisticated means for espionage. In addition American surprise over Sputnik led to a massive federal investment in education in the form of the National Defense Education Act and further reform and expansion of American public education. The importance of this contest was also seen in President Eisenhower's 1958 creation of the National Aeronautics and Space Administration (NASA) to oversee exploration and development.

Animals and humans soon followed the satellites into space. The Soviet Union's Yuri Gagarin in 1961 became the first human in space orbit. This feat was matched in 1962 by the United States' John Glenn. These flights marked the beginning of numerous human space explorations that characterized the 1960s, eventually leading to manned and unmanned lunar exploration. Both Presidents Kennedy and Johnson were committed to the space project as a means of demonstrating American superiority, and the American Apollo Project became the means for this endeavor.

By 1968 American Apollo missions had successfully orbited the moon and in July 1969, supported by Buzz Aldrin and Michael Collins, Neil Armstrong walked on the moon's surface, establishing an American first, and the prestige that went with it. Other planetary explorations followed, including the building of space stations to enable further space study. The July 1975 rendezvous in space of the American Apollo and Soviet Soyuz spacecraft symbolized the end of the formal space race, however military research and weapons applications continued.

McCARTHYISM AND DOMESTIC ANTI-COMMUNISM

The anxieties over potential nuclear war and Communist subversion reflected the public's insecurities and fears, which undermined a future that was supposed to be positive and prosperous. This climate of uncertainty and pessimism during this period would have a significant impact upon America's life and politics. Domestic subversion by Communist agents and their fellow travelers became a major concern. Loyalty programs were instituted at both federal and state levels of government. Beginning in 1947 the House Committee on Un-American Activities investigated the film industry for Communist infiltration, which led to blacklists of suspect individuals. The 1948 exposure of Alger Hiss, a ranking State Department official and President Roosevelt's advisor at the 1945 Yalta Conference, as a reputed Communist spy, and his 1950 conviction for perjury, made Americans increasingly suspect of Communist intrigue and threats.

This suspicion became a springboard that launched the rise to prominence of the Junior Senator from Wisconsin, Senator Joseph McCarthy (1908–57), who gained national publicity and influence with his claims that the nation and the federal government, particularly the State Department, were awash with hundreds of Communist agents and sympathizers. After the Republicans gained control of the Senate in 1952, McCarthy became a Committee Chairman and this increased his power and influence, as well as his ability to intimidate. In addition, the rise of television allowed McCarthy's hearings to enter the homes of many Americans, who became transfixed by his accusatory style and dramatics. However McCarthy's popularity was fleeting. He proved useful to the Republican Party when he was lambasting Democrats as traitors, but when his investigations turned to establishment institutions such as the U.S. Army he overstepped the boundaries of acceptability in Washington. His behavior and unproven attacks were eventually condemned and his conduct censured by a Senate vote of 67 to 22. His star declined as rapidly as it had risen, and McCarthy died aged 48 in 1957 of hepatitis, although many believe his condition was brought on by alcoholism.

The era of McCarthyism reflected an extension of Cold War suspicions into mainstream American thought and politics, and marked an unfortunate political episode where unsubstantiated accusation and guilt by association damaged many reputations and triumphed over freedom of expression and thought. This recriminatory style embarrassed the nation and ultimately uncovered relatively few Communist spies, although the threat, as later information has revealed, was real. The Ethel and Julius Rosenberg convictions and their later executions in 1953 for espionage furthered the public's unease. Some critics saw the postwar Communist scare as a continuation of America's battles with foreign ideology that began with the rise of Socialism in the 19th century. The height of these earlier concerns came after World War I and the Russian Revolution, and was best represented then by Attorney General A. Mitchell Palmer's deportations, and in the Red Scare atmosphere of 1919.

THE CIA AND THE FBI

The fear of Communism did not breed a sophisticated domestic debate or allow shades of gray in the discussions that did take place. A more complicated and intellectually involved anti-Communist crusade was led by the CIA, which was founded in 1947 and evolved from the Office of Strategic Services set up in World War II. The CIA was both a covert and overt organization, independent of the Department of State and the Federal Bureau of Investigation (FBI). Its operations, although conceived and planned at its headquarters in Langley, Virginia, were directed abroad. These efforts involved a variety of clandestine operations, and also forged links with other anti-Communist forces internationally.

Occasionally, as in the formation of the Congress of Cultural Freedom in Berlin in 1950, the CIA could cleverly use and subsidize front organizations to promote American ideas and values as a liberal counterweight to Communist propaganda. The engagement of many prominent intellectuals in the Congress of Cultural Freedom was a case in point. Journals such as *Encounter* promoted friendly pro-American viewpoints and American and European democratic ideals. CIA involvement in this organization did not finally surface until 1967, to the embarrassment of many associated with the program.

At the domestic level the fight against sedition and subversion was headed by J. Edgar Hoover's (1895–1972) FBI, which during the 1950s pursued domestic Communists, making use of the Smith Act of 1940 and the McCarran Act of 1950 (Internal Security Act of 1950), which allowed prosecutions for those advocating the violent overthrow of the U.S. government or its subversion. However, in the late 1950s, many convictions were reversed by the Supreme Court. During the presidencies of Johnson and Nixon in the 1960s, the domestic Communist Party had lost ground to new radical movements broadly labeled the New Left. The antiwar struggle gave rise to more violent anarchist ideologies and produced new subversive threats that occupied much FBI time. Groups such as the Weathermen and the Black Panthers were prominent examples of the new more violent radicalism. As the era ended, bombings against government offices and research establishments became more frequent.

ECONOMIC GROWTH AND PROSPERITY

American economic prosperity during this period was linked to substantial growth in productive capacity. Between 1940 and 1960 American Gross National Product (GNP) more than doubled and American employment increased, bringing higher incomes to more Americans. The effect of this prosperity was the creation of a vibrant and growing middle-class identity with all its associated aspirations. The growth was initially associated with the massively increased public expenditures during World War II, and America's role as the arsenal of democracy. Rising salaries during the 1950s increased consumption as a peacetime economy produced the goods desired by a growing population.

Automobile production led the way, and home construction followed as new homes and suburbs were created to house demobilized soldiers who now

Along with the growth of the suburbs, the spread of television began to reshape American life in the early 1950s. Here, President Dwight D. Eisenhower and First Lady Mamie Eisenhower posed around a television in July 1952 during the Republican National Convention.

had access to low-cost mortgages, as well as a G.I. Bill that expanded higher education opportunities and enabled the employment possibilities that followed. Americans could leave the inner cities, taking their families to the new suburbs that were rapidly constructed outside the major urban areas. The children of these growing young families soon became known as the Baby Boom generation.

To further facilitate this demographic transition, and make commuting a practical reality, the Highway Act of 1956 was passed and became the most expensive public works initiative in American history. The wave of road and highway construction was accompanied by the growth in suburban shopping center development, which allowed the suburbs to become in time self-contained islands surrounding America's cities. In addition, these new suburban communities benefited from construction techniques that sped building times with more prefabricated and streamlined production.

This also resulted in a growing suburban conformity in both appearance and social composition.

During this period American corporations grew larger as their operations and investments expanded at home and abroad and they searched for cheaper labor for their manufacturing enterprises. In addition new wealth was being created in the service industries as opposed to the production of manufactured goods, a trend that would set the stage for a rapid move toward white-collar occupations. By the mid-1950s the occupational transformation was nearly complete, as the majority of occupations became white-collar with office jobs, sales, and management as well as the professions gaining more and more dominance in the workplace.

The established trend of a steadily declining rural population, which was clear by 1920, continued even more dramatically after 1950. More and more family farms became too small to compete successfully with the investment, economies of scale, and resources that corporate farming possessed. The agribusiness sector enlarged operations, increased productivity, and gained extensive control over the food market.

In addition to these changing work patterns, the move to new housing, and the growth of corporate America, American geography was also changing, as populations moved both to the newly formed suburbs as well as to new areas entirely such as the West coast and the Southwest. These areas became known as the Sunbelt and set a population trend that continued to grow throughout the period 1950 to 1969 and beyond. Los Angeles symbolized the reality of both internal and external migration, surpassing Philadelphia and Chicago in size. Such population growth contributed heavily to California's emergence by 1970 as the most populous state. Other cities such as Miami, Houston, and Phoenix reflected similar growth patterns. Old urban America, dominated by the Northeast and Midwest, was losing ground as employment opportunities and local industries relocated or became obsolete.

DOMESTIC POLITICS

During the Eisenhower presidency from 1952 until 1960, domestic politics took on a more conservative slant. Although the administration did not attempt to reverse New Deal initiatives completely, Eisenhower did hope to balance the budget, contain inflation, cut taxes, and reduce federal spending, as well as transfer more powers to the states. Monetary security was always reassuring to Republican backers in the business community. For all the proposed frugality, defense spending increased dramatically, as well as corporate power and influence in military contracts and production. This development created unease with President Eisenhower, for he saw a mushrooming military-industrial complex as a threat to the normal patterns of government and democracy. Other than in this spending area, lack of

The Unisphere, centerpiece of the 1964 New York World's Fair, in Queens, New York. This World's Fair, like others before it, influenced technology and reshaped Americans' expectations for the future.

consistent government stimulus contributed to a series of mini-recessions that temporarily increased unemployment and forged a boom or bust pattern to American economic growth patterns in these decades.

When John F. Kennedy took office in 1961 the biggest tax cut in U.S. history occurred, and along with other spending initiatives, Gross Domestic Product (GDP) and other indicators of prosperity grew rapidly, giving the 1960s a solid economic foundation. The benefits affected every element of society, and also represented the high point of American labor union membership. Growth continued during the Johnson presidency and financed not only the Vietnam War, but also the creation of a "Great Society" with new social initiatives aimed at ending poverty, such as Medicaid and Medicare. Prosperity seemed guaranteed, with productivity reaching record levels in 1968 and 1969.

SCIENCE AND TECHNOLOGY
Triumphs in American science and technology were most clearly illustrated in the development of atomic weapons, in aeronautical industries, and in the intercontinental ballistic missile capacities needed for both weapons and the conquest of space. However, scientific and technical change filtered through all areas of American life, dramatically changing the way Americans lived and prospered 1950–69.

In 1952, wartime experiments with early computers led to the first successful commercial computer, the UNIVAC, which marked the initial step toward the three generations of computers that this period witnessed. From complex and time-consuming machine code, there came new computer languages such as IBM's FORTRAN in 1956 and BASIC in 1964 that made programming more accessible. In addition greater software language efficiencies led to more computer applications that solved everyday commercial needs. The IBM Corporation became a symbol of this new technology, as well as American business success.

Improvements in medicine and in basic university research also offered insights into the building blocks of life pioneered by the discovery of DNA in 1950 by Francis Crick, James Watson, and Rosalind Franklin at Cambridge University. New vaccines were developed beginning in 1955 with the Salk vaccine for polio, and later the Sabin oral vaccine. Organ transplants and new medicines provided new possibilities for extending life expectancy. Transistors changed communications, and laser technology furnished further new possibilities. Video cameras arrived and would evolve beyond recognition in the decades ahead. The introduction of the birth control pill in 1960 offered new control over reproduction and wrought fundamental changes in sexual relationships.

In the agricultural sector, better plants and livestock were developed. The Agricultural Research Service established in 1953 helped create better insect controls through new insecticides. Many research efforts improved products such as frozen foods and added new commercial applications. Productivity increases meant that by 1961 one farmer could feed 27 people as opposed to 11 in 1940. Food surpluses were also used to feed the world beginning with the 1954 Food for Peace program.

Improvements in food technology during the 1960s continued to produce impressive results leading to more new products such as permanent press cottons and medicines to better control animal diseases and plant infestations. The creation of new, more productive and resistant plant seeds, and shorter growth cycles, led to the Green Revolution of the 1960s, which reduced the threat of world famine. Food surpluses also allowed for food stamp programs that were designed to eliminate hunger and improve nutrition for Americans in need as well as school-age children.

CIVIL RIGHTS 1950–69

The immediate postwar years also witnessed the nation's first strides in addressing a variety of social issues that had been submerged for most of the century, most prominently the levels of discrimination suffered by the African-American population. The situation was also one of embarrassment when contrasted with America's professed ideals. Furthermore it was an issue easily exploited by the Communists when they contrasted America's image as a democratic force for good with certain social realities.

Marchers carrying flags during one of the several attempts civil rights demonstrators made to march from Selma to Montgomery, Alabama, in March 1965.

The Selma to Montgomery March

For many the 1965 Selma March symbolized the height of civil rights activity directed at securing full voting rights in the South for African Americans. The proposed march from Selma to the Alabama state capital, Montgomery, was to highlight the need for full political rights. The marches stretched over three weeks and were marked by local opposition, which became most violent on "Bloody Sunday" on March 7, 1965, when 600 civil rights activists were intercepted on U.S. Route 80 when they approached the Edmund Pettus Bridge. Here state and local police physically intervened using clubs and tear gas, and pushed the marchers back toward Selma in an effort to disperse the crowd. Many leading civil rights leaders such as Martin Luther King, Jr., James Bevel, and Hosea Williams were involved in this protest, which was initially the work of Amelia Boynton and her husband.

On March 9, 1965, Martin Luther King, Jr. led a further march to the bridge that became a symbol for the struggle. In order to gain safety, civil rights leaders appealed to the courts for protection. Federal District Court Judge Frank M. Johnson heard the petition and weighed the issues of the right to contain mobility versus the right to march. The judge ruled in favor of the marchers, concluding that grievances can be expressed by large groups and "these rights can be exercised by marching, even along public highways." Following this March 21 ruling, 3,200 campaigners began their journey to Montgomery, walking 12 miles a day. They gathered additional supporters along the way, finally arriving at the state capitol on March 25 with over 25,000 people.

Within months of this march, President Lyndon Johnson signed the Voting Rights Act of 1965, which provided voting access for all Americans. In 1996 the route of the march became the Selma to Montgomery Historic Trail under the National Trails System Act of 1968.

Some racial improvements had been made during Roosevelt's New Deal, but greater undertakings occurred in 1948 during the Truman administration when he banned discrimination in federal hiring, and ended the segregation of the military. Early in his administration Truman investigated violence and discrimination against African Americans, which led to a significant 1947 report, "To Secure These Rights," which became an important first step in the drive for civil rights that soon came to dominate the postwar years. However Truman's civil rights program, a key feature of the Fair Deal, was blocked by southern Democrats and led to the Dixiecrat election revolt of 1948, which was championed by South Carolina's Senator Strom Thurmond (1902–2003).

The campaign to end segregation was most helped by the 1954 Supreme Court decision of *Brown v. Board of Education,* which reversed the legal justification for racial separation in schools. This decision started the drive to end separation in all areas of life. Integration became a central plank of change in the 1950s and 1960s, and President Eisenhower enforced the *Brown* ruling most dramatically by ordering federal troops to Little Rock, Arkansas, to ensure the protection of African-American students who were entering the previously all-white Little Rock Central High School.

In 1955 Rosa Parks in Montgomery, Alabama, a member of the NAACP (the National Association for Advancement of Colored People) launched a significant attack on discrimination when she sat in the bus's reserved white seats and refused to move to the "colored" section. Her protest led to a major boycott of the entire bus system. Leadership in this protest moved to a young local minister, Martin Luther King, Jr. (1929–68) whose advocacy gained national support and made him an important symbol of the civil rights struggle.

Soon after these protests the Supreme Court again intervened to declare bus segregation unconstitutional. Still, segregation was but one of a multitude of civil rights issues that hindered African-American life. Voting

A Black Panther convention on the steps of the Lincoln Memorial on June 19, 1970.

Robert F. Kennedy speaking at a rally of the Congress of Racial Equality in June 1963.

rights were another prominent concern. Although the Fifteenth Amendment to the Constitution supposedly secured these rights, southern states had enacted many restrictions on voting rights, such as voting taxes and literacy tests, to frustrate African-American participation. President Eisenhower, working with the Senate and, in particular, Democratic Majority Leader Lyndon Johnson, produced the Civil Rights Act of 1957 to better ensure voting rights. This act was followed by the Civil Rights Act of 1960, which added penalties for voting infringements.

The narrow election victory of John F. Kennedy and Lyndon Johnson in 1960 returned the Democrats to power and launched other legislative drives to end state-based discrimination. In addition to voting rights, housing and jobs, even outside the South, were plagued by unfair practices. The important Civil Rights Act of 1964 outlawed employment and public accommodation discrimination, the 1965 Voting Rights Act strengthened voting protections, and immigration from non-European countries was made easier by the Immigration and National Services Act of 1965. Additional protections in the areas of housing sales and rentals came with the Civil Rights Acts of 1968.

As the Civil Rights movement progressed in the 1960s, besides the enactments of new legislation and Supreme Court interventions, the tactical styles and organization groupings within the movement also evolved. The movement effectively made use of mass protests and staged publicity, including the use of nonviolent civil disobedience in the form of "sits ins" and "freedom rides" that drew broad public support. Organizations such as the SCLC (Southern Christian Leadership Conference), CORE (Congress of Racial Equality), and SNCC (Student Non-Violent Coordinating Committee) became well-known nationally.

However as the decade unfolded, the racial mood also shifted. Some groups called for more militant responses and more violent forms of action in the pursuit of a variety of racial demands. This uneasy mood was reflected in race-based riots, which numbered over 700 across the country between 1964 and 1971. The most serious were the Los Angeles Watts Riot of 1965 and Detroit's 1967 riot, which required military intervention to restore order. These riots caused deaths, destroyed community property, and afterward negatively affected African Americans' property values as well as employment prospects. They also created fears and insecurities in the majority white community, which undermined some aspects of the progress made from the 1950s in bridging racial divides. The rhetoric and actions of the Nation of Islam, Black Panthers, and the influence of the increasingly militant Black Power movement had an additionally disquieting effect in the wider community.

The return of Republican control of the presidency in 1968 following the election of Richard Nixon did not reverse the gains of the Civil Rights movement, even in the face of Nixon's Southern Strategy to turn the South Republican. In practice President Nixon maintained the drive toward desegregation, particularly following the 1969 *Alexander v. Holmes County Board of Education* Supreme Court decision that ordered faster school desegregation. Most notably the Nixon administration expanded the Equal Employment Opportunity Commission and Affirmative Action program.

The end of the 1960s also saw the emergence of a growing feminist movement with the founding of NOW (the National Organization for Women) in 1966. The women's movement extended the battle for economic and social equality to new areas. This marked a significant civil rights development that grew more vocal in the 1970s and remains an important social force. This era also witnessed the appearance of a Chicano Movement (El Movimiento) that addressed issues involving Latino rights, initially mainly those of Mexican migrants. Other nationalist causes also became more vocal, such as that of the American Indian Movement, which campaigned to redress a number of historic grievances.

POSTWAR CULTURE

Much of American life during the 1950s reflected the increasing homogenization of the country in a general climate of uniformity and conformity. America was becoming a consumer or "throwaway" society dominated by middle-class values and assumptions. However, there were some in the arts who saw this nuclear age differently. They rebelled from the common acceptability and argued for greater experimentation with new forms in all the arts. These developments challenged the accepted norms both socially and culturally.

During the 1950s the Beat Generation arose, which was out of step with current notions of conformity. They confronted certain aspects of respectable behavior and broke with established methods whenever the opportunity and means presented itself, forming a subculture within the larger culture. Here began a critical, introspective, individualistic examination of

American society led by numerous writers such as Jack Kerouac and the poet Allen Ginsberg.

The triumph of Abstract Expressionism in the visual arts also shook the complacent. Artists such as Jackson Pollock, Mark Rothko, Willem de Kooning, and Joseph Albers shocked and mystified their audiences and built enormous reputations for themselves both domestically and internationally, making New York City the art capital of the world. In popular music the 1950s also witnessed a rock and roll explosion that seemed to reflect the many enthusiasms of an ever-growing teenage population. Performers such as Elvis Presley became icons of teenage rebellion. In film, the actors Marlon Brando, James Dean, and Montgomery Clift also personified new acting styles that stressed a personal, unconventional individualism that often bucked the status quo.

This ferment in the arts continued into the 1960s and grew stronger, moving in directions that were even more challenging to conventional society. Visual art reflected the rise of a manufactured mass culture, and Op Art became a byword for the era. Artists such as Andy Warhol became star public performers outside the mainstream. A spirit of rebellion and change characterized much of American life in the period and made new ways of living and experiencing life seem possible. Demographically an expanding youth population of over 70 million made such developments possible. Labels grew to identify the various and constantly changing 1960s youth cultural movements. There were also substantial changes in communications made possible by new technologies that helped make the world a "global village."

Developments in the arts and popular culture in the 1950s and 1960s exemplify the way these two seemingly distinct decades flowed together. The Beats had presaged the hippies, just as the Korean War and McCarthyism presaged Vietnam and the upheavals of the late 1960s. The Civil Rights movement, as much as it defined the era, also emerged from earlier, smaller moves toward change. By the end of the era, postwar optimism had long since descended into pessimism, especially with the long Vietnam War, but there had also been lasting positive moves toward racial equality and striking American achievements in science and technology, including the first moon landing.

THEODORE W. EVERSOLE

Further Reading

Agar, Herbert. *The Price of Power: America Since 1945*. Chicago, IL: University of Chicago Press, 1957.

Carson, Clayborne. *In Struggle: SNCC and the Black Awakening of the 1960s*. Cambridge, MA: Harvard University Press, 1995.

Chafe, William H., Harvard Sitkoff, and Beth Bailey, eds. *Readings on Postwar America*. New York: Oxford University Press, 2007.

Chalmers, David. *And the Crooked Places Made Straight: The Struggle for Social Change in the 1960s*. Baltimore, MD: John Hopkins University Press, 1996.

Cohen, Lizabeth. *A Consumers Republic: The Politics of Mass Consumption in Postwar America*. New York: Alfred A. Knopf, 2003.

Collins, Robert M. *More: The Politics of Economic Growth in Postwar America*. New York: Oxford University Press, 2002.

Dickstein, Morris. *Leopards in the Temple: Transformation of American Fiction, 1945–1970*. Cambridge, MA: Harvard University Press, 2002.

Donaldson, Gary A. *Abundance and Anxiety, America 1945–1960*. New York: Praeger, 1997.

Early, Gerald L. *This is Where I Came In: Black America in the 1960s*. Lincoln, NE: Bison Books, 2003.

Gaddis, John L. *The Cold War: A New History*. New York: Penguin Press, 2007.

Haynes, John E. *Red Scare or Red Menace? American Communism and Anti-Communism in the Cold War Era*. Chicago, IL: Ivan R. Dee Publishing, 1996.

Heinz, James. *Perspectives on American Music Since 1950*. Oxford: Routledge, 1999.

Isserman, Maurice and Michael Kazin. *America Divided: The Civil War of the 1960s*. New York: Oxford University Press, 2004.

Jones, Caroline A. *Machine in the Studio: Understanding the Postwar American Artist*. Chicago, IL: University of Chicago Press, 1996.

Melley, Timothy. *Empire of Conspiracy: The Culture of Paranoia in Postwar America*. Ithaca, NY: Cornell University Press, 2000.

Purcell, Carroll. *Technology in Postwar America: A History.* New York: Columbia University Press, 2007.

Reed, Ueda. *Postwar Immigrant America: A Social History*. New York: St. Martin's Press, 1994.

Sitkoff, Harvard. *The Struggle for Black Equality, 1954–1992* New York: Hill and Wang, 1993.

Woods, Randall B. *Quest For Identity: America Since 1945*. New York: Cambridge University Press, 2005.

Chapter 2

Family and Daily Life

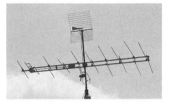

*"When you look at your life, the greatest happinesses
are family happinesses."*
—Dr. Joyce Brothers

IN POSTWAR AMERICA family and daily life underwent phenomenal changes as the United States became the leading world power, and Communism and the Cold War replaced fascism and world war as the greatest threats to American security. In the 1950s daily life for most Americans focused on economic growth and consumption, family life, and participation in community activities. The postwar years were the most affluent in American history. Salaries rose in the 1950s, and by 1960, the Gross National Product had more than doubled in comparison to 1940. By 1962 median family income reached $5,700, and the average college graduate earned $7,260 annually. This meant that many more American families joined the middle class and were able to raise larger families, become homeowners, and purchase a growing range of consumer products. Of those products, the automobile and television brought the most change to family life.

As prosperous as the country was, underlying social problems and discontent that may have fallen to the wayside during the war years resurfaced in the 1960s. Radio, television, and popular music may have brought increased cultural conformity, but they also strengthened connections and fostered youth movements. As the 1950s evolved into the 1960s, 70 million Baby Boomers reached their teenage or early adult years. This change produced an entire generation ready to rebel against the restrictions of the 1950s, leading to a

21

major generation gap, and leaving conservative parents frustrated and angry that they could not understand their children or the world they were creating. The revolutions produced by the 1960s affected all aspects of American life, and broke down centuries-old barriers that had prevented women and minorities from being treated as valuable members of society.

THE SILENT GENERATION

The "Silent Generation" of the 1950s generally saw nothing wrong with their country, which had recently survived the worst depression in history and two world wars. Most Americans, other than those directly affected, were able to pretend that poverty and racism did not exist in the United States. The Cold War made it seem unpatriotic to question decisions made by political leaders. Senator Joseph McCarthy was able to increase America's fear of Communism by launching an extensive and largely unjustified campaign to rid the country of suspected communists in government, academia, and the arts. In an interview for Tom Brokaw's *Boom! Voices of the Sixties*, Howard Pope told the newsman that he believed the Silent Generation had been deeply scarred by McCarthyism, to the point that they were content to follow, but never to lead.

Adults in the 1950s, especially men, were a generation of joiners. The many who were World War II veterans joined the American Legion and Veterans of Foreign Wars, but they also joined religious and community organizations with equal fervor. Some 7.9 percent of adult American males belonged to the Masons in 1955, and 2.3 percent to the Benevolent and Protective Order of the Elks. Males of the 1950s also joined the Order of the Eastern Star, Fraternal Order of Eagles, Loyal Order of Moose, Knights of Columbus, Nobles of the Mystic Shrine (Shriners), Kiwanis, Lions, and the Rotary Club. Others volunteered for the Red Cross or joined a chamber of commerce.

While children of the 1950s had gone far beyond the "children must be seen and not heard" mentality, they were very much a product of the need to conform, which had been considered necessary under McCarthyism. Inside schoolrooms, the emphasis was on producing model citizens who never questioned authority. School curricula frequently included lessons on manners, safety, and thrift. Church membership and attendance rose significantly in the 1950s, and religious values were represented in school days that began with prayers, Bible readings, and saluting the American flag. Some teachers kept records of which students attended church regularly.

GENDER ROLES

In the late 1940s many of the women who had entered the workplace during World War II returned home, and men took back the majority of the jobs. Some women began returning to the workplace in the 1950s, but they were relegated to working as secretaries or nurses, or in other low-paying or part-time positions. Nevertheless, women of the postwar years were much more likely to be employed than their mothers. By 1957 females made up more than one-third of the workforce, and more than half of all working women were married. The higher-paying, often industrial positions that had so empowered women on the home front in World War II, however, were once again held by men and largely out of reach.

Betty Friedan, the mother of the second wave of the women's movement, contended that women of the 1950s never knew they were being oppressed. During the process of trying to identify the reasons she was still unhappy after realizing the much-desired American dream, Friedan wrote *The Feminine Mystique* (1963) and gave birth to modern feminism. Riding on the coattails of the Civil Rights movement, feminists attempted to break down legal and social barriers to equal treatment for women. Consciousness-raising groups attempted to educate women about their rights and their bodies. They lobbied for an Equal Rights Amendment to the U.S. Constitution, for inclusion in the Civil Rights Act of 1964, and for the Equal Pay Act of 1963.

Toys such as this 1960s Barbie set continued to instill traditional gender roles in postwar children.

While few women actually burned their bras, they did begin wearing pants in public and claimed the right to decide whether or not to marry, and if and when to have children. They also won the right to choose to work or to remain at home without feeling guilty about either decision. Some scholars later claimed that feminism had failed, because men did not change along with the women in their lives. However, feminists of the 1960s raised children, both female and male, who questioned and transformed the traditional familial and societal roles of both sexes.

LIFESTYLE CHANGES

Returning veterans used G.I. benefits to improve the quality of life for themselves and their families. At the turn of the century only 27,000 Americans had attended college. By the 1960s 392,000 Americans were enrolled in such institutions, and large numbers were veterans. Between 1945 and 1955 15 million new houses were built in the United States. Instead of having to pay half the cost at the time of purchase as previously required, veterans could buy homes without a down payment. Generous terms, including four percent interest, allowed families to buy homes over a 30-year period instead of the 10 years required before the war. Other families also took advantage of the economic and housing booms. The move to the suburbs accelerated after 1954 in

The rise of tract house subdivisions was one of the foremost developments of the postwar era. The first Levittown quickly became home to 82,000 people.

Levittowns

The housing shortage of the postwar years was solved to a large extent by constructing sprawling developments on the edges of large cities. Between 1945 and 1954 more than nine million Americans moved to the suburbs. These developments were generally made up of white middle-class families with similar backgrounds. There was little mixing of races and ethnicities as was common in urban areas. The first of the model suburban developments, which came to be known as Levittowns, was built on Long Island, New York. Erected by Levitt and Sons, the 4,000-acre development was composed of previously assembled, mass-produced homes. At their peak, Levitt and Sons assembled 30 houses a day. As might be expected, these houses were similar in design. The two-bedroom Cape Cod with a kitchen, bath, and fireplace in the living room was the most popular. These Levittown homes included washing machines, outdoor barbeques, and built-in televisions. The homes were located on large lots, which gave families unprecedented privacy.

The first Levittown home sold for $7,900 and required no down payment. Because loans were guaranteed by the Federal Housing Authority, payments for veterans averaged $60 a month at a time when New Yorkers were paying from $90 to $100 per month for a small apartment. In a relatively short period of time, 17,000 units were sold, providing homes for 82,000 people. In addition to family dwellings, the planned communities of Levittowns included public meeting areas, swimming pools, public parks, and recreational facilities. By the early 1960s mobile home parks were offering low-income Americans alternatives to home ownership. By 1964 there were 16,000 trailer parks in the United States, and more than 1,000 were being manufactured each year.

response to highway modernization programs that reduced commuting time. By 1960 60 percent of families owned their own homes. Many Americans lived in suburbs, where they resided in identical homes on small, treeless lots with a one-car detached garage.

In the postwar years a new emphasis was placed on encouraging America's children to engage in physical and social activities. The yards of middle-class neighborhoods were filled with swing sets, sandboxes, tricycles, bicycles, balls, bats, frisbees, and hula hoops. After-school activities became popular, and American children joined Boy Scouts, Girl Scouts, Cub Scouts, Brownies, and 4-H Clubs in droves. Many also participated in organized church, sports, and community activities.

In the 1930s one-third of women in their childbearing years had never become mothers. By the 1950s only 11 percent of women in this group remained childless. During the 1960s young Americans married in unprecedented numbers. At the beginning of the decade 70 percent of all married women had become wives by the age of 24, as compared to 42 percent in 1920.

The birth rate continued to increase in the postwar years, giving rise to the Baby Boom generation. Between 1940 and 1957 the birth rate for third children doubled, and the rate for fourth children tripled. By 1960 90.9 percent of all American families contained at least one child. In 1967, as the first Baby Boomers matured, the birth rate began a steady decline, while the number of marriages increased. In 1968 two million marriage licenses were issued. Between 1955 and 1963 parents of Baby Boomers tended to stay together to an unprecedented degree, and the divorce rate was the lowest recorded since 1948, fluctuating between 2.1 and 2.3 per 1,000/population. By 1966, as early Baby Boomers grew up and left home, the divorce rate began to rise, reaching 2.5 percent. In 1957 the birthrate for women between the ages of 15 and 19 was 97 per 1,000/population. Because illegitimacy was highly unacceptable, infants born outside of wedlock were usually put up for adoption. Between 1944 and 1955 the rate of adoption increased by 80 percent. Abortion was illegal at the time, although that did not stop women from seeking "back alley" abortionists, and sometimes dying as a result.

Since working women continued to bear the chief responsibility for family and home, food manufacturers focused marketing efforts on frozen, boxed, and canned convenience foods. Convenience was also a major criterion for selling baby products. By 1957 baby food and diapers were generating $50

A 1965 edition of the Boy Scout Handbook.

million annually. Pampers began test-marketing disposable diapers in 1961. At a cost of $.10 each, most mothers considered them too expensive. By 1970 disposable diapers were considered a necessity, but the advisability of using them continued to be hotly debated because of the environmental threat posed by nondegradable plastic.

Convenience also became the order of the day in shopping. Supermarket chains enlarged and offered more products. In 1955 there were 1,800 shopping centers in the United States. In 1962 self-service discount stores such as Target, Wal-Mart, and K-Mart opened. Within three years, sales among discount stores totaled more than those of all other stores combined. By 1968 Target had eight stores, Wal-Mart 19, and K-Mart 250.

Suburban families considered leisure time as family time. In many homes, the recreational or family room, containing toys, televisions, stereos, books, games, and sports equipment became the center of activity. Milton Bradley and Parker Brothers dominated the board game industry, with offerings ranging from the traditional to those based on television shows and cultural icons. American families enjoyed such fads as hula hoops, rocking chairs, pill box hats, transistor radios, pop art, worry beads, permanent waves, Ben Franklin glasses, Batman, hippies, Twiggy, astrology, yoga, and transcendental meditation.

This 1962 living room, complete with wire chairs and a wood-framed television, has been preserved at Cape Canaveral, Florida.

TEENAGE CULTURE

The 1950s were known as the age of conformity, and high schools through-out the United States promoted uniformity by enforcing dress codes, which included no jeans for boys, and only skirts or dresses for females. Even young boys wore button-down shirts like their fathers, and girls dressed in crinolines and calf-length skirts and dresses like their mothers. Many female college students wore stockings with garter belts or girdles. Girls wore their hair tightly permed or in pony tails, while boys favored crew cuts like their fathers. Behavioral restrictions were particularly well-defined for girls who were expected to "act like ladies," and a double standard was informally enforced in regards to sexual behavior. Females who entered the field of higher education were channeled into professions such as nursing, teaching, and home economics.

Teenage girls spent $8.2 million a year on lipstick, $25 million on deodorants, and $9 million on permanent waves. The Breck Girls from the shampoo ads were seen as the ideal American teenage girls. Ninety percent of boys aged 12–27 used hair products to obtain the "wet look." Teenagers reported that their favorite foods included hamburgers, spaghetti, hot dogs, and macaroni and cheese. Between 1952 and 1955, consumption of soft drinks rose by 300 percent. Teenagers also drank 3.5 billion quarts of milk a year, and ate 1.5 million tons of ice cream. By 1965 teenagers were making half a billion telephone calls a year. Some 600,000 teenagers married in 1959, and a Gallup Poll of that year revealed that most teenage girls planned to be married by the age of 22 and expected to have four children. Many colleges instituted co-ed dormitories. The number of young, unmarried cohabitating couples rose constantly. By 1965 six million females were on the pill, and many of them were teenage girls.

Gasoline was cheap and most teenage boys owned their own cars. In 1963 gas rose to $.21 per gallon, but was still inexpensive enough for teenagers to engage in their favorite activities, riding around town and meeting up with their friends, or cruising for members of the opposite sex. Some teenagers owned Volkswagen Beetles and joined the craze of seeing how many friends could be stuffed into one small car. Others attempted the same thing with telephone booths. Most dates involved seeing a movie, socializing with friends, or attending church or a local sporting event. There were 7,000 drive-in movies in the United States, which were viewed as "safe" places for making out. Only teenagers who thought they were "cool" smoked in public in the 1950s; but by the 1960s, 53 percent of 16–19 year olds admitted they smoked. Between 1956 and 1965, the teenage crime rate doubled. In high school, only "greasers" admitted they drank alcohol on a regular basis. Going steady was popular throughout the 1950s and 1960s, and girls wore boys' class rings or "dog tags" to signify ownership. By the 1960s, parents and PTAs were expressing concern about the number of 12 year olds who were going steady and/or wearing makeup.

Although the majority of teenagers in the 1950s never challenged parental authority directly, they managed to do so through fads and music. Rock and roll paved the way for the rock explosion of the 1960s and 1970s that shouted rebellion at every turn. That rebellion included challenging existing mores on hair styles, clothing, and social behaviors. In San Antonio, Texas, school officials felt compelled to ban tight blue jeans and duck-tail haircuts, insisting that they led to discipline problems. The folk music craze exploded in 1958, and towns throughout the United States hosted hootenannies.

Many teenagers of the 1960s joined in the societal battle to end poverty, war, and injustice. Many of them looked to writer/psychologist Timothy Leary, a leading figure in America's counterculture movement who encouraged teenagers "to turn on, tune in, and drop out." The Port Huron Statement, issued by the Students for a Democratic Society (SDS) in 1962, became the manifesto for the growing student protest movement. The document stated that humans were "infinitely precious and possessed of unfulfilled capacities for reason, freedom and love" and rejected the notion that "man in the 20th century is a thing to be manipulated" and reduced "to the status of things."

ENTERTAINMENT AND THE FAMILY

Although radio was being replaced by television as the major form of entertainment, most Americans continued to purchase radios. Between 1950 and 1962 the number of radios in American homes increased from 98 million to 176 million, partly in response to the introduction of the transistor radio and rock music. In 1950 only 10 percent of Americans owned televisions, and 38 percent had never even seen a TV program. By 1950 there were 98 television stations and four million TV sets in the United States. Television was quickly becoming part of daily life; and by 1952 1,000 new appliance stores were opening each month to meet the demand. By 1962 90 percent of American families owned at least one television. That same year, *TV Guide* became the top-selling weekly magazine. Although the first color television sets were introduced in 1951, they did not become common in American homes until the 1960s when networks first began broadcasting some shows in color.

A television designed around 1958. By 1962 90 percent of American families owned at least one television.

Broadcasters of the postwar years discovered that family-oriented shows garnered enormous profits. The most popular show of the 1950s was *I Love*

Lucy, which broke new ground by pairing comedian Lucille Ball with her real-life husband Latino bandleader Desi Arnaz. Already an established comedienne, Ball was given control that was unprecedented for female entertainers. By 1952 her show was drawing a weekly audience of 10.6 million households, increasing to 50 million over the next two years and earning a profit for CBS for the first time in its history.

Expanding popularity allowed television to exercise a substantial influence on how American families viewed themselves. Situation comedies such as the *Adventures of Ozzie and Harriet* (1952–66), *Father Knows Best* (1954–60), *Leave It to Beaver* (1957–63), and *The Donna Reed Show* (1958–66) promoted an image of affluent, stable nuclear families. Each family had a mother who remained at home looking picture perfect in high heels and jewelry, and parents on TV never yelled at their children. While sit-coms dealt with family issues, they rarely addressed broader social issues such as poverty, racism, and sex. *The Honeymooners*, in which the main male character, Ralph Kramden, drove a bus and his best friend, Ed Norton, worked in the city sewers, was a rarity, as was *Our Miss Brooks*, a show about a single high school teacher searching for romance. The only African Americans on television were either stereotypically portrayed, as with *Amos 'N' Andy*, or in domestic roles. There were few old people, no openly acknowledged gays, and no single-parent families.

By 1953–54, I Love Lucy was drawing a weekly audience of 50 million viewers.

By 1960 nine out of every 10 children under 6 years old in the United States watched television every day. By the age of 12 youngsters were watching an average of four hours a day. Children usually watched television with their parents, but Saturday mornings and weekday afternoons were devoted almost exclusively to children's programming. From 1947 to the 1960s, the marionette Howdy Doody was a particular favorite. Young children were entertained by *Captain Kangaroo* from 1955 to the 1980s. Children of all ages tuned in on weekday afternoons to watch Disney's *Mickey Mouse Club* (1955–59).

Raccoon-style hats like this were an early television-driven fad.

Manufacturers were quick to see the advantage of television-related products and began offering a plethora of items. Few products could match the popularity of the coonskin cap worn by Fess Parker in a Disney series loosely based on the real life of Davy Crockett, a Tennessee politician killed at the Alamo. The sale of Davy Crockett items totaled $100 million before the craze ended. By 1959 sales from products advertised on Saturday morning television were recorded at $75 million per year.

As televisions became more common in American homes, movie attendance declined. In 1950 60 million Americans attended movies each week; by 1958 attendance had dropped to 42 million. Yet movies and celebrities continued to exercise a major influence on American society. When actor James Dean was killed in a motorcycle accident shortly before the release of *Rebel without A Cause* in 1955, he became an international symbol of the rebellious youth movement. The image of young people rejecting their parents' lifestyles was epitomized in *The Graduate* (1967), in which recent college graduate Benjamin Braddock (Dustin Hoffman) has an affair with Mrs. Robinson (Anne Bancroft), a friend of his parents. On the movie's soundtrack, Simon and Garfunkel used "Mrs. Robinson" to describe the American tendency to "hide it in the closet where no one ever goes" and the alienation felt by the young when idols came tumbling down: "Where have you gone, Joe DiMaggio, our nation turns its lonely eyes to you."

POPULAR MUSIC AND BOOKS

Americans of the postwar years were entertained by music of all kinds. In the early 1950s there were 32 professional orchestras, 343 community orchestras, and 231 college and amateur orchestras. Beginning in the 1940s and continuing into the early 1950s, soft-voiced crooners entertained with sentimental songs such as "How Much Is That Doggie in the Window" and "Oh, My Papa." Musicals continued to be popular in the postwar years, as evidenced by the success of *My Fair Lady*, *Mame*, *West Side Story*, and the *Music Man*.

The music scene changed drastically in the mid-1950s with the rise of Mississippi native Elvis Presley, who introduced white Americans to what had been exclusively black music. The rock and roll era was born after Presley appeared on shows hosted by Steve Allen and Ed Sullivan. Presley's pelvic movements were considered so suggestive that television cameras sometimes showed him only from the waist up when performing. Although 83 percent of teenagers supported rock music, many parents saw it as proof that teenagers were being

Woodstock

The final year of the postwar period introduced Woodstock into the American psyche. The joint concert and festival was held in a five-acre field attached to a dairy farm owned by Max Yasgar in Bethel, New York, on August 15–18, 1969. Woodstock has become synonymous in the minds of many Americans with the counterculture of free love, drugs, and heavy rock music of the late 1960s and early 1970s.

The event, which drew some 500,000 attendees, was so popular that it closed the New York State Thruway and caused the worst traffic jam in American history, stretching for 20 miles. Total costs of the event were estimated at $2.4 million.

Those who came to Woodstock were music lovers, liberals, activists, anti-establishment and war protestors, and conservatives who opposed everything the others stood for. The festival was fraught with drama. Two women gave birth at Woodstock. Out-of-control rioters led to fires, and the police reported two deaths. Yet scores of attendees remained for the entire three days despite heavy rain, dwindling food supplies, a lack of adequate sanitation facilities, and mounting use of drugs and alcohol.

Beginning shortly after 5 P.M. on Friday afternoon and continuing until Monday morning, Woodstock attracted a roster of musicians that reads like a Who's Who of classic rock and folk performers.

Performers at the Woodstock festival included Joan Baez, Joe Cocker, Arlo Guthrie, Jimi Hendrix, Janis Joplin, and Melanie. Popular bands on the program included Blood, Sweat, and Tears; Creedence Clearwater Revival; Crosby, Stills and Nash; the Grateful Dead; Jefferson Airplane; Santana; the Band; Sha-Na-Na; Sly and the Family Stone; and the Who.

When the event closed, many fans remained to help the crew in a five-day clean-up. Woodstock continues to draw visitors who come from all over the United States to view the site.

The site of Woodstock, where 500,000 people gathered in a defining event for the counterculture of the late 1960s.

corrupted, and it was banned around the country. Silly songs such as "Purple People Eater," "Bird Dog," and "Kookie, Kookie, Lend Me Your Comb" also had wide appeal.

In 1959 the first annual Grammy Awards were held, with awards going to perennial favorite Frank Sinatra and newcomer Bobby Darrin. Folk music rose to the forefront of the American music scene in the early 1960s, featuring the talents of Peter, Paul, and Mary; Joan Baez; and the Kingston Trio. A singing nun also had a major hit with the song "Dominique." By 1964 go-go clubs had appeared on the scene, and young Americans were spending their evenings dancing the Dog, the Monkey, the Chicken, the Watusi, and the Frog at clubs featuring scantily clad females in cages. In 1963 Beatlemania hit the United States. What became known as the British invasion abruptly ended the careers of most rock and roll idols. By 1966 heavy metal had also appeared on the music scene, with darker music increasingly depicting youth rebellion and sexual activity.

The American public continued to read. In 1951 11,000 separate book titles and 231,000 reprints were sold. In a little over a decade, the sale of paperbacks climbed to 310 million. Between 1939 and 1973 the most popular authors were Erskine Caldwell and Mickey Spillane. Books such as Ralph Ellison's *Invisible Man* (1952) and Harper Lee's *To Kill A Mockingbird* (1961) highlighted the plight of African Americans in a segregated society. Classics such as Ernest Hemingway's *The Old Man and the Sea* and John Steinbeck's *East of Eden* enthralled millions of readers. Religious books and nonfiction also had wide appeal. Among young readers, comic books remained popular. In 1955 one billion comic books were sold, generating sales of approximately $100 million.

Baseball continued to draw large numbers of fans. In 1955 Rocky Marciano won international attention as the world heavyweight champion. Two years later, Marciano shared that attention with Sugar Ray Robinson, the new middleweight champion. That same year, the Milwaukee Braves broke a National League record when 2.2 million fans attended a home game. In 1960 Floyd Patterson became the first American in history to regain the world heavyweight championship, which he lost the following year to Sonny Liston. The first Super Bowl began in 1967, giving football fans a chance to watch their favorite teams battle it out for the national title.

CONSUMER TECHNOLOGY

Research conducted during the war led to a plethora of new and improved products made from synthetic materials such as nylon and Dacron. By 1960 technology had exploded, providing Americans with improved frozen foods, plastic wrap, Xerox machines, all-in-one supermarkets, sprawling shopping malls, fast food chains, home air conditioning, Polaroid cameras, computers, transistor radios, ballpoint pens, power lawnmowers, tape recorders, hi-fi stereos, and long-playing record albums.

Automobiles increasingly became a part of daily life. Between 1951 and 1958 the number of families purchasing second cars doubled. This proliferation of car ownership came with a price. By 1959 the number of automobile-related deaths surpassed the number of Americans killed in all wars to that date. New technologies allowed manufacturers to offer more expensive automobiles with more options such as power steering, automatic transmission, air conditioning, and directional signals. After the Soviet Union successfully launched Sputnik into space, American technology focused on propelling the United States into the Space Age. In 1962 astronaut John Glenn became the first American to orbit the earth. By 1965 an American had completed the first spacewalk.

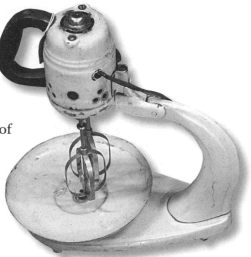

Postwar families invested in many appliances like this electric mixer from the early 1950s.

Families of the postwar years expended large portions of their incomes on household appliances. Between 1940 and 1963 the sale of electric stoves and washing machines quadrupled, and the sale of electric razors sextupled. Between 1950 and 1963 the sales of electric dishwashers and clothes driers quadrupled. In 1950 11,000 air conditioners were sold. By 1963 Americans were spending $2 million annually to air condition their homes. The sale of electric blankets rose from $800,000 in 1950 to $5.5 million in 1963. The first domestic microwaves were introduced in 1967, although they remained expensive and inefficient. Other domestic inventions included the electric mixer, the steam iron, the four-slice toaster, the electric can opener, electric shoe buffers, electric lawn equipment, electric coffee pots and grinders, electric grills, garbage disposals, portable dishwashers, and side-by-side refrigerator/freezer combinations. The new emphasis on convenience led to a constantly expanding market for frozen food. Between 1944 and 1962 the annual market grew from 600 million pounds to more than 10 billion pounds. The growing attachment to television led to the manufacture of frozen TV dinners, which could be quickly heated and then eaten before the television set.

Changes in home designs that had begun in the 1940s continued into the 1950s. Kitchens were designed in U- or L-shapes for convenience. The bright colors of the 1940s that had characterized walls, floors, furniture, and appliances gave way to soft pastels. Maytag introduced the two-speed washer, allowing consumers a choice of delicate or regular cycle, cold or hot wash/

rinse cycles, and push button operation. Stove manufacturers of the 1950s produced double ovens, finger-tip control, and self-cleaning ovens. Plastic tableware in a range of colors was introduced for everyday use. Popular colors of the 1960s included copper, avocado, and gold. Architectural house plans were introduced with open floor spaces in which kitchens and living areas were combined. The painted metal kitchen cabinets of the two preceding decades were replaced with wooden cabinets in various stains and finishes.

CONCLUSION

Technological improvements that brought more household appliances and a growing emphasis on convenience gave families more leisure time than in the past. As the consumer culture grew and people became more affluent, a new level of status consciousness crept into American culture. In 1953 there were only 27,000 millionaires in the United States, but by 1965 there were as many as 90,000. Families compared their circumstances to those of their neighbors, fueling further consumption as they tried to "keep up with the Joneses." By 1960 two-thirds of all American families were in debt.

In the postwar era the combination of new suburban developments with expanded highways and growing automobile ownership also meant that these families were more mobile than before. In some cases they left behind regional identities or moved far away from extended family. Into this breach came television, which was affecting how Americans saw themselves and their families, and was becoming a powerful force for homogenization. This homogenization was not necessarily negative; it had the potential to make people feel even more a part of their peer group or generation, which could lead to a growing common interest in social change.

ELIZABETH R. PURDY

Further Readings

Anderson, Terry. *The Sixties*. New York: Pearson Longman, 2007.

Archer, Jules. *Breaking Barriers: The Feminist Revolution from Susan B. Anthony to Betty Freidan*. New York: Viking, 1991.

Brokaw, Tom. *Boom! Voices of the Sixties*. New York: Random House, 2007.

Carson, Allan. *The "American Way": Family and Community in the Shaping of the American Identity*. Wilmington, DE: ISI Books, 2003.

Chapman, Tony. *Gender and Domestic Life: Changing Practices in Families and Households*. New York: Palgrave, 2004.

Clark, Gerald. "The Silent Generation Revisited." *Time* (June 29, 1970).

Du Noyer, Paul. *The Story of Rock and Roll: The Year-by-Year Illustrated Chronicle*. New York: Carlton Books, 1995.

Glick, Paul C. *American Families*. New York: John Wiley and Sons, 1957.

Goffman, Ken and Dan Joy. *Counterculture through the Ages: From Abraham to Acid House*. New York: Villard, 2004.

Hendler, Herb. *Year by Year in the Rock Era: Events and Conditions Shaping the Rock Generations That Reshaped America*. Westport, CT: Greenwood, 1983.

Kaledin, Eugenia. *Daily Life in the United States, 1940–1959: Shifting Worlds*. Westport, CT: Greenwood, 2000.

Kaledin, Eugenia. *Mothers and More: American Women in the 1950s*. Boston, MA: Twayne, 1984.

Mettler, Suzanne. *Soldiers to Citizens: The G.I. Bill and the Making of the Greatest Generation*. New York: Oxford University Press, 2005.

Morty, Myron A. *Daily Life in the United States, 1960–1990: Decades of Discord*. Westport, CT: Greenwood, 1997.

Pante, Ellen M. *The American Kitchen 1700 to the Present: From Hearth to High Rise*. New York: Facts on File, 1995.

Sherman, Janann, ed. *Interviews with Betty Friedan*. Jackson, MS: University of Mississippi Press, 2002.

Smith, Judith. *Visions of Belonging: Family Stories, Popular Culture, and Postwar Democracy, 1940–1960*. New York: Columbia University Press, 2004.

Students for a Democratic Society. "Port Huron Statement." Available online: http://coursesa.matrix.msu.edu/~hst306/documents/huron.html. Accessed October 2008.

West, Elliott. *Growing Up in Twentieth Century America: A History Reference Guide*. Westport, CT: Greenwood, 1996.

Woodstock Festival and Concert. Available online: http://www.woodstock69.com. Accessed May 2008.

Yalom, Marilyn. *A History of the Wife*. New York: Harper Collins, 2001.

Chapter 3

Material Culture

"There must be more to life than having everything."
—Maurice Sendak

MATERIAL LIFE IN the 1950s and early 1960s was centered on domesticity, consumerism, and the "good life." Most Americans turned their attention to home and family once the distractions of the Great Depression and World War II had ended and economic prosperity returned. Many Americans sought the domestic "American Dream" of marriage, family, and a new car and home in the quickly developing suburbs. Many families had saved money during the rationing and shortages of wartime and now sought to spend that money on the new consumer products and labor-saving devices that flooded the market. New types of entertainment helped shape architecture and fashion. Adolescents and young adults emerged as a new consumer force, launching a fashion revolution. The Modern style of previous decades intermingled with bright and kitschy architecture and décor.

COMMERCIAL AND DOMESTIC ARCHITECTURE

During the mid-20th century, the United States was considered a highly influential center of architectural innovation. The Modern architectural styles developed in the early 20th century remained popular into the 1950s and beyond. Stark, streamlined, and impersonal buildings with no unnecessary ornamentation continued to appear, and glass and steel skyscrapers continued to dominate the skylines of major American cities. The functionality of buildings remained a paramount goal of the architects who worked in the Modern style. Modern architects who had risen to prominence in the early 20th century, such as Ludwig Mies van der Rohe, Charles and Ray Eames, Eero Saarinen, Louis I. Kahn, Philip Johnson, I.M. Pei, Walter Gropius, Pietro Belluschi, Frank O. Gehry, and Edward Durrell Stone, remained influential. Noted buildings erected in the 1950s and 1960s include the Memorial Arch in St. Louis, the Kimball Art Museum in Fort Worth, the Pan Am (now Met Life) Building, the TWA Terminal at Kennedy Airport in New York, and the General Motors Technical Center in Michigan. In 1951 America's first all glass and steel apartment building, designed by Ludwig Mies van der Rohe, opened along Lake Shore Drive in Chicago. Better building technology allowed skyscrapers to rise in earthquake-prone areas like California.

While Modern architecture remained paramount in the late 1950s and 1960s, other styles continued or emerged as well. Postmodern architecture began to appear, with a growing recurrence of decorative design elements versus the stark and streamlined Modern style. Frank Lloyd Wright, with his emphasis on organic architecture that seamlessly blended with its surrounding environment, remained one of the country's pre-eminent architects. Morris Lapidus designed the renowned Fontainebleau Hotel in Miami Beach, Florida, while John Lautner designed houses that resembled flying saucers. Buckminster Fuller began designing his

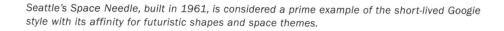

Seattle's Space Needle, built in 1961, is considered a prime example of the short-lived Googie style with its affinity for futuristic shapes and space themes.

Chain restaurants such as those evoked by this diner display in a museum spread rapidly in the 1950s, bringing futuristic architecture and more bold signs to the American landscape.

futuristic geodesic domes. The Sun House, erected by the Massachusetts Institute of Technology, utilized solar heat.

The so-called Googie School of Architecture, derisively named by its critics after the Googie Coffee Shop in Los Angeles, utilized abstract styles, bold colors, angular designs, clear plate glass windows, and neon to attract customers to the rapidly spreading suburban drive-in theaters, diners, supermarkets, bowling alleys, motels, and strip malls. Popular shapes included boomerangs, starbursts, spiked balls, arrows, geometric shapes, and space images. An iconic example is the Golden Arches, the trademark symbol of McDonalds.

One of the most influential architects and city planners of the period was Austrian immigrant Victor Gruen, who established Victor Gruen Associates in 1951. Many architectural historians consider him the father of the modern suburban shopping mall. His firm designed shopping centers to be easily accessible with numerous stores and additional attractions. One of his first storefronts was the Lederer leather goods shop located on New York's Fifth Avenue. His firm created some of the first enclosed shopping malls in the country. His well-known malls include the Northland Center and Eastland in suburban Detroit, the Southdale Center near Minneapolis, the Glendale in Indianapolis, the Valley and Bay Fairs in San Francisco, the Midtown Plaza in Rochester (the first inner-city enclosed shopping mall), and the Cherry Hill Mall in the New Jersey suburbs of Philadelphia. His firm helped develop city

The automobile and an improved highway system made the rapid growth of suburbs possible, and house designs reflected the importance of the automobile. This house, built around 1950, features an attached carport.

plans for Fort Worth, Texas; Kalamazoo, Michigan; Cincinnati, Ohio; and Fresno, California.

The return of American servicemen at the end of World War II and the resulting Baby Boom led to a rapidly growing demand for single-family housing at affordable prices, and the development of planned communities. Owning a house remained the American Dream, and housing purchases were a large part of 1950s consumer spending. New government-funded mortgage programs and cheaper construction materials and techniques put the dream in reach of many American families. The 1956 National Highway Act and subsequent development of the interstate highway system also fueled the growth of suburbs, as more families could afford to live outside the cities and commute to and from work. Urban flight and the resulting deterioration of inner cities became a widespread social trend of American society.

New materials, tools, and building methods led to the creation of houses that were larger and better constructed than those of earlier periods. Floor plans, hardware, and construction materials became more standardized, resulting in developments of similar houses in neat rows with well-manicured lawns and trees. As automobiles became common during these decades, more and more houses featured attached garages. Due to Cold War fears, a number of homeowners also added fully-stocked underground bomb shelters

Buckminster Fuller and the Geodesic Dome

Richard Buckminster Fuller (1895–1983), an innovative designer and builder, developed the geodesic dome as an inexpensive means of providing housing. Although not the dome's originator, he patented it in the United States. Fuller co-founded the Stockade Building Company in 1922 in an effort to mass-produce lightweight buildings and building materials. After losing his job in 1927, he went out on his own, continuing his quest for lightweight and inexpensive homes. Through his scientific research, he also developed plans for a variety of other products, including the Dymaxion Car and the Dymaxion World Map. His design philosophy was the idea of creating "more for less" and creating safe ways to maximize the planet's material resources in the least damaging way. He followed what he labeled four-dimensional (4D) design. He considered the fourth dimension to be time, considering the impact of the building on its environment over time. He won numerous awards and honorary degrees over the course of his lifetime, including a Nobel Peace Prize nomination in 1969. He taught at various universities, and his enthusiastic designs inspired many designers and architects.

Fuller first became known for his Dymaxion House in the late 1920s. The house was made of lightweight steel, aluminum, and plastic, and featured rooms that radiated from the center in a hexagonal pattern. He next began designing geodesic domes, structures that featured networks of intersecting circles that formed triangles. Geodesic domes were stable, strong, and resistant to extreme weather. The first geodesic structure appeared in Montreal, Canada, in 1950, and in 1952 Fuller displayed a geodesic dome at the Museum of Modern Art (MOMA) in New York. The earliest domes were used as commercial and industrial spaces, such as the Union Tank Car Company dome in Baton Rouge, Louisiana. However, Fuller hoped the idea would spread to include mass-produced, transportable, and affordable domestic housing. One of his most renowned plans was the design for a two-mile dome to be placed over Manhattan. Geodesic domes appeared at the 1964 World's Fair in New York, the Expo '67 in Montreal, the Ontario Place amusement park in Toronto, and the Spaceship Earth ride at EPCOT in Walt Disney World in Orlando, Florida. Fuller lived in a geodesic dome in Carbondale, Illinois.

to protect their families in the event of a nuclear war with the Soviet Union. The most famous developer of suburban planned communities was William J. Levitt, whose Levittown communities served as models for other communities that quickly sprang up across the United States. Millions of Americans moved to planned communities like Levittown during the 1950s.

Popular architectural styles for 1950s and 1960s domestic suburban dwellings include the manufactured home, Spanish Revival, the A-frame, and the

The tail fin fad for automobiles was at its peak when this 1957 Buick was built; the rocket-inspired look gradually disappeared in the 1960s.

different variations of the ranch style. Interest in the Spanish Revival style reflected the growing population of California and the southwestern states. It drew its inspiration from earlier historical Spanish Colonial and Mission style buildings found throughout the region. Spanish Revival houses combine such traditional elements as red tile roofs and adobe or stucco walls with more modern features. The exteriors are harmonious with the environment and often feature native plants. The interiors are warm, open, and comfortable. A-frame style homes also emphasize comfortable, cozy interiors and are distinguished by their dramatically sloping roofs that resemble the letter A. A-frame houses populated regions with heavy annual snowfall because their unique slanted roofs prevented snow from accumulating in heavy piles, the weight of which could result in structural damage.

One of the most popular and widely-recognized styles of domestic suburban architecture during this period was the uniquely American ranch style house, which developed in California and could be found throughout much of the suburban United States by the end of the 1950s. California architects and developers most commonly associated with the development of the ranch style include Cliff May, William Wurster, and Joseph Eichler. Ranch style houses came in several different varieties, including the Western Ranch, American Ranch, California Rambler, and Raised (or Split Level) Ranch. Most ranches were one-story houses with low-pitched gable roofs and large eaves. They were long and low to the ground, with large windows and a lack of exterior decorative ornamentation. Most followed an asymmetrical design centered on livability. Additional features included a patio and attached garage. The Raised Ranch featured a finished basement and raised roof that allowed for future expansion. The interior of a ranch-style house usually featured wood floors and vaulted ceilings with exposed wooden beams. Exteriors were usually wood or brick. Commercial architects adapted the ranch style for use in supermarkets, strip malls, and other suburban institutions.

HOUSEHOLD FURNISHINGS AND OTHER CONSUMER GOODS

The interiors of both commercial and domestic buildings of the time emphasized open, efficient floor plans and less individual demarcation between rooms. Most Americans preferred the simple, functional furniture style known as American Modern. Manufacturers mass-produced such furniture

Tupperware

Plastics innovator Earl Silas Tupper founded the Tupperware Plastics Company in 1938. He had begun his career at Du Pont and as a contractor for the U.S. military during World War II. Through experimentation, he created a method of transforming polyethylene slag, a byproduct of crude oil refinement, into a non-greasy, translucent, and odor-free plastic that would not break when dropped. In 1946 his Tupper Plastics products debuted on the consumer market. His famous plastic containers with lids were lightweight and non-breakable, with a patented Tupperware seal that kept stored food air- and water-tight. The line also contained cups, bowls, plates, cigarette cases, and bathroom tumblers. Products added to the line over the years included the Wonderlier Bowl, the Bell Tumbler, the Party Bowl, the Pie Taker, the Dip 'N Serve Tray, the Traveling Desk, and the Plastic Carrying Case. Tupperware products came in a range of colors.

Tupperware initially suffered from low sales as many consumers failed to understand how the innovative product worked without being shown. Tupper therefore joined with Stanley Home Products, a company that had successfully sold his product through in-house demonstrations, to launch Tupperware Home Parties. Florida housewife and Stanley employee Brownie Wise was instrumental in helping the parties become a marketing tool and employment opportunity for housewives. The home parties proved so successful that Tupperware was removed from store shelves and exclusively sold through the parties by 1951. The parties became a cultural phenomenon, and as Tupperware developed and changed over the years it became a worldwide presence and a household name. Tupper sold his company in 1958 for $16 million.

Among the many Tupperware designs were salt and pepper shakers, utensils, and even toys.

from synthetic materials like plastics and molded plywood, and often used bright colors. New plastics would also prove useful for dinnerware and lead to the development of the innovative new product Tupperware. Tubular metal furniture was popular. Well-known furniture companies and designers included Charles and Ray Eames, Herman Miller, Knoll Associates, and Verner Panton. Home furnishings tended to be minimal, and were often grouped by use as distinguishing features in the open floor plans common to the day. In contrast to the stark furniture, many 1950s homes also contained kitschy and colorful accessories such as bubble or hula girl lamps and wallpaper that featured wild patterns or colors. The Ball Clock produced by George Nelson and Company of New York, featuring twelve sticks with small balls on each end, was a bestseller.

Most American homes of the 1950s and 1960s included the latest gadgets and modern conveniences designed to ease the burdens of housework. Such labor-saving devices included automatic dishwashers, garbage disposals, clothes washers and dryers, and refrigerators. The widespread availability of such devices was seen as a symbol of American success. The model kitchen exhibit at the U.S. Trade and Cultural Fair in Moscow in 1959 featured such devices, and led to the famous impromptu debate over capitalism versus Communism between Soviet Premier Nikita Khrushchev and visiting U.S. President Richard Nixon that became known as the "kitchen debate." Black-and-white television sets, developed by RCA in 1939, had also become common in many American homes. The popularity of rock and roll and other forms of music meant that most homes also contained a radio and a record player.

A bedroom chest with rounded corners in the "waterfall" style, which was briefly popular in the 1950s.

Modern technology also changed the way Americans ate in the 1950s. TV dinners, complete frozen meals that were ready to eat after heating, made their debut in American refrigerators in the mid-1950s, quickly rising to the status of cultural icon. The invention of the TV dinner is variously credited to a number of companies and individuals who played key roles in its development. Maxson was the first company to manufacture complete frozen meals in 1945, producing their Strato-Plates for use on military and commercial airplane flights. Strato-Plates featured the TV dinner hallmark of meat, potato, and vegetable components in separate compartments, but never marketed the product for consumer use. In the late 1940s,

Jack Fisher began selling a similar product, called FridgiDinners, to bar owners. Albert and Meyer Bernstein formed Frozen Dinners, Inc. around the same time, later to become the Quaker State Food Corporation, and sold frozen dinners in compartmentalized aluminum trays in the Pennsylvania area. The Swanson Brothers, however, are most widely credited with mass-producing and advertising the idea on a national scale. They were also the first to call the product the TV dinner.

For many Americans, their cars ranked right next to their houses as symbols of individual success and American prosperity. By the 1950s most families could now afford to own at least one car, and the creation of the

Fashion icon Jackie Kennedy tossing her bouquet after her first wedding on September 12, 1953.

interstate highway system and the explosion of the suburbs increased reliance on cars as the main form of transportation. The station wagon would become a symbol of family and suburban life. The American car culture was born, and the National Auto Show reappeared in 1956 after a 16-year absence. American-made cars dominated the market in the 1950s, and the emphasis in car design was on large engines and style over fuel-efficiency and practicality. 1950s cars were characterized by ice cream colors, fancy grilles, spacious interiors, and tail fins that gave cars the appearance of airplanes or rockets. The tail fin fad would reach its height by the late 1950s, and their presence grew smaller and gradually disappeared over the course of the 1960s. The 1960s marked the era of the American muscle cars, such as the Ford Mustang and Chevy Corvette. One popular auto that defied the American trend of bigger is better was the Volkswagen Beetle, a tiny German import.

CLOTHING AND FASHION

The affluence and consumer culture of the 1950s also helped continue the revitalization of the fashion industry, and introduced new fashion markets aimed at children and teenagers. Man-made synthetic fibers also revolutionized the fashion industry, becoming increasingly common during the 1950s. Synthetic fibers such as polyester, rayon, acetate, nylon, and Dacron were lighter-weight

The American photographer Toni Frissell, who had been one of just a small number of women to work as war correspondents during World War II, made this fashion photograph featuring a streamlined skirt suit and beret inside Victoria Station, London, for the U.S. magazine Harper's Bazaar *in 1951.*

and more wrinkle-resistant, making them popular among consumers. Manufacturers often blended them with cotton and other natural fibers. Velcro was patented in 1955, introducing a new option for clothing and shoe closures. Plastic began appearing in women's shoes.

The New Look pioneered by Christian Dior after World War II, which emphasized the femininity and romanticism that had been repressed during the Great Depression and wartime, remained popular. Elegant Hollywood stars like Grace Kelly served as models for the glamorous look. French fashion designers such as Dior, Givenchy, and Chanel served as inspiration for American styles.

Women's dress emphasized a well-groomed and tailored appearance. Narrow waists, full or long skirts, and fitted bodices characterized women's dresses of the 1950s. Women used undergarments to create the popular form-flattering and long-legged silhouettes of the day. Daywear for working women included separates, mid-calf length dresses, and suits with slim skirts, straight short jackets, and silk blouses. Shoes, usually satin pumps, matched the outfit. Most women continued to wear gloves and hats; especially popular were pillbox hats and berets. Brightly colored lizard skin handbags were popular, as were fur stoles and capes. Eveningwear took the form of either full-skirted romantic dresses or tight, body-clinging sheath dresses popularized by Hollywood stars Marilyn Monroe and Jane Russell. Evening dresses were often sequined and strapless, with plunging neck and back lines.

1950s fashion also introduced new trends in women's appearances. Nylon stockings once again became common, and the decade saw the introduction of seamless stockings. High stiletto heels became popular. Short hairstyles and cosmetics regained popularity. Christian Dior debuted several new styles,

Claire McCardell and the Development of the American Look

Claire McCardell is known as the pioneer of the American Look, helping the United States become the fashion capital for sportswear and leisurewear in the 1950s and 1960s. She graduated from the New York School of Fine and Applied Arts (now known as the Parsons School of Design) in 1927. She felt that the comfort of daytime fashions suffered because of the emphasis solely on style. She sought to blend the two concepts to create comfortable and functional clothing that also flattered its wearer. She also designed clothes to be mass-produced for affordability. She worked at a succession of jobs for various companies after her graduation before becoming a vice-president and partner in Townley in 1952.

McCardell designed swimsuits, dresses, resort clothes, and pajamas. Her trademark looks included clothes whose shapes could be adjusted through the use of drawstrings, sashes, and belts as well as deep armholes, large pockets with top stitching, and details inspired by menswear. She worked with comfortable fabrics such as denim, corduroy, wool, calico, and velveteen. Some of the fashion innovations she is known for include the robe-like Monastic dress, the wrap-around Pop Over dress, harem pajamas, and the diaper bathing suit. In addition to women's clothes, she designed sunglasses, children's and infants shoes and clothing, and jewelry. She won numerous design awards, including the American Designers Coty Award, the Women's National Press Club Award, and the Neiman-Marcus Award. She is also honored with a bronze plaque on 7th Avenue along New York's Fashion Walk of Fame.

including the boyish H-look featuring straight dresses with lowered waist-lines, and the chemise, or sack, dress that proved to be a comfortable daytime choice. Fellow French designer Yves St. Laurent debuted the Trapeze dress by decade's end. Trend-setting fashion icons of the late 1950s and 1960s included Audrey Hepburn, known for her black sweaters, flats, gold hoop earrings, and short hair, and First Lady Jackie Kennedy, known for her elegant and sophisticated wardrobe. A fan of French designers, she began working with Kennedy family friend and American designer Oleg Cassini during the Kennedy presidency. She also became famous for her restoration of the White House, which was shown on television to the American public on February 14, 1962. The Kennedy style demonstrated the power of image, and would influence an entire generation of Americans.

1950s menswear was generally conservative, with styles that did not change as often as women's styles. The Eisenhower jacket, originally designed by General Dwight Eisenhower for use by U.S. troops in World War II, became popular among civilian males in the postwar period. It featured a shortened coat ending in a waistband, and was meant to be both stylish and comfortable. It was the ubiquitous gray flannel suit, however, that became the basic 1950s fashion uniform and cultural symbol of conformity in men's apparel. The suit became narrower than those of the preceding decade, with fitted single-breasted jackets featuring narrow lapels and pocket flaps and tapered trousers. Underneath the jacket was a dress shirt with a button down collar, most often in white. A tie, black leather shoes, and a raincoat or overcoat completed the ensemble. Flat tops and crew cuts were the most popular men's hairstyles. The cultural symbolism of the look was captured in Sloan Wilson's novel *The Man in the Gray Flannel Suit*, which followed suburban businessman Tom Rath and his wife Betsy as they searched for happiness in business and consumer culture of 1950s society. In 1956 the novel became a movie starring Gregory Peck and Jennifer Jones.

Poodle skirts like this one were a craze among teenage girls in the 1950s.

American fashion designers led the way in the growing popularity of the sports and leisurewear market, introducing the comfortable styles that became known as the American Look. Key designers included Claire McCardell, Norman Norell, Anne Klein, Kaspar, and James Galanos. Fashion historians credit McCardell as a pioneer of the American Look. The key to ready-to-wear leisurewear design was consumer

The swirling colors and symbols on author Ken Kesey's famous painted bus, in which he and his Merry Pranksters toured, are emblematic of the hippie aesthetic that arose in the 1960s.

demand for casual looks that were comfortable, functional, and inexpensive without sacrificing style. Women's leisurewear included mix-and-match separates, golf and shirtwaist dresses, housecoats, jumpers, slacks, and dungarees. Pearls were the jewelry of choice, even for casual dressing. The exploding popularity of Bermuda shorts marked men's leisurewear of the 1950s. Men often topped them with "Aloha" shirts featuring Hawaiian-style prints during weekend barbeques and backyard gatherings. Casual shoe styles included sandals, sneakers, and loafers. The Preppy look also gained popularity and the Izod shirt with alligator logo became a status symbol in America.

Another fashion revolution of the 1950s and 1960s was the rise of fashion designed for children and adolescents. Adolescents became a major consumer force openly cultivated by designers and manufacturers. For many adolescents and young adults, fashion became a symbol through which to express rebellion against adult society and conventions. Fashion was a way to set oneself apart from the adult world and mainstream conventions. Beginning in the 1940s, teenaged fans of singer Frank Sinatra began wearing bobby sox under felt poodle skirts or pants with the cuffs rolled up. The short white ankle socks were named for the slang term for British police officers, and became popular beginning with the nylon shortage of World War II. Sweaters, ponytails, and saddle shoes or penny loafers completed the look.

Those young girls in relationships wore a boy's class ring around their neck, or fraternity pin on their sweater. Other movie or music stars that inspired 1950s and 1960s teen fashion include Elvis Presley, James Dean, the Beatles, and the Rolling Stones.

For many young people, dress became a symbol of nonconformity and a social protest statement. Many adolescents abandoned normal and traditional dress in favor of informal and often outlandish styles. Blue jeans became common. Rebellious fashions of the 1950s included the rock and roll or "greaser" look, featuring tight jeans, leather jackets, T-shirts with packs of cigarettes rolled in the cuffs, boots, sideburns, and long hair greased back into a ducktail hairstyle with Vaseline or hair gel. Beatniks expressed their contempt for mainstream society in part through their dress, most often featuring khaki pants, black sweaters, and sandals. The hippies of the 1960s counterculture wore tattered jeans, sandals, love beads, long hair and beards, long robes, peace symbols, and flowers. Feminists deliberately violated traditional standards of women's dress by not wearing bras, high heels, corsets, or makeup, and by not shaving their legs or underarms. Many of these protest fashions would be adopted into the mainstream culture in subsequent decades.

Shorter hemlines, bright colors, ethnic styles, an anything goes attitude, and revealing garments also characterized the fashion revolution of the 1960s. Public demand, rather than the guidance of top haute couture designers, became the key force in determining the direction of consumer fashion. Miniskirts, hot pants, bikinis, and other revealing articles of clothing began to appear more frequently. Other popular 1960s women's styles included peasant skirts, granny style dresses, bell-bottoms, t-shirts, shirtwaist dresses, chunky sweaters, turtlenecks, stilettos, and chunky platform shoes. Popular men's styles included plaid button-down shirts, double-breasted sports jackets, polyester pants suits, and wide, patterned ties. Unisex, androgynous styles and women wearing pants became more acceptable. Men wore longer hair, beards, and moustaches, while women wore bouffant styles or very short or long hair. 1960s clothing often featured a mix of bright colors, designs, and geometric patterns.

CONCLUSION

The youth-oriented 1960s fashion revolution, with its emphasis on consumer desires, would continue into the 1970s. Material culture from the late 1960s is strikingly different from the 1950s, but the differences belie the many links between the decades. While the fashions were mostly fleeting, some of the more lasting developments from both decades were a highly status-conscious consumerism and an attitude of rebellion, real or contrived, that became a recurrent motif in American arts and culture.

MARCELLA TREVINO

Further Readings

Brouws, Jeffrey T. *Readymades: American Roadside Artifacts*. San Francisco, CA: Chronicle Books, 2003.

Colomina, Beatriz, Annmarie Brennan, and Jeannie Kim. *Cold War Hothouses: Inventing Postwar Culture, From Cockpit to Playboy*. New York: Princeton Architectural Press, 2004.

Dubrow, Eileen. *Styles of American Furniture, 1860–1960*. Atglen, PA: Schiffer Publications, 2007.

Farrell-Beck, Jane and Jean Parsons. *Twentieth Century Dress in the United States*. New York: Fairchild, 2007.

Gould, Richard A. and Michael B. Schiffer. *Modern Material Culture: The Archaeology of Us*. New York: Academic Press, 1981.

Hall, Lee. *Common Threads: A Parade of American Clothing*. Boston, MA: Little, Brown, 1992.

Horn, Richard. *1950s Style Then and Now*. New York: Beech Tree, 1985.

Kuchler, Susanne and Daniel Miller. *Clothing as Material Culture*. New York: Berg Publishers, 2005.

LeBlanc, Sydney. *Twentieth Century American Architecture: 200 Key Buildings*. New York: Whitney Library of Design, 1993.

Martin, Richard and Harold Koda. *Jocks and Nerds: Men's Style in the Twentieth Century*. New York: Rizzoli, 1989.

Mayo, Edith. *American Material Culture: The Shape of Things Around Us*. Bowling Green, OH: Bowling Green State University Popular Press, 1984.

Schlereth, Thomas J. *Cultural History and Material Culture: Everyday Life, Landscapes, Museums*. Charlottesville, VA: University Press of Virginia, 1992.

Strasser, Susan, Charles McGovern, and Judy Matthias. *Getting and Spending: European and American Consumer Societies in the Twentieth Century*. New York: Cambridge University Press, 1998.

Susman, Warren I. *Culture as History: The Transformation of American Society in the Twentieth Century*. New York: Pantheon Books, 1984.

Welters, Linda and Patricia A. Cunningham, eds. *Twentieth Century American Fashion*. New York: Berg Publishers, 2005.

Chapter 4

Social Attitudes

"The life of the Negro is still sadly crippled by the manacles
of segregation and the chains of discrimination."
—Dr. Martin Luther King, Jr.

THE 1950s AND 1960s have been painted very simply in the American imagination: the 1950s were black-and-white, bland, conservative, and straight-laced; the 1960s were a tumultuous, psychedelic time of long hair, protests, and social upheaval. This caricature is not just an exaggeration—it is plainly incorrect. Not only were the 1950s the era of the Beat Generation and the start of the Civil Rights movement, but also the campus-based protest culture so associated in the popular mind with the 1960s did not become prevalent until the end of the decade, in part in response to the escalation of the Vietnam War. There is no doubt that these two decades were a turbulent time, but the positioning of each against the other is more a product of the contemporary "culture wars" that portray one decade as conservative, and the next as liberal.

Above all else, this was the age of the Cold War, which remained prominent in the public mind throughout the era, coloring everything from politics to science to the protest culture, as the seemingly irrelevant battleground of Vietnam was transformed into an epic and ongoing war—the longest in which the United States has been involved—because of the broader context of the "spread of Communism" and Cold War foreign policy. Americans enjoyed a higher quality of life than ever before, thanks to the G.I. Bill, the housing boom, the economic recovery brought about by World War II and the Cold

War, and other factors. But at the same time, a devastating war had just been fought, during which civilians on the home front had worried about enemy saboteurs and seemingly inevitable attacks on the American mainland. Volunteer lookouts were even posted in the Great Plains, dutifully watching skies that no enemy aircraft could possibly have reached. The end of World War II's Pacific theater, with the detonation of atomic bombs over Hiroshima and Nagasaki, seemed to foreshadow how much worse the next war would be—and while old imperial Europe was a thing of the past, the postwar world quickly fell into opposing capitalist and Communist camps. Americans wondered if the United Nations would be enough to prevent all-out World War III.

ANXIETY AND PARANOIA

Cold War anxieties inform not only the whole of the era, but the entire second half of the 20th century. They are at their purest, so to speak, their least complicated and most concentrated, in the 1950s and 1960s, when the bulk of the population remembered World War II and wrung their hands during the early days of the space race, and worried that the Soviet Union's successful launch of the Sputnik satellite could lead to space-based weaponry. While the general public may have supported the build-up of atomic weapons in response to the apparent Soviet threat, fears of radiation were obvious and widespread. Monster movies began to supplant the more traditional thrillers, with giant mutated bugs and other strange creatures that had resulted from contamination by radiation. By the early 1960s, radiation figured into the origins of most of the major Marvel Comics superheroes—Bruce Banner was turned into the Incredible Hulk at the test detonation of his new gamma bomb (a new nuclear weapon), the Fantastic Four developed their powers after exposure to radiation in space, Peter Parker was bitten by a radioactive spider, and the X-Men were mutants whose altered genes were thought to be the result of an increased amount of radiation in the world. It was truly the Atomic Age.

The feasibility of reaching space also awakened interest in the possibility of extraterrestrial life. UFO sightings—often the classic flying saucer or cigar types—skyrocketed in the decades after World War II, which may have been in part a result of government testing of various manned and unmanned aircraft, which certainly was rampant at the time. More and more movies and science fiction novels began to deal with alien encounters and "space invaders," and the aliens quite often resembled the popular idea of the Communist: little emotion, inscrutable, devoid of individuality, and a devotee of a strange alien culture.

McCARTHYISM

The most obvious and overt example of Cold War anxiety is McCarthyism, an umbrella term named for Senator Joseph McCarthy, who used his position

During the Cold War, Minuteman missiles were kept ready in silos like this one at the Ellsworth Air Force Base Delta Flight Launch Facility in South Dakota, which was built in 1961 and converted into the Minuteman Missile National Historic Site in 1999.

as senator to lead a vicious, paranoid, and unfounded witch hunting campaign seeking to root out Communists in the federal government and American military. The first "Red Scare" had occurred in the years after World War I, when Communism first became a serious force in world politics; labor unions, socialists, and others came under suspicion in an era when all Communists were assumed to be loyal to the Soviet Union (as, in a sense, many were—though that became less and less true fairly rapidly). The early 1950s saw fears of Soviet expansion rise sharply, when in the course of two years, the Soviets developed their first atomic bomb; the Communists took power in China; and U.S. State Department official Alger Hiss was found guilty of espionage for spying on behalf of the Soviets. Fears of Soviet activity seemed very reasonable.

However reasonable these fears were, they were co-opted by paranoiacs. McCarthy made a name for himself with his anti-Communism tirades, which were punctuated by claims he was never able to support, beginning most prominently in 1950 with what he claimed was a list of 205 employees of the State Department who were not only members of the Communist Party, but also known to be such by the Secretary of State. Both of these claims were wildly untrue, in fact so untrue that it is unlikely McCarthy had merely misunderstood the facts—if he was not consciously lying, he was certainly aware of his exaggeration and misrepresentation. But he succeeded in inflaming fears. By 1954 more than 100 investigations of potential communist activity had been carried out by the House Un-American Activities Committee (HUAC), which had originally been focused on the Ku Klux Klan and Nazi sympathizers, and by other congressional committees.

While anti-Communism had traditionally been a conservative Republican concern, as it mounted, liberals and Democrats faced accusations of being "soft on Communism," which in some districts could be as politically damaging as actually being a member of the Communist Party (which in truth had next to no political sway anyway). President Truman, a Democrat himself, called for a loyalty review of federal employees in order to weed out any Communist elements; Eisenhower strengthened the program when he took office in 1953, and some private industries soon followed. At the peak of anti-Communist panic in the 1950s, one in five American employees were subject to a loyalty review of some kind. Failure of such loyalty reviews made it difficult to find a new job, even with an employer who conducted no such reviews. Such failure often came about because of membership—or merely contact—with one of the groups on the Justice Department's list of suspect organizations (a third of which were not identified as Communist groups, simply groups that were guilty by association because Communists often joined them). Many Americans echoed the sentiments of actor Adolphe Menjou, who said that Communists should "go back to Russia" (never minding the fact that few of them had come from there).

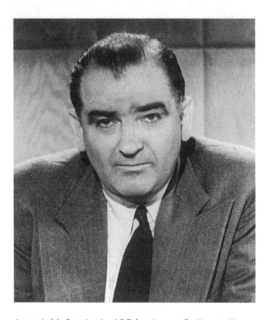

Joseph McCarthy in 1954, when a Gallup poll found that half the country felt there was some truth to his claims. His support soon evaporated.

THE HOLLYWOOD BLACKLIST

As a result of HUAC's investigation into the film industry, the Hollywood blacklist was established voluntarily by the movie studios. The Hollywood Ten—10 writers and directors charged with contempt of Congress for refusing to testify on the matter of Communism in Hollywood—had been fired in 1947, and lists continued to be compiled throughout the 1950s. Membership in the Communist Party or any other Communist group—even, in many cases, attending a single meeting—led to being blacklisted, meaning no Hollywood studio would hire you. Future president Ronald Reagan was among the actors who testified before HUAC, supporting their aims and condemning any of his colleagues who refused to "name names" and reveal those they knew to be Communists or Communist sympathizers. It is

This 1950 anti-communist booklet attacked 151 radio and television entertainers.

important to remember that these were legal organizations—such people were not accused of being spies, of working for foreign governments, or of working for the overthrow of the American government. They were plainly accused of having the wrong political beliefs, regardless of how they acted on them.

No one wanted to be accused of being "soft on Communism," because sympathizing with Communism was almost as bad as being a Communist—just as being a Communist was almost as bad as being a Soviet spy. That old American attitude wherein the slightest hint of an unwanted element taints the whole—one rotten spot spoiling the apple—had been revived. As with the part-Japanese American-born orphans who were interned in camps during World War II so that they could not collaborate with the enemy Japanese government, as with the Americans considered black because of "a drop of African blood" in their family tree, Communism was treated as something that could fully corrupt a person simply by attending a single meeting. The underlying fear in this paranoia is clear: only a very powerful belief system could be so persuasive, and ultimately when Americans feared Soviet might in space, Soviet power in nuclear weapons, they were also fearing the confusing and inexplicable popularity of Communism in other parts of the world—and the confidence Communist leaders had in their expectation that the rest of the world would soon be converted.

Many Americans believed—after the first few months—that McCarthy exaggerated his claims. But in a 1954 Gallup poll, half the country believed there was "no smoke without fire"—in other words, that the Senator was not manufacturing a problem, but was only overreacting to it. This belief has persisted among some factions of the far right in American politics, but it is important to note that this is not a political issue. Both Republicans and Democrats agree that it is a matter of fact that McCarthy was consistently wrong, lied outright to the media, and despite all his hearings and witch hunts, uncovered few Communists and no security breaches. Some 10,000 people lost their jobs, most of them in positions that would not have been security risks even if they had been Soviet spies. The Hollywood blacklist is one obvious example of hunting for witches in a place where they could have done little harm, but again it points to the idea of Communism as a force of seduction.

McCarthy's power waned quickly when he went after alleged Communists in the military. His hard-right support fell away, and he found the army an even less tractable target than the State Department had been. McCarthyist sentiments persisted—arguably through the 1980s in some respects, though they waned during the 1960s before flaring back up in the Reagan era. The Supreme Court in the late 1950s issued several decisions curtailing discrimination against those who had come, or could have come, under suspicion for various reasons, and in 1960, screenwriter Dalton Trumbo was the first of the Hollywood Ten to successfully return to work.

ATTACKING THE COLOR BAR

Almost from the beginning of America, one of its persistent realities had been racial discrimination. From outright slavery to segregation under the notorious Jim Crow laws, one of the fundamental assumptions of American society was the subordination of people of African ancestry. Harsh "one-drop" laws sought to prevent people of mixed race from securing the privileges reserved for white people on the basis of physical appearance.

In the aftermath of World War II those assumptions were beginning to lose their power. After having witnessed the horrors of the Holocaust firsthand, returning servicemen no longer found such things as segregated restrooms and drinking fountains to be background noise, an invisible part of daily life. However, after the titanic struggle against Naziism, the veterans just wanted to settle into civilian life, not fight a fresh war on the home front.

Still, the hypocrisy of condemning racial mass murder abroad while maintaining segregation at home was becoming insupportable. Even in the 1940s President Harry Truman abolished separate units for black soldiers over the objections of old-school generals, many of them Southern, who felt that integrating the armed forces would destroy discipline and diminish combat readiness. The next blow to legalized segregation came in 1954, when the Supreme Court struck down laws requiring that public schools be segregated.

However, Southern states, where most of the country's black population still lived even after the migrations to northern cities, fought desegregation with an astonishing ferocity. Only a months-long total boycott of buses in Montgomery, Alabama, won African Americans the right to sit in any seat they chose, beside whomever they chose. By 1960 the pressure to change was becoming strong enough to over-turn even the strongest of barri-ers. The younger generation was entering the fight; they no longer believed that waiting patiently was the solution. Such approach-es could only gain privileges, not the acknowledgement of inalien-able rights too long denied. At the same time they had no desire to ignite a second civil war or alien-ate the silent majority who were no longer comfortable about seg-regation but who did not want violent social upheaval disrupting their lives or prosperity.

Police carrying a young African-American demonstrator in Brooklyn, New York, in 1963.

These idealistic young people looked to the successes of Indian leaders such as Mohandas Gandhi against British rule using nonvio-lent confrontations to prick the consciences of the silent majority. Although Gandhi's methods were based upon Hindu concepts of *ahisma* or non-harm, the leaders of the Student Non-violent Coordinating Committee believed that the example of Dr. Martin Luther King, Jr. in the Montgomery bus boycott showed that Christian ideals of turning the other cheek could work just as ef-fectively to embarrass fence-sitters into insisting that changes be made.

Hundreds of idealistic young people went into Southern communities to integrate facilities such as buses and lunch counters. They braved the wrath of bigoted whites without an angry word, and the images of them being attacked by police dogs while offering no resistance flashed across televisions all over the nation and the world. While they provoked indignation among Northern liberals, they caused a loss of prestige in the eyes of foreigners confronted with undeniable evidence of the mismatch between word and deed in a nation that championed freedom abroad while suppressing it at home.

All those efforts were just a prologue for Freedom Summer, in which vol-unteers crisscrossed the South registering poor African Americans to vote. This time they encountered not just brutality, but murder. However, the effect was to give a voice to people who had been denied a part in the American political process since the end of Reconstruction.

THE COUNTERCULTURE
The American counterculture began to surface in the 1950s, and its birth is often attributed to the publication of Canadian-American writer Jack Kerouac's

The Town and the City (1951). Six years later in *On the Road,* Kerouac coined the term Beat Generation. This autobiographical novel told of an identity quest: "... all my New York friends were in the negative, nightmare position of putting down society and giving their tired bookish or political or psychoanalytical reasons ..." Stereotypically, members of the counterculture were identified by their love of all things bohemian, and many used drugs to release their "inner spirits." Another turning point in the rise of the counterculture came with Allen Ginsberg's reading of *Howl* at Six Gallery in San Francisco in 1955. Ginsberg opened the poem by proclaiming:

> *I saw the best minds of my generation destroyed by*
> *madness, starving hysterical naked,*
> *dragging themselves through the negro streets at dawn*
> *looking for an angry fix ...*

Members of the counterculture often blamed older generations for wars and destruction, and decried the use of the atomic bomb to end World War II. Even J. Robert Oppenheimer, the father of the bomb, quoted this line from the *Bhagavad Gita*: "I am become death, the destroyer of worlds." The reach of the counterculture expanded in the 1960s, as dissatisfaction with American society deepened. Vietnam War protestors chanted, "Hey, Hey, LBJ, how many kids have you killed today?" The Civil Rights movement, after gaining speed with the addition of contingents of black college students conducting nonviolent sit-ins, began to be co-opted by the Black Power movement, which viewed all whites as enemies. Women also joined the counterculture movement, fighting for political and social rights, which included the right to control their own reproductive lives.

Members of the counterculture were intent on breaking down all social barriers that interfered with their right to live their own lives. Swear words became part of everyday life. When a case begun in the 1960s reached the Supreme Court early in the following decade, Justice John Marshall upheld the use of the "F-word," noting that "one man's vulgarity is another's lyric" (*Cohen v. California*, 403, U.S. 15, 1971). Sex and violence became common fare in American films, and movies such

Allen Ginsberg (right) with fellow Beat Generation poet Gregory Corso.

as *Rebel without a Cause* (1955) and *The Wild One* (1953) personified youth rebellion. The counterculture also found its voice in rock and roll and folk music. In 1957 the singer Chuck Berry proclaimed, "Hail, hail, rock and roll. Deliver me from the days of old."

THE SEXUAL REVOLUTION AND SEXUAL EQUALITY

In the popular mind, the sexual revolution and women's liberation or feminism are linked. Certainly they had a relationship. Feminism encouraged women to pursue their own fulfillment, whether in a career or in the bedroom, while both movements appreciated the benefits of the birth control pill and more widespread use of condoms. Some of the groundwork for the sexual revolution was laid by science. Advances in contraception and the birth control pill would have led to social change no matter what climate into which they were introduced. But much of it was also laid by the Kinsey reports, the first of which—*Sexual Behavior of the Human Male*—had been released in the late 1940s, and the second of which covering the human female was issued in the early 1950s. The Kinsey reports, compiled from extensive survey data, revealed that a great deal of the sexual activity that Americans considered extremely rare was actually fairly common. Premarital sex was nearly universal among men and common among women, homosexual activity was far from rare, and a significant number of Americans reported enjoying biting and other light-pain activities.

Though they were not written with a general audience in mind and presented little narrative—simply the facts and findings of the surveys—the Kinsey reports were rampant bestsellers. Their success and the academic acclaim Kinsey enjoyed enabled William Howell Masters, a gynecologist at the Washington University Medical School in St. Louis, to get funding for sex research as well. Virginia Johnson, an entertainer with no academic degree, joined him in order to provide a female presence for their interviews. Masters and Johnson published their findings in 1966.

The birth control pill was introduced in the United States in 1960. Various state laws outlawed them (until 1965, when Connecticut's law, the last holdout, was reversed) or limited them to married women (until 1972), and the age of majority was still 21, which prevented most college-age women from getting a prescription; the age of parents signing a consent form for their daughters' birth control was yet years off. It would not be until the 1970s that the pill really became widespread. It did not matter; the country was not ready for

By 1966 six million American women were reported to be on the pill.

Divorce, American Style

As common as divorce is today, only a generation ago it was still rare and stigmatized, and a generation before that it could prove exceptionally difficult to get divorced, even if both people wanted to. Divorce was possible only by showing fault on the part of one spouse, usually one of the three As: abuse, adultery, or abandonment. Though a civil case, there is a reason we say that someone "sues for divorce"—one party had to show damages, little different in many respects from the way we handle a fender-bender. And just as, in a civil suit, one party can countersue the other in order to demonstrate that they have suffered damages themselves, in a divorce case the defendant could plead recrimination. A husband could argue that he had had an affair only because his wife cheated on him first or withheld sex. A wife could argue that she had had her affair only after being abandoned; and so on. In any case, it was not merely a matter of deciding whose fault it was—the judge could, and often did, rule that both parties were at fault, and refuse to grant them a divorce—almost like saying "the two of you deserve each other."

This led increasingly to spouses collaborating to lie in court in order to obtain a divorce they both wanted. In states where cruelty was an acceptable reason for divorce, wives would recite a litany of boilerplate acts of cruelty, claiming their husbands had sworn at them, called them names, perhaps hit them. It was more and more obvious that many of these cases of cruelty were manufactured, while others could have been prevented had the couple been granted a divorce before they had become so intolerable to one another. Lawyers, law professors, even judges began arguing that there should be some means of divorce when no party has done wrong, provided both parties want to end the relationship. It hardly sounds radical now, but in the 1960s the idea of the "no-fault divorce" was as controversial and divisive as gay marriage is now. In the eyes of many conservative commentators, it violated the sanctity of marriage to allow spouses to simply walk away.

Nevertheless, at the very end of the decade, California—often the first state to adopt a legal reform—instituted the no-fault divorce, signed into law on September 4, 1969, by Governor Ronald Reagan, the ultraconservative former Democrat and future Republican president who had himself been divorced following arguments over politics with his first wife. He met his second wife, Nancy Davis, when her name accidentally appeared on a Hollywood blacklist. Further adding to all this irony is the fact that the first no-fault divorce law was instituted by the Communist Bolsheviks as part of their first social reforms in Russia. The new law allowed divorce in the case of mutually acknowledged "irreconcilable differences" and the rest of the country followed over the next 15 years.

it anyway. The mere fact of the pill, its existence, gave the country a dozen years to get ready for it—to work up to the possibilities of more common premarital sex (and, especially, fewer marriages arranged because of an accidental pregnancy), and in general, sex between two people who had no desire to raise a family together. Of course, married parents benefited too, and family sizes have gradually decreased since the advent of the pill and other forms of contraception.

CENSORSHIP

In 1965, the obscenity case *Memoirs v. Massachusetts*, 383 U.S. 413, reached the Supreme Court. Publisher G.B. Putnam had two years earlier published an edition of John Cleland's 1748 novel *Fanny Hill*, which had previously been banned in the United States in the early 19th century. The novel is the first erotic novel in the English language, an account of the adventures of a teenage girl tricked into working at a brothel. The new edition was banned as well, and attorney Charles Rembar, who had previously won an obscenity case on behalf of the publisher of D.H. Lawrence's *Lady Chatterley's Lover*, appealed the case until it reached the Supreme Court, which ruled in Putnam's favor. Sexual content did not automatically constitute obscenity, the court declared. To be obscene, something had to be "patently offensive" and "utterly without redeeming social value," fairly vague descriptors which necessitated that the Court review a great many reputedly obscene books and movies on a case-by-case basis. But it opened the floodgates for a large amount of material to be printed in the United States that previously had been available only in Europe.

Marilyn Monroe in costume for the 1957 film The Prince and the Showgirl.

This also led to the gradual proliferation of pornographic magazines, but they remained an underground phenomenon. Some "men's interest" magazines, combining tasteful, casual-looking nude pictorials and pin-up shots with articles on cars, current issues, health, literature, and high-end audio equipment, were much more common—and thanks to Hugh Hefner, quickly mainstreamed. Hefner published the first issue of *Playboy* in 1953, featuring a nude pictorial of Marilyn Monroe, who had just had her first major feature starring role in the movie *Niagara*. The photos had been taken some years earlier and sold to Hefner, helping to sell the magazine out in a few weeks (most issues of most magazines never sell out at all). Monroe took it well, and when asked by reporters what she was wearing during the photo shoot, answered, "Chanel No. 5."

FREE LOVE

In hindsight, little is so associated with the sexual revolution as "free love," a phrase that has been widely misunderstood. The free love movement actually began in the 19th century, during the same wave of political and religious activity that led to the Progressive movement, the Social Gospel, and other shifts in social attitudes, though it enjoyed no mainstream participation in the United States. Free love thinkers, especially in those early years, advocated not promiscuity, but rather the abolition of marriage, which was seen as an antiquated social contract that restricted the rights and privileges of women both directly and indirectly (in its use as justification to restrict women's property and voting rights, for instance, as well as the inability of some districts to recognize spousal rape). The simplest form of free love philosophy is that romantic and sexual relationships should not be regulated by law. That would include not only marriage—a legal agreement—but laws against adultery, "sodomy" (which in many legal districts refers simply to "unlawful acts of sexual intercourse," covering a great many specifics), prostitution, and homosexuality. In modern parlance, free love movements can be said to support the right to sexual relationships that are "safe, sane, and consensual"—and so they still recognize the need for an age of consent and do not oppose long-term monogamous relationships, only laws governing or requiring them.

For feminists, the ideal of free love underscored the fact that a woman's body and sexuality was her own, that ownership of these things did not reside with a father to be passed on to a husband under the oversight of the state. For the writers and artists of the Beat Generation, free love meant freedom for homosexuality as well, and the cause was championed by William Burroughs and Allen Ginsberg. In the 1960s and especially the counterculture prevalent among young people at the end of the decade, the free love ideal represented a woman's freedom to pursue her own sexual pleasure, rather than defining her sexual identity as the provider of pleasure for her husband or boyfriend. Women enjoyed sex, Kinsey had affirmed. For most of American history they had been told that sexual pleasure was incidental, theirs most of all, but the young women who came of age in the 1960s rebelled against this, not in secret but vocally.

Free love remained principally the concern of the counterculture, but sexual liberation was a widespread phenomenon. Couples became gradually more open about their premarital relations, which in turn became less scandalous, especially among people under 30 or in the socially liberal bastions like California. "Living in sin" became more common, though as you can tell from the phrase, mainstream America did not exactly approve of unmarried couples living together. At the same time, married couples became more experimental in their sex lives, and while this was treated discreetly, there was less shame and sinfulness attached to it.

FEMINISM

Meanwhile, in the years leading up to that countercultural explosion, Betty Friedan published her book *The Feminine Mystique* in 1963. She had written the book after all the major women's magazines turned down her article about the dissatisfaction of the women at her 15-year college reunion, their feelings of isolation and envy of their husbands for having a work and social life out-side of the home; the magazines found it unbelievable or indefensible. Before World War II women's magazines had prominently focused on career women, but since then they had focused on the image of women as homemakers and mothers. Women were bristling under that harness, Friedan wrote, and—as with the findings of Kinsey and Masters and Johnson—they were not talking to each other enough to realize that they were not alone in their resentment.

Friedan helped draw attention to the circumstances of women, which prompted the President's Commission on the Status of Women, which is-sued a report in 1965 revealing a declining number of women in professional and executive jobs, as well as the fact that women earned on average half as much as men holding the same job. The National Organization for Women (NOW) was founded the following year at a meeting of the Commis-sion, with Friedan as its first presi-dent. She wrote the first draft of NOW's statement of purpose on a napkin at the conference:

To take action to bring women into full participation in the main-stream of American society now, exercising all the privileges and re-sponsibilities thereof in equal part-nership with men.

The organization's acronym was not accidental—equality was some-thing to be brought into being ac-tively, not merely hoped for or voted on. NOW worked to petition the government to act against gender

Betty Friedan, the influential feminist and first president of NOW, in 1960.

discrimination in hiring and payroll practices, and spent much of the next decade supporting the Equal Rights Amendment. With the passage of time, they have also focused on reproductive rights and domestic violence, and have joined other organizations in the fight against racism and homophobia.

CONCLUSION

The 1950s and 1960s brought Americans both the shining new houses of the suburbs and the fallout shelters in their backyards. Children emulated fearless superheroes and new astronauts, but also learned to "duck and cover" during civil defense drills in preparation for nuclear attack. For an era born in so much Cold War paranoia, positive social change in the form of growing gender and racial equality was an unexpected but welcome result for many. While McCarthyism in its most extreme form was short-lived, similar tendencies lie dormant in American culture, resurfacing in times of threat or trauma.

BILL KTE'PI
ELIZABETH R. PURDY

Further Readings

Best, Gary. *The Retreat from Liberalism*. New York: Praeger, 2002.

Caute, David. *The Great Fear*. New York: Simon and Schuster, 1978.

Doherty, Thomas. *Cold War, Cool Medium*. New York: Columbia University Press, 2003.

Fried, Albert. *McCarthyism*. Oxford: Oxford University Press, 1997.

Fried, Richard. *Nightmare in Red*. Oxford: Oxford University Press, 1990.

Friedan, Betty. *The Feminine Mystique*. New York: W.W. Norton & Company, 2001.

Gair, Christopher. *The American Counterculture*. Edinburgh: Edinburg University Press, 2007.

Ginsberg, Allen. *Howl and Other Poems*. San Francisco, CA: City Lights Books, 1959.

Goffman, Ken and Dan Joy. *Counterculture through the Ages: From Abraham to Acid House*. New York: Villard, 2004.

Haynes, John. *Red Scare or Red Menace?* Chicago, IL: Ivan R. Dee, 1996.

Jong, Erica. *Fear of Flying*. New York: Holt, Rinehart and Winston, 1973.

Lytle, Mark Hamilton. *America's Uncivil Wars: The Sixties Era from Elvis to the Fall of Richard Nixon*. New York: Oxford University Press, 2006.

Navasky, Victor. *Naming Names*. New York: Hill and Wang, 2003.

Skolnick, Jerome H. *The Politics of Protest*. New York: Ballantine Books, 1996.

Chapter 5

Cities and Urban Life

*"Suburbia is where the developer bulldozes out the trees,
then names the streets after them."*
—Bill Vaughn

A NUMBER OF factors altered the characteristics of cities and urban life in the United States during the 1950s and 1960s. The postindustrial city experienced new patterns of growth and development. The stark, modern glass-and-steel skyscrapers that had come to dominate the urban skyline were joined by the appearance of postmodern buildings with more emphasis on history, the environment, and decorative stylistic elements. The growth of automobile ownership, development of the interstate highway system, and the "American Dream" of single-family home ownership expanded cities outward and fostered suburban sprawl. The growth of largely white, middle-class suburbs, in turn, led to declining inner-city tax bases, the changing racial and class compositions of inner-city neighborhoods, and the process of urban decay. Social protest movements such as the counterculture, anti–Vietnam War, and Civil Rights movements all contained urban elements. The rise of the Sunbelt cities of the Southern and Western United States shifted the urban population from older industrial Northeastern and Midwestern cities, although New York–Northern New Jersey, Chicago–Northwestern Illinois, Philadelphia, and Detroit remained four of the five largest urban areas according to the 1960 U.S. Census.

The Sunbelt gained widespread attention in the 1960s with the rapid growth of cities like Los Angeles, Phoenix, Houston, Dallas, Atlanta, and Miami. Sunbelt cities attracted residents and workers because of the concentration of key growth industries such as defense, aerospace, and information technology in those areas, and the growth of a leisure economy based on tourism and its concomitant service-based industries that required many workers. Los Angeles–Long Beach had become one of the top five urban areas according to the 1960 U.S. Census. The popularity of Sunbelt cities was further enhanced by the introduction of affordable central air conditioning in many businesses and residences. Air conditioning changed the daily life of urban and suburban areas, as people no longer had to head outside on hot evenings and could find comfort inside even in the heat of the day. Americans' growing reliance on air conditioning and its beneficial health impacts could be seen by the death tolls among those without it during periodic heat waves. Meanwhile, older industrial cities like Detroit were losing jobs.

THE DEVELOPMENT OF URBAN SPRAWL

The traditional industrial American city pattern, featuring a core of business, financial, and working-class residential districts, began to shift in the post-industrial 1950s and 1960s. The post–World War II American Dream centered on the nuclear family and the ownership of a single-family home with a white picket fence, green lawn, and garage. This desire heightened the exodus of middle-class urban residents to the rapidly expanding suburbs, as they sought to

Split-level homes like this one were a variation on the one-floor ranch home that became common in the 1960s.

escape from the problems of inner-city life in a process known as urban (or white) flight. The automobile and interstate highway system, and the aid of federal government programs such as the G.I. Bill of Rights, made it possible for the upper and middle classes to escape the overcrowding, pollution, and crime of the inner cities. At the same time, urban flight reduced the tax bases of inner-city neighborhoods with the loss of higher-income residents, which negatively impacted the funding available for public schools and municipal services, and exacerbated the very problems suburban residents sought to escape.

Urban (or suburban) sprawl describes the effects of the automobile on the outward growth of cities and their rapidly developing suburbs. The federal Highway Act of 1956 launched the creation of the interstate highway system linking major cities with each other and with outlying residential areas. "Edge cities," new municipalities on the outskirts of existing metropolitan areas, rapidly multiplied in the 1950s and 1960s. Suburban developments featured low-density land use, a prevalence of single-family homes with large lot sizes, lawns, and garages, rather than the apartment buildings prevalent in urban residential areas. Suburban residents depended on their automobiles to commute to work, strip malls and shopping centers, fast food chains and restaurants, and recreational activities.

Many suburban dwellers exhibited an anti-urban attitude, claiming that suburban life provided benefits such as lower population densities, lower crime rates and noise levels, increased privacy, better schools and municipal services, and a slower-paced, less stressful lifestyle than that found in urban areas. Critics argued that sprawl resulted in the loss of green spaces as more and more land was developed. Sprawl also increased pollution and traffic deaths from the rise in automobile use, contributed to the decline of interaction with one's neighbors and resulting social isolation, and increased infrastructural costs of providing basic services such as public transportation, water, sewage treatment, and electricity.

URBAN DECAY

Suburban advocates, on the other hand, emphasized the problems of life in inner-city neighborhoods suffering from the process termed *urban decay*. During the spread of drug use and the growing "war on drugs," the popular stereotypes of drug users and dealers centered on urban ghettos and youth gangs, even as the 1960s counterculture helped spread drug use to the suburbs and rural areas. In addition to the illicit drug trade, urban gangs were linked to graffiti, gang wars, urban violence, and rising crime rates. They painted a negative portrait of inner cities plagued by broken families, high unemployment, generations of poverty, and blighted communities that offered their residents nothing but despair. Slumlords charged high rates for apartments that were often dilapidated, and repairs and insect or rodent infestations went unfixed, while public housing projects were not much better. The growing

The Failure of High-Rise Public Housing

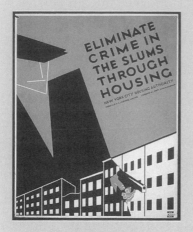

This poster advocated replacing tenements with new housing projects to reduce crime.

During the height of the African-American exodus to the northern cities, policy makers were confronted with the problem of how to house all these people at a reasonable standard of living. Traditionally black neighborhoods in cities such as Chicago were rapidly turning into overcrowded slums, and even as white flight made additional neighborhoods available to the internal immigration, African Americans rarely got to enjoy the same standard of living, since rental agents would often cut the large houses up into tiny "kitchenette" apartments.

Hoping to break the cycle of deterioration of neighborhoods into slums, officials in several Northern cities drew upon federal urban renewal funds to clear the worst slums and build new, clean, and sanitary housing for the poor. The choice of high-rise apartment buildings for these housing units was partly the result of the high cost of land, particularly in Chicago. However, the 1950s and early 1960s, when high-rise apartment complexes such as the Robert Taylor Homes, the Ida B. Wells Homes, and the Cabrini-Green Homes were built, were a time when technology was equated with progress, and the skyscraper was seen as one of the symbols of American technological progress.

In theory, potential residents of the high-rise public housing complexes were to be carefully screened in order to exclude potential troublemakers. In practice, the sheer number of units to be filled overwhelmed social workers associated with the Chicago Housing Authority, and increasing pressure from civil rights activists made it progressively more difficult to exclude applicants on the basis of marital status and other "moral" grounds. As a result, conditions within what had originally been showpieces quickly deteriorated. In the absence of the authority of stable adult males, street gangs soon took over, using various methods of intimidation to break down what authority could be exerted by single mothers. Gang activity led maintenance people to become afraid to enter the area, with the result that vandalism and breakdowns went untended, leading to further deterioration as it became obvious that no one in authority cared. By the end of the 20th century, high-rise apartment complexes were being condemned as "warehouses for people" that encouraged depersonalization of inhabitants by their structural features. In several Chicago housing complexes, the high-rises were being demolished and replaced by smaller four- and five-floor buildings.

multitudes of homeless men, women, and families were forced to frequent shelters, panhandle, or sleep in cars or on streets or park benches.

Urban supporters countered that suburban dwellers missed out on the vibrancy of inner-city, mixed-use neighborhoods, with their multicultural-ism, active lifestyle, and close proximity to a wide variety of social, recre-ational, and dining activities. Large cities often provided various forms of public transportation for those areas not within walking distance. They also emphasized the benefits of more social interaction with neighbors and ac-quaintances, or "social capital," due to the emphasis on walking, and habits like sitting outside on the porch steps during hot summer evenings. They also noted that cities have a sense of history often lacking in the newer and more homogenous suburbs. Immigrant neighborhoods such as San Francis-co's Chinatown or Baltimore's Little Italy provided urban character, added to the diversity of urban life, and served as tourist attractions. The problems of urban decay were the result of conditions that could and should be fixed, such as racism, political disenfranchisement, and the lack of economic and educational opportunities.

CITIES AND SOCIAL UNREST

The social protest movements of the 1950s and especially the 1960s impacted urban life. In the 1950s, the Beats criticized mainstream American society from the cafes of city neighborhoods such as Greenwich Village in New York City. Members of the Hippie counterculture populated the Haight-Ashbury district in San Francisco. Anti–Vietnam War protests broke out on urban as well as rural college campuses. Americans watched on national television as protesters violently clashed with police officers on the streets outside the 1968 Democratic National Convention in Chicago. Some of the most visible Civil Rights movement struggles occurred in cities such as Little Rock, Arkansas; Greensboro, North Carolina; Montgomery and Birmingham, Alabama; and Memphis, Tennessee.

An urban branch of the Civil Rights movement became especially prev-alent in the mid to late 1960s, sparked by urban African-American leaders frustrated by the slow pace of change, continued discrimination, and the im-poverishment of inner-city neighborhoods. The practice of redlining, denying loans to certain categories of potential homeowners, had legally helped create segregated residential and business districts throughout much of the 1950s and 1960s. Militant African-American activists such as Malcolm X felt that minorities would never receive fair treatment from white-controlled institu-tions and advocated that African-American leaders find ways to take control of their own neighborhoods and future.

Throughout the mid- to late-1960s, race riots occurred in numerous cit-ies across the United States as minority inner-city residents reacted to the frustration over persistent racial inequality and the slow pace of change in

The Watts Riot

The Watts riot was one of the first major race riots of the 1960s. It began with the August 11, 1965, arrest of 21-year-old African-American motorist Marquette Frye by California Highway Patrolman Lee W. Minikus, a Caucasian, for suspected intoxication (drunk driving) near Watts, a mostly African-American neighborhood in South Central Los Angeles. Frye was arrested after failing a standard sobriety test. Frye's brother Ronald was a passenger in the car. The Fryes lived a short distance from the location and their mother soon arrived on the scene. Many residents were outdoors due to the warm weather generated by a heat wave, and a crowd quickly gathered at the scene. Minikus had called in backup when placing Frye under arrest, and additional Los Angeles police were called to the scene when Frye began resisting arrest. The crowd became increasingly hostile, and some eyewitnesses later claimed that one of the officers had used his police baton to strike members of the crowd. There were also accounts that officers were spat on and a police car was stoned as they were leaving the scene. Rumors quickly began spreading through the neighborhood, heightening pre-existing racial tensions.

That evening, crowds continued to stone cars, beat white motorists driving through the area, and loot and burn local stores. Police established a field command post in the area, and over 20 people were arrested during the first evening of the riots. Governor Edmund "Pat" Brown was out of the country at the time, so Lieutenant Governor Glenn Anderson took charge of the situation. Brown would return to California by Saturday, but his political career was damaged by the riots, and he lost his subsequent re-election bid to upcoming challenger Ronald Reagan.

The next day the Los Angeles County Human Relations Commission called a meeting attended by neighborhood groups, local African-American leaders, elected officials, and members of the Los Angeles Police Department. The meeting failed to restore order, however, and police established a perimeter around the riot-stricken area in an attempt to keep the trouble from spreading. The California National Guard was placed on alert, and an Emergency Control Center at Police Headquarters was established. The National Guard troops were called to action on Friday, August 13, which proved to be the most intense night of rioting. On Saturday, August 14, an 8:00 P.M. curfew was imposed in the riot area. It would be lifted the following Tuesday. In total, the rioting lasted five days and spread to nearby areas such as San Diego, Pasadena, Pacoima, Monrovia, Long Beach, and San Pedro–Wilmington. An estimated 35,000 people participated in the riots and thousands were arrested, most for theft and burglary. Thirty-four people were killed, including 25 African Americans, over 1,000 were wounded, and more than 600 buildings were damaged or destroyed for a total of over $40 million in property damage. The riots resulted in lasting anger, fear, and tensions.

Soldiers watch the street in front of smoldering ruins in Washington, D.C., on April 8, 1968, after the riots incited by the assassination of Martin Luther King, Jr.

response to the Civil Rights movement. Other areas of frustration included perceived abuse and discrimination by police officers, a lack of affordable housing and equal housing opportunities, high rates of unemployment and poverty, lack of political representation, and opposition to the Vietnam War. In 1962 President John F. Kennedy sent troops to quell riots that began after the court-ordered admission of African-American student James Meredith to the University of Mississippi. The 1965 Watts Riot in Los Angeles resulted in 34 deaths and millions of dollars in property damage. 1967 was a key year, with the country enduring over 30 race riots and many lesser incidents.

Two of the most serious riots that year took place in Newark, New Jersey, and Detroit, Michigan. Both cities called in National Guard troops to help local police departments stop the violence, looting, and fires. In Newark, over 20 people were killed, with thousands more injured and arrested. In Detroit, over 40 people were killed, with thousands more injured and arrested. In both cities, thousands of buildings were destroyed, resulting in millions of dollars in property damages. Other noted riots included the 1964 riots in Harlem and in Rochester, New York, and the riots in 125 cities after the April 4, 1968, assassination of Martin Luther King, Jr. in Memphis, Tennessee. The Washington, D.C., riots following the King assassination resulted in the closing of routes to and from the city, and the stationing of armed guards in front of the Capitol.

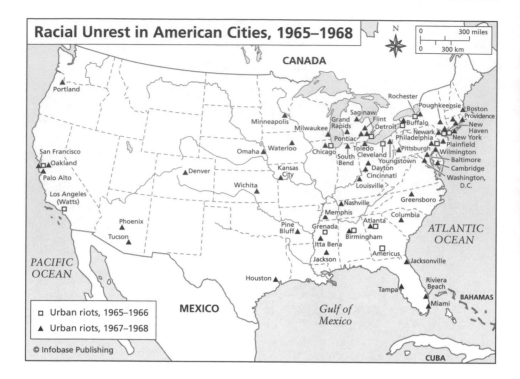

Racial Unrest in American Cities, 1965–1968

Militant Civil Rights leaders such as Stokely Carmichael and Floyd McKissick of the Congress of Racial Equality (CORE), and Huey Newton and Bobby Seale of the Black Panthers, endorsed the riots as part of a needed violent revolution in response to the perceived failures of the earlier Civil Rights movement, with its emphasis on nonviolent civil disobedience and interracial cooperation. Some people argued that race riots confirmed the fears of the violent nature of inner-city minorities, while others argued that they were understandable responses to centuries of racism and discrimination.

In 1967 President Lyndon Johnson formed the National Advisory Committee on Civil Disorders headed by Illinois Governor Otto Kerner, also known as the Kerner Commission, to investigate the causes of the race riots that had broken out across the country in that year and solutions to prevent future riots. The Kerner Commission issued a 1968 report, commonly known as the Kerner Report, whose most well-known conclusion stated that the United States was separating into two unequal societies along racial lines, and that white institutions were responsible for creating, maintaining, and condoning urban ghettoes. The federal government officially recognized the existence of racism and the damage it was inflicting on American society. Among the commission's recommended changes were the creation of new jobs and housing, a change in the settlement patterns of urban neighborhoods, an end to de-facto (customary) segregation, and improvements in minority education

"The Cycle of Despair: The Negro and the City"

John W. Gardner, the former secretary of health, education, and welfare, contributed the following to the March 8, 1968, issue of *Life* magazine as part of a special report titled "The Cycle of Despair: the Negro and the City."

The comfortable American does not enjoy thinking about the human misery festering at the other end of town. He does not enjoy knowing that many of his fellow citizens live in conditions that breed every variety of social evil. It is not easy for him to acknowledge that his own infant, dropped into that ruinous environment, would just as surely fall victim to it....

In the absence of medical attention, physical deficiencies that could be corrected early become lifelong handicaps. In the absence of early mental stimulation, minds that could be awakened settle into lifelong dullness. Crime, drugs, prostitution claim their victims. So do apathy, degradation, and despair. Ultimately, all Americans bear the cost....

What can save us is, first of all, a great effort on the part of white Americans to understand and extend a hand across the gulf of fear and anger. They must make a full commitment to right injustices and build a better future. What is also needed is a recognition on the part of the Negro community that the better future cannot be built instantly. The wrongs of centuries cannot be righted in a day or a year. But a common commitment to act now can create the climate in which solutions are possible.

We must begin with a massive resolve on the part of the great, politically moderate majority of whites and blacks—to transform destructive emotion into constructive action. The time has come when the full weight of community opinion, white and Negro, should be felt against those within their own ranks who hate and destroy....

We cannot have two nations, one white and one black. Every time we salute the flag we pledge allegiance to "one nation indivisible."

One nation indivisible it must remain.

and economic opportunities. The Voting Rights Act of 1965 helped by registering thousands of minority voters, who helped elect African-American mayors in a number of cities.

GOVERNMENTAL RESPONSE TO URBAN FLIGHT AND DECAY

The federal government passed new housing legislation to aid inner-city residents in response to the processes of urban flight, social unrest, and urban decay that had begun in earnest in the post–World War II period. Earlier efforts had occurred mostly at the state and local levels. The federal Housing Acts of 1949 and 1954 and subsequent amendments provided guidelines

Construction of Boston's 1969 Government Center, a federally aided urban renewal project, eliminated most of the old neighborhood of Scollay Square, with its smaller-scale housing, in favor of monumental buildings and vast concrete plazas.

and federal resources to begin the sometimes-controversial process of urban renewal. The Housing Act of 1949 was the first major federal response to urban flight and the deterioration of inner cities. Title I created the Urban Renewal Authority and provided federal loans and grants for the clearance and redevelopment of slum areas. The authority approved redevelopment plans and monitored their implementation. The act's overall goal was to attract private investors willing to redevelop blighted urban areas by providing them with public assistance. Redeveloped sites had to be primarily residential either before or after development, meaning that many areas either targeted for redevelopment or removed for the construction of freeways were areas of low-cost housing. Cities' power of eminent domain, the ability to seize property for public purposes, was expanded.

The federal government passed various adaptations and amendments during the next several decades in response to criticisms of the more controversial aspects of urban renewal. Many residents were forced to relocate from areas targeted for redevelopment, and the lost low-income housing was often replaced with luxury high rise apartments, retail centers, parks, or office buildings, resulting in an overall loss of low-income housing and overcrowding in other areas. Critics noted that low-income and minority residents were most affected by the changes because they formed the bulk of the displaced populations, often referring to urban renewal as "negro removal." Other critics noted that urban renewal often resulted in the loss of the vibrant, mixed-use neighborhoods that had characterized inner-city life. Amendments under the Housing Act of 1954 sought to shift the focus of urban renewal from wholesale slum clearance and demolition to the conservation and rehabilitation of such

The War on Poverty and Urban Renewal

The War on Poverty was part of President Lyndon Johnson's domestic agenda known as the Great Society. Johnson sought to empower poor communities to aid themselves and break the cycle of poverty by making federal resources available through a variety of programs. Head Start sought to improve poor and minority education through federally funded programs that would provide preschool aged children with nutritious meals and an educational foundation.

The Job Corps provided job skills training to help the poor and minorities have access to higher-paying careers. The Demonstration Cities and Metropolitan Development Act of 1966 created the Model Cities Program, providing additional sources of federal aid to urban areas. The Office of Economic Opportunity (OEO) administered many of these programs created under the War on Poverty. President Richard Nixon would later end the OEO in 1973, transferring many of its programs to other federal agencies. The War on Poverty and urban renewal were linked to the Civil Rights movement that increasingly affected urban areas in the mid to late 1960s. Cities across the country created Community Action Agencies (CAAs) under the Economic Opportunity Act of 1964.

These nonprofit private and public organizations offered a variety of programs and services to poor urban residents. African-American activists in urban areas saw the Community Action Program as a tool by which they could help gain control of their own communities, as Malcolm X had stated, by taking a leading role in the CAAs and other War on Poverty programs. African-American participation in War on Poverty programs also provided lasting political experience that aided future political leaders such as mayors and congressmen.

areas instead. An emphasis on social services and community participation was also added. The program also expended to include nonresidential urban renewal. For example, many cities rehabilitated central business districts and downtown areas to attract the middle class and tourists back to cities. The Housing Act of 1956 sought to extend special protection to the elderly, and to provide financial relocation assistance to displaced residents.

Federal legislation was further expanded in the 1960s in response to the growing Civil Rights movement and President Lyndon Johnson's Great Society Programs, including the War on Poverty. In 1965 the older Housing and Home Finance Agency (HHFA) was replaced with the new Cabinet-level Department of Housing and Urban Development (HUD). Title VII of the Civil Rights Act of 1968 and the Fair Housing Act sought to ensure equality of opportunity in housing, outlawing redlining and other methods of housing discrimination. War on Poverty programs designed to empower poor communities to help themselves with the aid of federal resources included the Office of Economic Opportunity (OEO), Head Start, the Job Corps, the Model Cities Program, the Community Action Program, and the Economic Opportunity Act of 1964. Other relevant legislation included the Demonstration Cities and Metropolitan Development Act of 1966; the Housing and Urban Development Act of 1968, which created the Neighborhood Development Program; and the Uniform Relocation Assistance and Real Property Acquisition Policies Act of 1970.

CONCLUSION

Changes in cities begun in the 1950s and 1960s set in motion processes of decay, renewal, and gentrification that are still at work in many urban neighborhoods. Urban renewal legislation would continue to undergo modification in the late 20th century, most notably with the development of the long-lasting Community Development Block Grant program in 1974. Urban renewal also fostered gentrification, which is characterized by the renovation of older residential and business districts, the conversion of warehouses into popular residential spaces, and the return of middle-class residents to inner-city neighborhoods. Many of these returning residents would add another facet to the diversity of city life, as they were often young and either single or childless married couples.

Another significant change in city life has stemmed from the return of immigrants in large numbers that began in the late 1960s. Immigration had slowed after the immigration quotas of the 1920s, but urban immigrant populations once again began to climb after the Immigration and Nationality Act of 1965 eased restrictions. These immigrants added another dimension to urban neighborhoods, at times living beside both the returning middle-class residents, and the long-time residents most affected by gentrification.

MARCELLA TREVINO

Further Readings

Bartlett, Randall. *The Crisis of America's Cities*. Armonk, NY: M.E. Sharpe, 1998.

Bernard, R. *Snowbelt Cities: Metropolitan Politics in the Northeast and Midwest Since World War II*. Bloomington, IN. Indiana University Press, 1990.

Findlay, John M. *Magic Lands: Western Cityscapes and American Culture After 1940*. Berkeley, CA: University of California Press, 1992.

Fox, Kenneth. *Metropolitan America: Urban Life and Urban Policy in the United States, 1940–1980*. Piscataway, NJ: Rutgers University Press, 1990.

Goings, K.W. and R.A. Mohl, eds. *The New African-American Urban History*. Thousand Oaks, CA: Sage, 1996.

Greenstone, J.D. and P. Peterson. *Race and Authority in Urban Politics: Community Participation and the War on Poverty*. Chicago, IL: University of Chicago Press, 1976.

Hayden, Dolores. *Building Suburbia: Green Fields and Urban Growth, 1820–2000*. New York: Pantheon Books, 2003.

Isenberg, Alison. *Downtown America: A History of the Place and the People Who Made It*. Chicago, IL: University of Chicago Press, 2004.

Jackson, Kenneth T. *Crabgrass Frontier: The Suburbanization of the United States*. New York: Oxford University Press, 1985.

Jacobs, B. *The Political Economy of Organizational Change: Urban Institutional Response to the War on Poverty*. New York: Academic Press, 1981.

Katz, Michael B. *The "Underclass Debate": Views From History*. Princeton, NJ: Princeton University Press, 1993.

Melosi, M.V. *The Sanitary City: Urban Infrastructure In America From Colonial Times to the Present*. Baltimore, MD: Johns Hopkins University Press, 2000.

Mohl, Raymond A. *The Making of Urban America*. 2nd ed. Wilmington, DE: Scholarly Resources, 1997.

Monkkonen, E.H. *America Becomes Urban: The Development of U.S. Cities and Towns, 1780–1980*. Berkeley, CA: University of California Press, 1988.

Monti, Daniel J. *The American City: A Social and Cultural History*. Malden, MA: Blackwell, 1999.

Trotter, J.W., E. Lewis, and T.W. Hunter, eds. *The African-American Urban Experience: Perspectives From the Colonial Period to the Present*. New York: Palgrave Macmillan, 2004.

Von Hoffman, A. *House by House, Block by Block: The Rebirth of America's Neighborhoods*. New York: Oxford University Press, 2003.

Wright, G. *Building the Dream: A Social History of Housing in America*. Cambridge, MA: MIT Press, 1983.

Chapter 6

Rural Life

"Ironically, rural America has become viewed by a growing number of Americans as having a higher quality of life . . . because of what it does not have!"
—Don A. Dillman

LIFE IN RURAL areas in the postwar years varied from extremes of isolation, deprivation, and discrimination to the purposeful retreat of urban idealists to the countryside. Continuing a trend from previous decades, technology such as the radio and telephone and utilities such as electricity and indoor plumbing reached even further into rural areas, changing and usually improving the lives of residents. While some rural women's roles remained traditional, appliances had the potential to reduce their work loads, and a growing move toward employment off the family farm opened up new possibilities. While many of these improvements in rural areas were of little help for those who did not own farms, such as Mexican migrant laborers or African-American sharecroppers, other developments, such as the farm labor movement and the Civil Rights movement, held out some hope of alleviating rural poverty for them as well.

ELECTRIFICATION
Electricity shaped rural life in the 1950s and 1960s to a degree that it had not in earlier years. In the early decades of the 20th century only a minority of rural homes had electricity, in contrast to the cities where electricity had spread rapidly early in the century. Congress had created the Rural Electrification Administration (REA), a New Deal agency, in 1935 to accelerate the spread

Farmers often banded together in nonprofit cooperatives to buy electrical service. These meters at the U.S. Rural Electrification Administration cooperative headquarters in Hayti, Missouri, were being prepared for distribution to members of farm cooperatives in July 1942.

of electricity in the countryside. The REA made rapid progress after World War II so that in 1954 93 percent of rural homes had electricity. By 1956, the last year for which the REA kept records, 96 percent of rural homes had electricity. Remote areas in the West, including some parts of Native American reservations, still lacked electricity.

Those rural homes with electricity got it from power stations. Typically these stations converted mechanical energy into electricity via a generator. These stations produced an alternating current of electricity. Insulated copper wires carried a current from a power station to rural homes. Transformers reduced the high voltage in a line before electricity came into the home. Electricity powered lights, appliances, and gadgets of various kinds. Rural homes varied in their use of appliances. By tradition the husband decided how to spend the family's money. The wife, however, even when she did not have her own income, might have prevailed upon her husband to buy a washing machine or a dishwasher.

Women were not alone in wanting electric appliances to lighten the burden of housework. In an effort to encourage the purchase of appliances, and more generally to encourage the use of electricity, the REA publicized the names of rural people who bought electric appliances and who had used the most electricity in a month. In the halcyon days when energy was cheap and seemed

"Our Example Will Make Them Free": The Grape Boycott

The Delano, California, grape pickers' strike began in September 1965 and lasted for several years. In 1969 the Agricultural Workers Organizing Committee and the National Farm Workers' Union, the unions sponsoring the strike, called for a national boycott of grapes in their International Boycott Day Proclamation (excerpted from the April 15, 1969, *El Malcriado*).

We, the striking grape workers of California, join on this International Boycott Day with the consumers across the continent in planning the steps that lie ahead on the road to our liberation . . . We have been farm workers for hundreds of years and pioneers for seven. Mexicans, Filipinos, Africans, and others, our ancestors were among those who founded this land and tamed its natural wilderness . . . If this road we chart leads to the rights and reforms we demand, if it leads to just wages, humane working conditions, protection from the misuse of pesticides, and to the fundamental right of collective bargaining, if it changes the social order that relegates us to the bottom reaches of society, then in our wake will follow thousands of American farm workers. Our example will make them free. But if our road does not bring us to victory and social change, it will not be because our direction is mistaken or our resolve too weak, but only because our bodies are mortal and our journey hard. For we are in the midst of a great social movement, and we will not stop struggling 'till we die, or win! . . .

We marched alone at the beginning, but today we count men of all creeds, nationalities, and occupations in our number. Between us and the justice we seek now stand the large and powerful grocers who, in continuing to buy table grapes, betray the boycott their own customers have built . . .

Grapes must remain an unenjoyed luxury for all as long as the barest human needs and basic human rights are still luxuries for farm workers. The grapes grow sweet and heavy on the vines, but they will have to wait while we reach out first for our freedom. The time is ripe for our liberation.

A Mexican migrant picking tomatoes in Santa Clara Valley, California.

A promotional photo from the Rural Electrification Administration depicts a young farm woman mending clothes with an electric sewing machine.

inexhaustible, the REA gave no thought to conservation. In 1953 the Socorro Electric Cooperative in New Mexico adopted the slogan "use more electricity." The REA was eager to demonstrate the utility of electric appliances. At a county fair in North Carolina a woman employed by the REA demonstrated the ease of using an electric range and oven to bake cakes, pies, and cookies. REA field representatives crisscrossed the countryside, making house calls. They carried 100-watt light bulbs and, whenever they found a 60-watt bulb in a house, they replaced it with a 100-watt bulb, showing a housewife how much better she could illuminate the home with extra wattage. Schools that lit their rooms with electric lights transfixed students. Those who had never seen an electric light begged their teacher to keep the lights on all day.

The adoption of electric appliances varied by geography. Rural people in the South bought more refrigerators than washing machines, whereas those in the North bought more washing machines than refrigerators. Everywhere rural people doubted the value of some appliances and were slow to buy electric clocks, coffee makers, portable fans, hot pads, hot plates, razors, grills, sewing machines, and vacuum cleaners. Some families balked at the cost of an electric range and oven; others questioned the need for a dishwasher. Agricultural Research Service housing equipment specialist Nada Poole wrote in the 1965 *Yearbook of Agriculture* that rural women "do not really need a dishwasher." Other appliances made headway quickly. Rural women adopted the electric iron because it was several pounds lighter than the flatiron. Rural women also welcomed washing machines for easing the chore of washing clothes. The purchase of a freezer encouraged women and girls to freeze vegetables from the garden for later use. The rural homes that adopted electric appliances and electric lighting saved women at least some of the drudgery of housework. No longer did they need to clean kerosene lamps, bring coal or wood into the home to fire the stove, or clean up ashes from the stove or furnace. Other women preferred the coal or wood burning stove to the electric range and oven they had bought at their daughters' urging.

Rural people adopted radio and the new medium of television. By 1950 more than 80 percent of rural homes had a radio. Portable radios allowed men and women to listen to them while milking the cows. Rural people used radio for news and market reports. In the South religious broadcasts were popular. Television did not reach the ubiquity of radio during the 1950s and 1960s, but it spread rapidly. Whereas only 2.4 percent of rural homes had television in 1950, the percentage leapt to 36 in 1954. Television was most prevalent in the Midwest and West. Rural people watched soap operas, which had migrated from radio to television in the 1950s, and comedies. They also used television as an electronic babysitter, keeping their children occupied while they worked in the home.

Electricity was so basic to rural life that tenants did not want to work for landowners who did not have electricity and electric appliances in the tenant dwelling. Rural schools found many uses for electricity, using it to power slide projectors, movies, intercoms, microphones, lights, and large refrigerators that stored perishable food. These refrigerators made it possible for schools to serve a greater variety of food for lunch. At times the demand for electricity exceeded the generating capacity of power plants. During peak demand, outages were common in the 1950s and 1960s. Bereft of electricity, rural people had to return to using kerosene lamps and doing chores by hand.

In contrast to the rapidity with which rural people adopted radio and television, they were slow to adopt the telephone. Rural people claimed that they could use their neighbor's phone, making it unnecessary to install a phone of their own. Others cited cost: $5 to sign up for a phone and $10 for installation in 1951. Farmers sought to reduce expenses by classifying their phone as a residential unit, thereby avoiding the higher cost of a business line. Moreover, a party line was standard, making it possible for neighbors to listen to what would otherwise have been a private conversation. Remarkably, one survey found that half of rural respondents did not worry at the thought of losing their privacy when talking on the phone. Rural people used the telephone to report an emergency, make an appointment, call a store to check the price of an item, and to talk with relatives and friends. Rural women used the telephone

Dial telephones like this one from Bell superseded older hand-cranked models.

Earl Lauer Butz

The son of Harman Lee and Ada Tillie (Lower) Butz, Earl Lauer Butz was born on July 3, 1909, on a farm near Albion, Indiana. He graduated Wawaka High School in Wawaka, Indiana, in 1927 and, receiving a 4-H scholarship, enrolled in Purdue University. There he was editor of the school newspaper, a position that strengthened his communication skills. Throughout life Butz credited his communication skills with his success in academe and government. In 1932 he received a B.S. in agriculture from Purdue. Working a year on the family farm, Butz returned to Purdue as a graduate fellow. While in graduate school he was a research fellow with the Federal Land Bank in Louisville, Kentucky. In 1937 he received a Ph.D. in agricultural economics. Completing his doctorate, Butz married Mary Powell in 1937; they had met at a 4-H conference in Washington, D.C. They had two sons, William Powell and Thomas Earl Butz.

Butz remained at Purdue, where he taught agricultural economics. While a faculty member he was a research fellow with the Brookings Institute in Washington, D.C. In 1948 he became vice president of the American Agricultural Economics Association and in 1951 of the American Society of Farm Managers and Rural Appraisers. In 1951 he began his ascent through the ranks of government, becoming President Dwight D. Eisenhower's assistant secretary of agriculture. That year he became a member of the Board of Directors of the Commodity Credit Corporation, and was chairman of the U.S. Delegation to the U.N. Food and Agriculture Organization. In 1957 Butz returned to Purdue University as dean of the School of Agriculture, but in 1971 he returned to government when President Nixon appointed him secretary of agriculture.

A Republican, Butz believed that people and companies were most efficient in a free market. He opposed price supports as government intrusion in agriculture. Price supports, Butz believed, kept crop prices artificially high. By removing price supports and allowing prices to fall, U.S. food would be competitive on the open market. Foreign nations would buy food from the United States, giving farmers entrée into overseas markets. He encouraged farmers to take advantage of domestic and foreign markets by expanding production. Farmers heeded his advice, producing record surpluses in the 1970s. Yet these surpluses caused prices to fall in the 1980s, and were the cause of the farm crisis.

Butz's career faltered in 1974 when he mocked the Pope's opposition to birth control. The White House reprimanded Butz and forced him to apologize. Butz issued the apology, but was not chastened. When a slur against blacks became public, Butz resigned on October 4, 1976. Butz's reputation slid further when he pled guilty to tax evasion in 1981. Although he received a five-year sentence, the judge suspended all but 30 days. Butz retired to Purdue, where he kept an office. In 2008, at age 98, he was the oldest living former cabinet officer.

This photo shows a farmer using a small, portable electric motor to run a corn sheller; he could later use the same motor to run the feed mixer in the background.

more than men. Sociability motivated women to use the phone. They used the telephone to enhance relationships and emotional ties between people. After 1952 dial telephones began to replace hand cranked phones. By 1960 two-thirds of rural homes had a telephone.

GENDER IN RURAL AMERICA

Gender roles shaped rural life in the 1950s and 1960s. Where a family farmed, the husband cared for pigs, beef cattle, sheep, and crops. The wife cared for children, cooked, cleaned the home and clothes, raised vegetables, harvested them and canned the surplus, kept dairy cows for milk and raised poultry for meat and eggs. On occasion women even worked in the field beside their husbands. Some women preferred this work because it came to an end, whereas their work in the home was never done. The sale of poultry and eggs gave women income, but during the 1950s large agribusiness firms monopolized the growing of chickens and the production of eggs, costing women income. Bereft of this traditional source of income, many women took jobs off the farm. Education, skills, gender expectations and the local job market determined the work that women did. Some women picked fruit at nearby orchards. Others stayed home, taking in laundry. Restaurants and stores, other sources of

Angus cattle such as these originated in Scotland and had been in the United States since the 19th century, but their popularity as a source of beef grew in the 1960s.

employment, often paid little, though women nonetheless valued their jobs because they provided income that the family needed. Off-farm work gave women a sense of independence and self worth. Women with college degrees could aspire to be teachers or nurses.

One woman who became a teacher left the cooking to her husband. His dissatisfaction with this arrangement pointed to an undercurrent of resentment. Many rural men adhered to the traditional division of labor that allotted a job to men, and housework and childcare to women. Some men felt inadequate because a woman's having a job implied that her husband could not provide adequately for the family. Other men felt lonely without their mates to consult during the day and to share lunch. Men could not of course keep women home. Whereas only nine percent of rural women worked outside the home in 1940, the percentage rose to 25 in 1960.

The manufacturers of electric appliances touted their products as time and labor savers. Some rural women were skeptical of these claims. They were slow to buy vacuum cleaners, viewing them as luxuries. Nada Poole may have expressed the sentiments of many women when she declared that dishwashers were not necessities. Even when rural women bought them, appliances did not save time. Rather, expectations rose that women, in fulfilling their domestic role, would keep their homes cleaner. Some women, for example, cleaned their bathroom once or even twice daily. Rising expectations kept rural women at their household chores more than 50 hours per week in the 1950s and 1960s, a number that had not changed since 1924.

Not all rural women had a bathroom to clean. Some men, holding the traditional belief that people should discharge excreta outside, opposed the addition of a bathroom to the home. They believed that bathrooms were unsanitary, and that their use allowed disease to fester inside the home. Many rural women believed otherwise, viewing the outhouse as unsanitary. Some women added a bathroom to the home only after their husbands died. In other cases rural men continued to use the outhouse even after their wives installed a bathroom. Sometimes spending money on farm equipment took precedence over spending money on the home. In 1960 slightly more than half of rural homes had both a bathroom and running water. The installation of indoor plumbing saved rural women from the chore of hauling water into the home and disposing of dirty water. In 1954 nearly two-thirds of rural homes had running water; nevertheless, one year later only 14 percent of rural homes in southern Kentucky had running water.

Rural churches perpetuated traditional gender roles. Men often held positions of authority, serving on the church councils, and women often cooked for church dinners. At funerals women cooked for the bereaved family. In other instances women cared for children to give the bereaved family time to make arrangements for the deceased.

THE HOME
The home was the centerpiece of rural life. The farmhouse was different from other rural homes in its use of three rooms. Farmers had an office in which they kept records of purchases and sales. The washroom, inside the rear entrance to the home, gave farmers a place to keep boots and dirty clothes, and the kitchen was larger than in a typical rural home to give farm women space to can the surplus from the garden and to serve large meals. In some cases the kitchen was large enough for a dishwasher or a clothes washer. In other cases, farm women put a clothes washer in the basement. Home economist Nancy White advised rural people in 1965 to set aside one room in the home as a playroom for children. No longer was childhood an apprenticeship to become a farmer, rather it was a developmental stage where children used imagination and creativity to fashion a sanctuary of play.

White envisioned wood floors and carpet as part of the typical rural home, but by then rural people could, if they chose, lay linoleum on the floor. Housewives who favored linoleum over wood appreciated the ease with which linoleum could be cleaned. The rural home was wired for electricity in the 1950s and 1960s and had separate bedrooms for boys and girls, a dining room that was separate from the kitchen, and closets for the storage of clothes. In some locales the rural home resembled the suburban

The Commission on Rural Poverty

In September 1966 President Lyndon B. Johnson created the Commission on Rural Poverty as part of the War on Poverty. Its chairman was Kentucky's governor. Other members were four university presidents, representatives of farm workers, the editor in chief of *Harper's Magazine*, and a representative of CBS News. Interviewing poor people throughout the United States, the commission accumulated firsthand information of the scope and debilitating effects of poverty in the countryside.

In May 1967 the commission began drafting its report to Congress and the president, completing it in September. In contrast to the attention on urban poverty, the report criticized Americans for ignoring the rural poor. The report traced the source of poverty to the malaise in the countryside. The rural poor migrated to the city, swelling the number of poor city dwellers. Government and business could not end urban poverty without first confronting its rural source. Because poverty sank roots in the countryside, Congress should, the report maintained, create antipoverty programs in the countryside rather than overwhelmingly in the city. The report counted 14 million rural poor. In the face of these numbers the report urged Congress to act aggressively. In its most ambitious recommendation, the report urged the federal government to create a job for every poor rural American willing to work. The poor would work their way out of poverty. The report held that a dearth of jobs left people without work and thus poor.

The report of the Commission on Rural Poverty led Congress to increase funding for Aid to Families with Dependent Children, food stamps, and school lunches. These programs helped the rural poor, but government at all levels did not, as the report recommended, create jobs in the countryside. The government might have made more progress in fighting rural poverty if it were not for the deterioration of the cities. Race riots focused media attention on the pathology of urban life. The cities, it seemed, needed money more desperately than the countryside. Equally important, escalation of the Vietnam War claimed federal funds that might have gone to fight rural poverty. In the 1960s the promise of the report went largely unfulfilled.

home. In the late 1960s the last farmers in St. George, Vermont, sold their farms to make housing for suburbanites. In areas such as St. George the rural home and the suburban home overlapped geographically. In these cases suburbanites and rural people shared expectations. Like suburbanites, rural people prided themselves on keeping a green and healthy lawn. They used herbicides to kill weeds, and insecticides to kill grubs and Japanese beetles.

Inside the home rural people used DDT against bedbugs, fleas, cockroaches, and mosquitoes, though by 1950 entomologists had established that some insects were resistant to DDT.

Many farm homes had a barn for livestock and a shed for a tractor, a combine, a hay baler, and other types of machinery. The use of tractors and other machines lessened the demand for labor. No longer needing to do heavy physical labor, a farmer could retain control of a farm until late in life, postponing the day when he transferred it to his children. Because farms were growing larger in the 1950s and

By the 1950s and 1960s tractors, along with other heavy machinery, had become ubiquitous.

1960s, farmers were reluctant to divide their farms into small units to be inherited by all their children. Rather, farmers aimed to keep a farm intact and to pass it on to only one child. The rest had to seek off-farm work.

Machines replaced horses as a source of traction. One man recalled returning to the farm of his youth in 1952 to find all the horses gone. Machines were not always a benefit. They could be dangerous. Many farms in the 1950s had a Farmall tractor that, like a Model T, had a crank start. If the crank slipped, it recoiled on a farmer, possibly breaking his arm. A farmer who made the mistake of starting a tractor in gear risked being run over. Like machines, livestock posed dangers. On one farm a boar ate a small child. On another a farmer cut off his thumb while trying to kill a chicken with a small axe. He had hoped to have a physician reattach the thumb but was not quick enough in retrieving it. Instead a cat darted off with the thumb, intent on eating it.

In poor rural areas homes sometimes fell into disrepair. In 1959 the coal mine that had been the primary source of income in Stump Creek, Pennsylvania, closed. Miners left the town in search of work. Those who remained did not have the money to maintain their homes. Tax revenues plunged and the waterworks, short of money, failed to deliver running water to homes as pipes broke. Without running water, homes returned to the use of cisterns and wells.

THE COUNTERCULTURE OF THE 1960s AND RURAL LIFE

The counterculture of the 1960s grew out of dissatisfaction with America's corporate culture. The counterculture was a movement in which young people repudiated the values of thrift, sobriety, and pragmatism. Some people turned to illegal drugs in an attempt to alter their consciousness. One scholar found that people in rural Union County, Illinois, used marijuana and other illegal drugs in the 1960s. Some farmers grew marijuana as a cash crop, hiding it in a cornfield. In laboring to stamp out the use of marijuana, police inspected fields and, when they found marijuana, arrested the farmer who owned the land. Some farmers hired gunmen to turn away children and adults who strayed onto a stand of marijuana. Violence pervaded the culture of illegal drugs. One farmer mowed down a patch of marijuana, only to have his pigs poisoned in retaliation.

The counterculture also repudiated agribusiness with its use of chemicals and machines. Chemicals poisoned the land and water, and machines severed the relationship between humans and the earth. In 1962 biologist Rachel Carson sounded the alarm against agrochemicals, and young, well-educated people heeded her warning. In Round Valley, California, horticulturist Alan Chadwick created a cross between a commune and an organic farm. Attracting suburbanites, with their idyllic notions of farming, he accepted 25 apprentices each year. They lived and worked on his farm. Because he eschewed chemicals and machines, the apprentices grew crops and tended the soil with heavy labor. Life was austere and labor, from dawn to dusk, unremitting. Eating what they grew, the laborers had free food, and Chadwick charged no tuition. For Chadwick and the people who gathered around him, farming evoked a spiritual dimension alien from the purely economic focus of agribusiness. The earth was sacred and the source of everything that humans needed to thrive. At year's end most of the apprentices, sobered by a year of hard labor, returned to suburbia, though a few, persuaded of organic farming's value, stayed longer.

EDUCATION AND RURAL LIFE

Like Americans everywhere, rural people wanted the send their children to good schools. Many rural people believed that their schools would flourish only so long as they remained independent. Rural people labored to preserve the independence of their schools as a way of ensuring that they remained beholden to their wishes. In Waucoma, Iowa, rural people sent their children to the Waucoma Independent School District during the 1950s. Many teachers lived in Waucoma, some at the local hotel, integrating themselves into the community. Because families were stable, many of them living for generations in Waucoma, their children went through school as a single cohort, building close relationships over the years.

The loss of people through migration, and the resulting loss of tax revenues forced the school district to close in 1960. Teachers who had lived in Waucoma moved to town, where they could find lodging near the consolidated school. St. Mary's School, the only Catholic school in Waucoma, closed in

1968 for lack of enrollment. The last independent school in Waucoma, its closing left the region without a school of its own.

Other schools fared better. One school in a coal town in Appalachia boasted that two-thirds of graduates went to college in the 1960s. Few schools in Appalachia could match this performance. The worst schools produced graduates who could neither read nor write. Some adults were illiterate, as well as unable to drive a car. In one rural area in Appalachia women averaged only seven years of schooling. Affluent families sent their children to school in town, whereas poor miners sent their children to the underperforming schools in the countryside. In the 1960s and later, one-room schoolhouses, in which all the grades were taught by the same teacher, continued in Appalachia and other rural areas. In many of these schools, coal stoves were the only source of heat, windows were broken, and classrooms lacked textbooks.

RACE AND LIFE IN RURAL MISSISSIPPI

When they did not live in the city, blacks inhabited the countryside, often in the South. Their interactions with whites had long been tense. Whites expected obsequiousness from blacks, and racism condemned many blacks to poverty. The 1960 Census fixed the poverty rate in Dahlia, Mississippi, a rural area with large numbers of blacks, at 75 percent. Ninety percent of Dahlia's

The 86-acre Jeffries-Gardner farm in Lowndes County, Mississippi, is historically significant because it was farmed by two black families continuously from 1873 to at least 1978. Besides the main house (shown), outbuildings included a smokehouse, corn crib, and chicken house.

residents earned incomes below the national median. Blacks were dispropor-
tionately poor and had the lowest incomes in Dahlia. Many blacks lived in
shacks that had no bathroom and often lacked running water. Complaints
about poor conditions led landlords to tear them down, rather than make
improvements. The one room schoolhouse, yielding to consolidation in other
rural areas, continued to educate blacks in Dahlia.

In the mid 1950s, however, the county closed the one-room schoolhouse in
Dahlia. African Americans then attended Dahlia Vocational School, which ended at grade ten and did not therefore allow blacks to graduate high school. The
vocational school had one bathroom for 900 black students and one for faculty.
A poorly engineered building, it discharged sewage into the school. The white
teachers at Dahlia Vocational School had to teach students to look them in the
eye because blacks had been told, as a gesture of submission, to avert their eyes
from whites. Whites attended Dahlia Day School, a private academy built in the
1960s when whites feared that Mississippi might integrate its public schools. By
admitting only whites, Dahlia Day School preserved segregation even if Mississippi were to integrate schools. Whites rode a bus to school whereas blacks
walked. When blacks tried to integrate the swimming pool in the 1960s, the
county declared it a private pool, charging dues that blacks could not afford.
Dubbing it the public pool, the county then built a pool for blacks.

Rural Dahlia offered blacks only low wage labor. Men were farm laborers, janitors at the school, deboners at the catfish plant, or workers at the
textile mill. Women were domestics, cooks, or field hands, or also worked at
the catfish plant or textile mill. In a gesture of paternalism, white landowners
gave their black workers money during slack times, but whites were quick to
withdraw aid when they needed blacks in the fields. Whites expected a compliant labor force. They blacklisted those who participated in the Civil Rights
movement in the 1950s and 1960s. Those who signed petitions to integrate
the schools lost their jobs. In the 1960s the planter elite courted industry to
settle in Dahlia with the understanding that it would hire blacks, if at all, only
as janitors. In the 1960s the spread of a mechanical cotton picker threw blacks
out of work. They often turned to the black church for aid. The white churches
in Dahlia turned away poor blacks. These churches targeted charity to any-
body but blacks, sending volunteers to a Mexican village or giving money to
national programs to help foster children.

CONCLUSION

For the idealistic laborers on Alan Chadwick's organic farm, farming must have
felt like a return to an earlier, simpler time. For the isolated rural people who
were among the last Americans to live without electricity in the late 1950s,
their lifestyle may have felt like something very different indeed. Modern conveniences were belatedly arriving to improve their lives, but many of their
peers had made the choice to leave for urban areas already. For yet another

group deeply connected to farming, if infrequently benefitting from their own labor as sharecroppers and field laborers in the south, African Americans remaining in rural areas after the Great Migration lived in quite another reality, one beset by unrelenting racism as in previous decades, but brightened by the hope of the Civil Rights movement. All these groups experienced different versions of rural life in the 1950s and 1960s, versions that may seem to belong to different times. Divisions in society had long been obvious in urban areas, but extreme differences in lifestyles were just as possible in rural areas.

CHRISTOPHER CUMO

Further Readings

Adams, Jane. *The Transformation of Rural Life: Southern Illinois, 1890–1990*. Chapel Hill, NC: University of North Carolina Press, 1994.

Castle, Emery N., ed. *The Changing American Countryside: Rural People and Places*. Lawrence, KS: University Press of Kansas, 1995.

Danbom, David B. *Born in the Country: A History of Rural America*. Baltimore, MD: Johns Hopkins University Press, 1995.

Duncan, Cynthia. *Worlds Apart: Why Poverty Persists in Rural America*. New Haven, CT: Yale University Press, 1999.

Fish, Charles. *In Good Hands: The Keeping of a Family Farm*. New York: Kodansha International, 1995.

Kline, Ronald. *Consumers in the Country: Technology and Social Change in Rural America*. Baltimore, MD: Johns Hopkins University Press, 2000.

Luloff, A.E. and Louis E. Swanson, eds. *American Rural Communities*. Boulder, CO: Westview, 1990.

Pistorius, Alan. *Cutting Hill: A Chronicle of a Family Farm*. New York: Alfred A. Knopf, 1990.

Robertson, James. *The Small Towns Book: Show Me the Way to Go Home*. Garden City, NY: Anchor Press, 1978.

Schwartz, Dona. *Waucoma Twilight: Generations of the Farm*. Washington, D.C.: Smithsonian Institution Press, 1992.

Shover, John. *First Majority, Last Minority: The Transforming of Rural Life in America*. DeKalb, IL: Northern Illinois University Press, 1976.

Stewart, James B and Joyce E. Allen-Smith, eds. *Blacks in Rural America*. New Brunswick, NJ: Transaction, 1995.

U.S. Department of Agriculture. *Consumers All: The Yearbook of Agriculture*. Washington, D.C.: GPO, 1965.

Chapter 7

Religion

*"The framers of our Constitution meant we were to have
freedom of religion, not freedom from religion."*
—Reverend Billy Graham

THE DEVASTATION OF World War II caused the faithful all over America to question God's beneficence and the moral progress of man. Over 300,000 American soldiers had died in the war, with close to 700,000 wounded. Over 25 million servicemen on all sides of the conflict had died, along with an estimated 47 million civilians killed by war, famine, and disease.

Jewish theologians, in particular, had to find a way to help their faithful to reconcile the reality of the Holocaust and its six million victims with their belief in a merciful deity. There were no easy answers. Some came to believe that God, while a powerful force, was not omnipotent, and could not always stop evil in the world; others believed He chooses not to interfere in human events, willfully hiding Himself from view; a few, like Rabbi Richard Rubenstein, believed that God was dead, or at the very least, nonexistent in the modern world.

The beginning of the Cold War had a profound impact on American religion. Communist nations, such as the Soviet Union, not only held to an economic and political philosophy that ran counter to everything Americans held dear, they were officially atheists as well. It was very easy to contrast "godless" Communism with religious capitalism. It was in the early 1950s that the government began printing "In God We Trust" on the front of every coin, and in 1951 a Catholic fraternal organization called the Knights of Columbus added the words "under God" to the Pledge of Allegiance, an amendment later

With 60 percent of Americans attending church every week in the late 1950s, the parishioners of this church in Hershey, Pennsylvania, outgrew a 1921 building and moved to this one in 1962.

picked up by the American Legion and other groups, and eventually making its way into American classrooms.

This kind of basic, homogenized religious observance became the norm in the 1950s and early 1960s. Acting visibly religious was a way of acting visibly patriotic. By the late 1950s, 60 percent of all Americans attended church services on a weekly basis. "Liberal Protestants, post–Vatican II Catholics and Reform Jews carried their religion into corporate boardrooms and neighborhood barbecues," says religious historian Paul Harvey. All religious groups of the time were against the Communist threat, while Protestant denominations were most likely to be vocally anti-Communist in their rhetoric.

For most Americans, it must have seemed like God was smiling on their efforts. The United States was the only major country involved in World War II that did not suffer a major loss of infrastructure. The nation's economy roared into high gear immediately after the war, fueled by a worldwide demand for products and a booming population looking for good-paying jobs. Millions of returning servicemen were able to attend college on the G.I. Bill, giving them a leg up into the world of white collar professionalism. A house in the suburbs, a car in the driveway, a new TV in the living room, and a bunch of kids playing in the backyard was no longer just a dream for the majority of Americans.

But the "American way of life"—the idea that through hard work and talent, anyone could achieve success and a high standard of living—ignored the plight of millions who still lived on the margins of society. The needs of the poor and disadvantaged became a major focus of social and religious activists in the late 1950s and early 1960s.

RELIGION AND CIVIL RIGHTS

The Civil Rights movement was probably the most important of the religiously-based social movements of the period. Martin Luther King, Jr., then a charismatic 24-year-old preacher at the Dexter Avenue Baptist Church in Montgomery, Alabama, helped organize a boycott of the Montgomery transit system after an African-American woman named Rosa Parks had been arrested for refusing to give up her seat on a city bus to a white man. The boycott lasted 381 days, until a federal district court and the U.S. Supreme Court ruled that Alabama's segregation laws were unconstitutional. It was the first of many fights King would undertake over the next decade.

King had begun to form a sophisticated religious approach to the problem of racial segregation in his native South while still a student in college. As a graduate student, and later as a preacher, he turned again and again to the concept of *agape*, which theologians and philosophers across the centuries had defined as the highest form of love. Through his readings of Mahatma Gandhi, he came to believe that nonviolent resistance was the best method of civil disobedience. "At the center of nonviolence stands the principle of love," he said in a speech. "When we rise to love on the *agape* level, we love men

Dr. Martin Luther King, Jr., in 1964, the year he won the Nobel Peace Prize.

A stained glass window in the Hershey, Pennsylvania, St. Joan of Arc Church, which was built in the early 1960s. In the midst of postwar prosperity, social and religious activists in the late 1950s and early 1960s turned their attention to the poor and disadvantaged.

not because we like them, not because their attitudes and ways appeal to us, but we love them because God loves them." He was also steeped in the tradition of the African-American church, which had a long-standing strain of liberation theology, or a belief that God was on the side of the oppressed. King was also helped by the decision of the National Council on Churches to condemn segregation as un-Christian in 1952, and a similar statement by a group of Catholic bishops in 1958.

King's vehicle for his civil rights work was the Southern Christian Leadership Council (SCLC), which he organized with fellow activist Ralph David Abernathy and 60 other clergymen and activists in January 1957. Originally named the Negro Leadership Conference on Transportation and Nonviolent Integration, the SCLC grew into a clearinghouse and organizing body for the work done by small churches and civil rights groups across the South. Firmly committed to nonviolent direct action, the SCLC was, ideologically,

Billy Graham

"You have a voice that pulls," legendary evangelist Bob Jones told Billy Graham sometime in the late 1930s. "God can use that voice of yours. He can use it mightily." The son of a North Carolina dairy farmer, Graham had joined the evangelical movement as a teenager and became an ordained Baptist minister in 1939. He came to national prominence in 1949 during a revival meeting in Los Angeles that pulled in thousands of people. So popular was this "crusade" that the original three-week run was extended to eight weeks. Graham was young, handsome, charismatic, and patriotic—"Either communism must die or Christianity must die," he said in the 1950s—and preached a simple message of salvation through the acceptance of Jesus Christ. He quickly became one of the most well-known and well-respected people in the country.

The influential evangelist Billy Graham in April 1966.

Graham used radio and television to spread his message and reached out to youths and people of different faiths, rather than confining himself to like-minded Southern Baptists. Early in his career, he decided on simple methods to avoid the moral pitfalls that seemed to plague evangelical ministers: he would never be alone in a room with a woman other than his wife; his ministry, the Billy Graham Evangelistic Association, was run largely by an outside board of directors; he drew an annual salary and did not have access to his organization's accounts; and he opened up his organization's finances to interested parties. His ministry, which has lasted almost 55 years and reached more than 200 million people in 185 countries, has avoided scandals.

Although Graham was not an active participant in the Civil Rights movement of the 1950s, he did give it his quiet support. In 1953, he integrated his audience during a revival in Chattanooga, Tennessee. "When God looks at you, He doesn't look on the outward appearance," he told the tens of thousands who attended his sermons. "The Bible says he looks upon the heart." He became friends with Martin Luther King, Jr. during the Montgomery Bus Boycott, inviting him to share the stage at a revival in Madison Square Garden in the summer of 1957. King and Graham later fell out over the Vietnam War, which King opposed and Graham supported. But when King was assassinated in 1968, Graham mourned him as "a social leader and a prophet."

Both black and white marchers attempted to carry on King's antipoverty campaign after his assassination with the Poor People's March in Washington, D.C., on June 18, 1968.

far more radical than the NAACP, whose membership was older and more conservative. The SCLC was less radical than younger, more militant groups like the Student Nonviolent Coordinating Committee (SNCC)—which received an $800 start-up grant from the SCLC in 1960—or the Congress of Racial Equality (CORE). The SCLC helped coordinate a string of high-profile civil rights campaigns, including the Birmingham Campaign of 1963, and the March on Washington in August 1963, which culminated in King's magnificent "I Have a Dream" speech on the steps of the Lincoln Memorial. Other large-scale SCLC protests included the Selma Campaign on 1964 and the Grenada, Mississippi campaign of 1966.

By late 1967, King had begun to turn his attention to the plight of the poor, no matter what their color or ethnicity. At a November meeting of the SCLC, he announced that he planned to bring together a multiracial group of about 2,000 people, both urban and rural, to stage a march on Washington, D.C., to demand a living minimum wage, unemployment insurance, and better educational opportunities for the disadvantaged. Many within the SCLC were not particularly supportive of the proposed "poor people's campaign," but King was adamant, calling it "the beginning of a new understanding, and a determination by poor people of all colors and backgrounds to assert and win their right to a decent life and respect for their culture and dignity." He was busy planning out his campaign when he was assassinated.

The Nation of Islam

While Martin Luther King, Jr. was working to integrate African Americans into mainstream civic life, another African-American group was working to separate themselves altogether from white culture. The Nation of Islam was created by a shadowy figure called Wallace Fard Muhammed in Detroit around 1930. After Muhammed mysteriously vanished in 1934, leadership passed to his disciple, Elijah Muhammad, who would run the organization until his death in 1975. The group did not come to public attention until the 1950s, and what they believed was fairly shocking to the American consciousness.

Members of the Nation of Islam read the Qur'an and held that there is no God but Allah ("who came in the person of W.D. Fard"). They followed the Muslim discipline of daily prayer and rituals, food, dress, and rituals. They did not believe in war. But they also identified whites as "devils," believed that blacks were the original human beings on Earth, and that they were self-made, not made by God. They called for the separation of whites and blacks into different territories. They had their own mosques, schools, businesses, and publications. This was not a widespread population, with estimates of membership ranging from 10,000 to 250,000 people, mostly in the urban areas of the North.

There was tremendous criticism of the Nation of Islam during the 1960s —not just from white Americans, but also from African-American civil rights leaders, and from Muslim immigrants who felt that this was, at best, a corrupted form of mainstream Islam. While rank-and-file members were mostly well-meaning individuals who found dignity and beauty in their new religion, their leader, Elijah Muhammed, grew rich on the tithes of his followers. The charismatic hustler-turned-spokesperson Malcolm X generated a huge media following in the early 1960s, and when he seemed poised to challenge Muhammed for leadership, he was ejected from the movement. On February 21, 1965, as he was giving a speech in the Audubon Ballroom in New York City, Malcolm X was assassinated, shot 16 times by three assailants as a horrified audience looked on.

Malcolm X waiting at a Martin Luther King, Jr., press conference on March 26, 1964.

RELIGION AND THE WAR ON POVERTY

King was not the only person working on poverty issues in the 1960s. In 1962, author Michael Harrington published a book entitled *The Other America: Poverty in the United States*. Harrington was a socialist, but earlier in his life, he had been a Catholic Worker, part of a movement launched by Dorothy Day and Peter Maurin in 1933 to reach out to the poor and dispossessed through direct acts of assistance and mercy. As a Catholic Worker, Harrington had lived in the Bowery district of New York City, seeing up-close the "culture of poverty" that kept people trapped in hopelessness—in direct contradiction to the idea that anyone in America could work their way up from the bottom, through hard work, clean living, and the superiority of the free-market system. His investigations showed that the plight of the poor in post–World War II America was based on indifference by the public, and the government in particular. Unlike previous eras, he contended, the poor had become invisible, with the wealthy and expanding middle class able to ignore them because

The Evolution of Ram Dass

Dr. Richard Alpert had it all. He was a professor of psychology at Harvard University, a freewheeling bachelor with an apartment full of antiques, a boat, a Mercedes, a Triumph 500 CC motorcycle, and a Cessna airplane. He worked hard at his research and teaching. "I was really driven," he said of this time. "Until you know a good, Jewish middle class, upwardly mobile, anxiety-ridden neurotic, you haven't met a real achiever!"

He was also deeply unhappy. He spent years in psychoanalysis, and was an occasional user of psychedelic drugs, but none of it alleviated his dissatisfaction with his life. Then, in 1961, he became friends with fellow Harvard professor Timothy Leary. Over the next few years, he was an enthusiastic participant in Leary's experimentations with LSD. He and Leary were both kicked out of Harvard in 1963, and quickly became counterculture legends. Alpert enjoyed the expansion of consciousness he felt from the drug, but by 1967 felt that he was still missing something, still too dissatisfied with life. "So I left to go to India, and I took a bottle of LSD with me, with the idea that I'd meet holy men along the way, and I'd give them LSD and they'd tell me what LSD is," he said. "Maybe I'd learn the missing clue."

It did not work out that way. In India, he met his guru, Neem Karoli Baba, and began a study of Eastern philosophy and practice. By the time he returned to the United States, Dr. Richard Alpert was the guru Ram Dass—"servant of God." In 1971, he published his bestselling book *Be Here Now*, which for almost 40 years has led millions of Americans to a deeper understanding of the mind-expanding potential of Eastern metaphysics, yoga, and meditation.

they simply did not see them in their own communities. By 1960, 19 percent of Americans lived in this economic environment, from the decaying inner cities to isolated rural communities.

Both John F. Kennedy and Lyndon Johnson read Harrington's work, and were moved by his portrait of suffering. Kennedy was assassinated before he had a chance to develop antipoverty legislation, but in his first State of the Union address in January 1964, Lyndon Johnson announced the beginning of a War on Poverty as part of his Great Society program. Congress quickly passed his proposed Economic Opportunity Act and created an Office of Economic Opportunity, which in turn started programs such as Head Start, the Legal Services Corps, VISTA, and Job Corps. By the early 1970s, the national poverty rate had dropped to 11 percent.

Lyndon Johnson's attention was quickly drawn from domestic social issues toward America's expanding involvement in the Vietnam War. As the conflict dragged on, a growing number of Americans—theologians among them—began to question the morality of the country's actions in Vietnam. There were several interfaith antiwar groups formed during the middle and late 1960s that took part in demonstrations. In 1968, a group of men broke into a draft board office in Catonsville, Maryland, hauled 378 draft files out into the parking lot, and burned them with homemade napalm. All of the "Catonsville Nine" were Catholics, including priests (and brothers) Philip and Daniel Berrigan. "We confront the Roman Catholic Church, other Christian bodies, and the synagogues of America with their silence and cowardice in the face of our country's crimes," they said in a statement after the incident. "We are convinced that the religious bureaucracy in this country is racist, is an accomplice in this war, and is hostile to the poor."

DEATH OF GOD

"Is God Dead?" asked the *Time* magazine cover story of April 8, 1966, just in time for Easter. "The current death-of-God group believes that God is indeed absolutely dead," it said, "but proposes to carry on and write a theology without theos, without God." Science, capitalism, even the relatively new phenomenon of birth, illness, and death taking place in hospitals rather than the home, were increasingly removing a sense of wonder in the miracles and mysteries of life from the common man. Modern life, argued theologians like Thomas J. Altizer, Gabriel Vahanian, and

A church bell tower built in the 1960s.

The Byodo-In Buddhist Temple in Kaneohe, Hawaii, was built in 1968. In the late 1960s and early 1970s, interest in Eastern philosophy and religion grew in the United States.

Richard Rubenstein, had lost all sense of sacrament, and modern Americans had no transcendent purpose to their lives. Still, the magazine noted that polls showed 97 percent of Americans believed in God, 27 percent classified their faith as "deep," and 44 percent were attending church services weekly.

While the death-of-God crowd never had a strong following in this highly Christianized culture, their work, along with the social changes evident within minority communities, help opened up new vistas in religion. For example, in 1968, Mary Daly (a scholar at Jesuit-run Boston College) published *The Church and the Second Sex*, examining the misogyny woven into the traditions of the Catholic Church. This launched the new field of feminist theology, as other feminist writers began to pick apart the antifemale traditions of many mainline churches, to suggest ways in which these could become more woman-centered, or to build their own spirituality and worship by exploring pre-Christian traditions of goddess worship.

RELIGION IN AN AGE OF EXPERIMENTATION

Others began searching for higher forms of consciousness in the tradition of some Native American cultures—through the use of psychedelic drugs such as psilocybin, mushrooms, and mescaline. The most famous of these experiments took place at Harvard in the early 1960s, when psychology professor Timothy Leary headed the Harvard Psychedelic Drug Research Project at the university's Center for the Study of Personality. Over four years, about 1,000 people took part in the study, many of them taking the favorite psychedelic drug of the time, LSD. While Leary was not personally religious, he was fascinated by the spiritual aspects of psychedelic experiences. The project found that if the participants were put in a spiritual frame of mind or environment before ingesting the drugs, 90 percent reported life-changing religious experiences while under the influence. For those that were not put in that frame of mind, 40–75 percent reported a similar result.

In 1962, an M.D. and minister at Harvard Divinity School named Walter Panhnke conducted another experiment as part of a study in religious experience. On Good Friday, 20 theology students were split into two groups; one was given a capsule with psilocybin, the other a vitamin that caused nothing more than a slight tingling in the arms. The participants then sat through the two-and-a-half hour service, and afterward filled out a questionnaire. Nine out of 10 of the members of the psilocybin group said they had a heightened religious experience, compared to only one of the vitamin group. It was, said Panhnke's advisor, "the most cogent single piece of evidence that psychedelic chemicals do, under certain circumstances, release profound religious experience."

Leary and his associate Richard Alpert were dismissed from Harvard in May 1963, after word reached the administration that they were giving drugs to undergraduates. They moved their experimentation to the Millbrook estate in New York, where, for the next four years, the mansion served as "a monastery, school, research laboratory, religious commune, and opium den all rolled into one," says historian Robert Fuller. In September 1966, Leary started the League for Spiritual Discovery, claiming it was a religion with LSD usage as a sacrament. This attempt to cloak drug use as a freedom of religion issue did not fly with authorities, especially when LSD was added to the government's list of Schedule I drugs—making it illegal to create, possess, or distribute the substance—in October 1966.

Hippies—the young, white, middle-class Americans who "dropped out" of the mainstream and joined the counterculture—were enthusiastic participants in the drug culture of the 1960s and early 1970s. There was no small amount of hand-wringing at the time over how quickly these kids had rejected the strong religiosity of their upbringing in favor of "sex,

The nine-foot tall wooden Lotus Buddha inside the Byodo-In Temple in Hawaii.

drugs, and rock and roll." While a good percentage of hippies were simply acting out against parental authority, most observers did not see the strong undercurrent of spirituality behind much of the hippie movement. Many young people who grew up in the mass produced, bland safety of the suburbs in the 1950s and 1960s were repelled by the plastic sameness of it all. Their parents' robust Americanism, with all its religious capitalism and conformity, rang hollow to them. The back-to-the-land movement, organic farming, home-birthing, communal living, meditation—all of these counterculture practices were attempts to lead a more authentic, less materialistic lifestyle, and the basic principles of fairness and equality that guided those that chose to live that lifestyle were undeniably rooted in Judeo-Christian systems of thought.

CONCLUSION
Most young Americans did not join the counterculture, and a high percentage of them held on to the religious beliefs and practices of their youth. Americans of all ages ended the 1960s with a deep sense of uneasiness and spiritual confusion. This was reinforced in late July 1969, when Apollo 11 beamed back the first color photos of the earth from the surface of the moon. For centuries, people had looked up at the sky and built images of a celestial paradise in Heaven. The images of the earth from the heavens were beautiful, awe-inspiring, but also troubling. Human beings were alone on a small blue globe, spinning in the infinite blackness of space.

HEATHER K. MICHON

Further Readings

Alhstrom, Sydney E. *A Religious History of the American People*. New Haven and London: Yale University Press, 1972.

Allen, David. *Make Love Not War: The Sexual Revolution: An Unfettered History*. Boston, MA: Little, Brown, 2000.

Cavert, Samuel McCrea. *The American Churches in the Ecumenical Movement, 1900–1968*. New York: Association Press, 1968.

Dodds, John W. *Life in Twentieth Century America*. New York: Putnam's, 1973.

Kaledin, Eugenia. *Daily Life in the United States, 1940–1959: Shifting Worlds*. Westport, CT: Greenwood, 2000.

Morty, Myron A. *Daily Life in the United States, 1960–1990: Decades of Discord*. Westport, CT: Greenwood, 1997.

West, Elliott. *Growing Up in Twentieth Century America: A History Reference Guide*. Westport, CT: Greenwood, 1996.

Wiebe, Robert. *The Search for Order*. New York: Hill and Wang, 1966.

Chapter 8

Education

*"We conclude that in the field of public education,
the doctrine of 'separate but equal' has no place."*
—Supreme Court Chief Justice Earl Warren

THE DESEGREGATION OF public schools was by far the most important development in education in the 1950s and 1960s. In 1954 the landmark Supreme Court case *Brown v. Board of Education* transformed the public school landscape of America. By declaring "separate but equal" schools unconstitutional, the ruling opened the door to educational integration across the country. While the ideals outlined in the case were urgent and powerful, implementation of desegregation policies took decades to achieve. Other changes in the era were shifts in gender roles, teachers and unions agitating for improved wages and working conditions, and a federal move to try to influence how science was taught in the classroom.

DESEGREGATION

Desegregation took different forms in different parts of the country. Across the South, in 17 states, state laws required that elementary schools be segregated by race. It took over a decade for these laws to be overturned, and for integration programs to take root at all levels of education. Attempts by the federal government to force integration efforts often brought violence and struggle, as in Little Rock, Arkansas, in 1958.

Higher education in the South also faced challenges in desegregating peacefully. In 1962, James H. Meredith, an African American, sought to register at the University of Mississippi as a transfer student. The state government tried a variety of approaches to block his admission, but the federal courts overruled them and ordered that he be allowed to register. On September 30, Meredith arrived on the Oxford campus with a federal entourage of over 120 U.S. marshals to ensure his safety. The result was a nightlong riot that resulted in two deaths, 175 injuries, and 212 arrests. Meredith enrolled the next day, and graduated with his bachelor's degree the following summer. In 1963 the University of Alabama was also forced to integrate, despite Governor George Wallace's election claim that he would maintain "segregation now, segregation tomorrow, segregation forever." On June 11, the governor personally barred the path of two African-American students, James A. Hood and Vivian J. Malone, who attempted to register. The governor was flanked by armed state troopers. President Kennedy federalized the Alabama National Guard to come to the students' aid, and the governor was forced to stand aside while the students enrolled.

In most northern industrial states, schools were not segregated by district or state regulation. Instead, they were segregated because of the racial composition of residential neighborhoods themselves. In 1966 a report by James Coleman entitled "Equality of Educational Opportunity" described a study of over 600,000 children, which found that African-American children did best

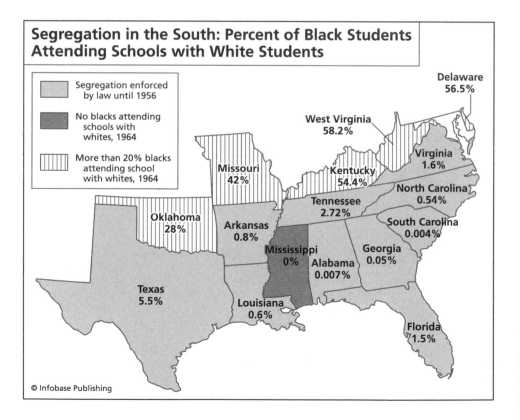

Segregation in the South: Percent of Black Students Attending Schools with White Students

Segregation enforced by law until 1956

No blacks attending schools with whites, 1964

More than 20% blacks attending school with whites, 1964

Delaware 56.5%
West Virginia 58.2%
Virginia 1.6%
Missouri 42%
Kentucky 54.4%
North Carolina 0.54%
Tennessee 2.72%
Oklahoma 28%
Arkansas 0.8%
South Carolina 0.004%
Mississippi 0%
Alabama 0.007%
Georgia 0.05%
Texas 5.5%
Louisiana 0.6%
Florida 1.5%

© Infobase Publishing

Signs like this one, which hung at a bus station in Rome, Georgia, were common in the South during segregation.

Brown v. Board of Education

Before 1954 daily life for many African Americans was marked by rampant discrimination. In the South, Jim Crow laws, a form of legal discrimination, allowed state and local governments to prevent blacks from voting to change the laws that had implemented the separate but equal doctrine that had been upheld by the Supreme Court since *Plessy v. Ferguson* (163 U.S. 537) in 1896. Jim Crow laws mandated separation in public transportation, public parks, hotels, restaurants, and libraries. "Whites Only" signs were common, and African Americans were forced to drink from designated water fountains.

The separate but equal doctrine also extended to public schools, where black children were sometimes educated in ill-equipped, unheated new schools with unprepared teachers. Proportionally, states spent far less per student in black schools than in white. In 1954 the Supreme Court agreed to hear five challenges to segregated educational facilities: *Brown v. Board of Education* (Kansas), *Briggs v. Elliott* (South Carolina), *Davis v. Prince Edward County* (Virginia), *Gephardt v. Beldon* (Delaware), and *Bolling v. Sharpe* (Washington, D.C.). The cases were collectively known as *Brown v. Board of Education*.

In all cases except *Bolling*, the court held that segregated schools violated the Equal Protection Clause of the Fourteenth Amendment to the U.S. Constitution. In determining that the Fourteenth Amendment applied only to states and not the nation's capital, the justices determined in *Bolling* that the city had violated the due process of the Fifteenth Amendment by preventing black children from attending all-white schools. Concluding that the separate but equal doctrine always resulted in inherent inequality, in 1955 the court decided to hear arguments in *Brown II* (349 U.S. 294), considering ways in which integration could be implemented. The justices rejected attorney Thurgood Marshall's pleas for immediate integration and compromised on demanding that desegregation take place with "all deliberate speed." When white supremacists in segregated states tried to block integration, the court decided that immediate integration was necessary.

Governor Orval Faubus addressing an anti-integration rally in Little Rock, Arkansas, on August 20, 1959, two years after the initial crisis.

Eisenhower and the Little Rock Crisis

After the U.S. Supreme Court determined in *Brown v. Board of Education* in 1954 that separate but equal had no place in public education, many southern states attempted to block integration by claiming that states had complete authority over their own schools. In 1957 Arkansas Governor Orval Faubus entered the fray in an unsuccessful attempt to block the entry of nine African-American students into Central High School in Little Rock by calling out the National Guard. On September 5, 1957, President Dwight Eisenhower responded to a telegram from Faubus requesting federal assistance by reasserting his intention to honor his oath of office. Assured by a two-hour meeting with Faubus, President Eisenhower concluded that the governor recognized that national law had precedence over state law. On September 21, Eisenhower issued a statement from Newport, Rhode Island, informing the nation that the National Guard had been withdrawn from Central High and that law and order would be maintained in Little Rock as integration continued. The president praised the "sincere and conscientious efforts of the citizens of Little Rock" to comply with the federal mandate to "preserve and respect the law—whether or not they personally agree with it," and expressed confidence that Arkansans would "oppose any violence by extremists."

It became clear, however, that white supremacists in Arkansas were determined to block entry of the Arkansas Nine; President Eisenhower responded on September 23 with Proclamation 3204, commanding "all persons engaged in . . . obstruction of justice to cease and desist therefrom and to disperse forthwith." In a note to himself, Eisenhower acknowledged the need for federal action "not to enforce integration but to prevent opposition by violence to orders of a court." On September 24 at 9 P.M. the president addressed the nation from the Oval Office, announcing that he had "issued an Executive Order directing the use of troops under Federal authority to aid in the execution of Federal Law at Little Rock." With the 101st Airborne standing guard, the Arkansas Nine were finally able to attend classes at Central High.

academically in integrated schools. This study supported reformers' attempts to eliminate informal segregation through policy means. Attempts to address segregation in locations like Detroit came in the form of forced public busing, where black children were bused to white-majority schools and white children were bused to black-majority schools. Busing solutions were often unpopular with parents of all races, who sharply opposed sending their children out of their local neighborhoods. Several other approaches to desegregation met with varied success. Rezoning enabled neighborhood schools to draw on mixed-race populations. Some districts closed effectively segregated schools, and then reorganized them to serve different purposes. For example, in Morristown, New Jersey, a local segregated grade school was closed, then turned into a junior high school that served a larger area in order to draw on a more diverse population. In other locations, student transfers between schools were eliminated to keep resegregation from occurring.

It took further legislation passed by Congress to provide the motivation for many regions to address the challenges of desegregation. Title VI of the 1964 Civil Rights Act stated that federal funding could be removed from school districts if the programs that funding supported were racially discriminatory. This threat of reduced funding, combined with the previous decade of reforms occasionally supported by military force, aided the desegregation movement, which took root across the United States by the end of the 1960s.

African-American students pass through a phalanx of white boys during a tense period of school integration in Clinton, Tennessee, in December 1956.

TEACHERS AND TEACHING

The gender divide in teaching fields was slightly altered in these two decades, as men returning from World War II received the benefits of the G.I. Bill and were encouraged to go into teaching careers. In 1950 21.3 percent of K–12 teachers were male; by 1968 that proportion rose to 31.3 percent. Men remained far more likely to teach at the high school levels, while lower-paid elementary and middle school positions remained the province of female teachers. Another postwar change affected the number of women attracted to teaching professions. Because of a shortage of teachers across the nation in wartime, "marriage bars" (laws outlawing married female teachers) were declared illegal in 1944. After that time, increasing numbers of married women entered and stayed in the field of education. By 1960 42 percent of female teachers were married.

By 1960 the era of the two-year teacher's college came to an end. The vast majority of elementary, middle, and high schools required a four-year degree for teacher certification. Many of these colleges either closed their doors or combined with other local colleges and universities to create four-year teacher education programs. One of the few such colleges to keep its name in the United States was Teacher's College at Columbia University, which still provides undergraduate and graduate programs in education. Reform organizations developed to ease this transitional process from isolated teachers' program to part of college curricula. One such program was Trainers of Teacher Trainers (TTT), founded in 1967 and disbanded by 1973. In its brief existence, the projects sponsored by TTT at many liberal-arts colleges spawned innovative teaching methods that education graduates successfully brought into public schools.

Other programs sought to retrain college graduates to become teachers. One of these was the National Teacher Corps (NTC), founded in 1965 on the model of the Peace Corps. One of its core ideas was to train teachers effectively for urban school positions so that they could reach low-income and minority children. For two years, participants with bachelor's degrees in other fields taught two classes and then attended after-school seminars taught by high school teachers and local professors in order to gain a master's degree in education. A bachelor's degree program was also available in some areas of the country. While the NTC structure remained similar across program locations, curricula and pedagogy were developed differently in each program. This kept the NTC from developing a coherent educational philosophy, and caused backlash among existing school personnel. Teachers and administrators questioned the wisdom of sending untrained interns into schools to teach without prior classroom experience or background in educational theories. Participants felt isolated in settings where they were not treated as qualified teachers, and their initial enthusiasm often turned to frustration when they could not enact educational innovations due to local resistance. The program eventually disbanded in 1981.

A private Christian academy that opened in 1954. One attempt to stop integration in Virginia gave tuition grants to white children so that they could attend private schools known as "segregation academies."

THE RISE OF THE TEACHER'S UNION

Local resistance to tax increases brought on the organization of numerous teachers' strikes in the late 1940s and early 1950s. In cities like Buffalo, Detroit, and Minneapolis, teachers demanded pay increases or work reductions in response to citizens' refusal to fund local education. Outside these local areas, teachers turned to two major national organizations for support for their demands as workers. While the National Education Association (NEA) had existed since 1857, a gradual shift in teachers' working conditions led to a major challenge to its leadership abilities as the premier teachers' professional association. The NEA had once served as a national network for administrators to compare management methods and strategies, and continued to have a membership composed of both teachers and administrators. As an organization, its mixed membership resulted in muted responses to school funding crises across the country in the 1950s, because administrators' goals were often at cross-purposes with those of teachers.

By contrast, the American Federation of Teachers (AFT) was composed solely of teachers, and was much better-placed to encourage teacher activism. The AFT is the branch of the American Federation of Labor (AFL-CIO) for education workers. During the 1960s, the AFT became a hotbed for activism as teachers unionized in order to engage in collective bargaining

Prayer in Public Schools

The Supreme Court in 1962 ruled in *Engel v. Vitale* in a 6-1 decision that a prayer mandated by the Board of Education of Union Free School District No. 9, in New Hyde Park, New York, was illegal under the First Amendment of the Constitution. The Senate Committee on the Judiciary responded in the summer of 1962 by holding hearings to amend the Constitution to make school prayers legal. The group Protestants and Other Americans issued the following statement on July 26 for the separation of church and state in support of the Supreme Court's ruling.

The attempt by a group of New York public officials to prescribe a prayer for schoolchildren in that state has been pronounced unconstitutional by a 6 to 1 decision of the U.S. Supreme Court. All persons who believe in prayer as the authentic thrust of the human spirit toward its Maker should welcome the decision. We predict that when the current wave of emotion has subsided the Court's decision in Engel v. Vitale *will loom as a landmark of religious freedom. . .*

The principle enunciated by the Court in this opinion is eminently sound. It reiterates the deeply cherished American principle of the separation of church and state. As Justice Black correctly notes: ". . .In this country it is not part of the business of government to compose official prayers for any group of the American people to recite as part of a religious program carried on by government."

. . .The regents' prayer and the public school religion of which it is an example are a religion of the least common denominator. This is the standard brand of religion that public officials could be counted on to provide if this matter were placed in their domain. The objection to their product is not that it is too religious but that it is not religious enough. We are not convinced that there has been a collapse of the church and the home as to necessitate a transfer of religious responsibility to public officials. The fact that such a transfer has been seriously proposed and urged, and to some extent accepted, is in itself a symptom of spiritual sickness which only a genuine spiritual revival can cure. Surely government intervention is not the answer here. The state's edict cannot produce the sincere seeker and the contrite heart.

Engel v. Vitale marked the beginning of a series of Supreme Court cases that had the effect of removing Christian prayer from public schools. In 1963 the *Abington School District v. Schempp* ruling outlawed recitations of Bible passages and the Lord's Prayer in Pennsylvania. Later cases outlawed prayers at public-school commencements and student-led prayers at school events. The groundwork for this move toward secular public schools began in the 1960s, a time when society questioned long-held beliefs and religious and other minorities began to gain access to the power of the court system.

and ask for better wages, safer and better-equipped schools, and other employee benefits. The AFT had chapters in every state, and organized its members around specific goals, including teacher pay and worker protections such as grievance procedures. It also hired lobbyists to work in Washington, D.C. and advocate for teachers' rights and protections at the federal government level. From 1960 to 1970, AFT membership grew from 60,000 to over 200,000.

As unionization of teachers grew over these two decades, changes that resulted had both positive and negative impacts. Teachers won collective bargaining rights in many parts of the country, enabling wage and benefits negotiations. As a result, school districts had to bear the costs of pay raises and insurance, and deal with additional professional regulations that denied administrative flexibility. For example, new grievance procedures gave teachers an important means to appeal negative parent or administrator evaluations, but made it much harder for school administrators to fire incompetent teachers. Basing pay raises and promotions on seniority improved teacher retention, but kept administrators from rewarding and promoting teachers based on achievements and qualifications. The best practices in relations between teachers and school administration remain controversial to the present day.

HEAD START

Project Head Start began in 1965 as part of President Lyndon Johnson's War on Poverty. Aimed at children from three years to school entry age, the program's mission was to provide quality preschool education in order "to increase the social competence of children from low-income families." The Office of Economic Opportunity worked with a panel of child development experts led by Dr. Robert Cooke to establish seven goals in their initial framework for the Head Start program:

1. Improving the child's physical health and physical abilities.

2. Helping the emotional and social development of the child by encouraging self-confidence, spontaneity, curiosity, and self-discipline.

3. Improving the child's mental processes and skills, with particular attention to conceptual and verbal skills.

4. Establishing patterns and expectations of success for the child that will create a climate of confidence for future learning efforts.

5. Increasing the child's capacity to relate positively to family members and others, while at the same time strengthening the family's ability to relate positively to the child and his problems.

6. Developing in the child and his family a responsible attitude toward society, and encouraging society to work with the poor in solving their problems.

7. Increasing the sense of dignity and self-worth within the child and his family.

Children's Literature and Reading

Dr. Seuss drawing an illustration of the Grinch for How the Grinch Stole Christmas.

Sally, Dick, and Jane first made their way into the hands of American school children in 1930. The books were a series of adventures that followed three young siblings, Dick, the loyal older brother, Jane, the middle child, and Sally, a precocious tot. The books were in publication by Scott Foresman and Co. until 1965 and were widely popular. Each reader was designed to teach students to read by using simply constructed sentences, repetition, and only introducing one new word per page. Reading instruction focused on sight reading, which is the recognition of whole words rather than phonetic structure. After increased awareness of the necessity of phonetic instruction in the early 1970s, the Dick and Jane books fell out of favor with educators. Dick and Jane reflected the racial and societal inequities due to their middle class, Caucasian lives. Not only did they reinforce the racial divide, but women's roles in society were narrowly depicted.

Dr. Seuss was born Theodor Seuss Geisel in 1904. He began his career not as a children's writer, but as an illustrator for Standard Oil advertisements. His first children's book, *And to Think That I Saw It on Mulberry Street*, was published in 1937.

As World War II approached he began to focus more on political cartoons, creating over 400 that were published in a New York magazine titled *PM*. Dr. Seuss wrote some of the most beloved children's classics ever published, including *How the Grinch Stole Christmas*, *The Sneeches*, *If I Ran the Zoo*, and *The Cat and The Hat*.

Head Start programs quickly became an essential part of public education. In later decades, the program expanded to cover children from birth to age three in select regions of the country. The program continues to work with young children and their parents today. One reason for the program's long-lasting appeal is its direct involvement of parents in their children's education. A second reason is its appeal to policymakers and government funding sources. Research demonstrates that the advantages of Head Start carry into the school years to increase the likelihood of academic success in elementary school and beyond.

HIGH SCHOOLS

U.S. Census Bureau data shows that in 1950, 59 out of 100 U.S. 17-year-olds graduated from high school. By 1969 that number rose to 77 out of 100. This significant increase took place over the specific period that desegregation increased access to public schools, suggesting that unequal school quality might have played a significant role in minorities' lower graduation rates.

Examination of a typical high school curriculum shows many similarities to current programs. Graduation and college entrance requirements were less standardized in the 1950s and 1960s, but many of the core subject areas taught remain the same. Biology, chemistry, and physics were standard science courses. Math requirements included algebra and geometry, while more advanced courses such as trigonometry were electives. History, English, physical education, and government classes were also usually included in graduation requirements. By the late 1960s, electronics classes became the precursor to computer science courses. Other common elective courses

When Little Rock, Arkansas, closed public high schools during the 1958–59 school year rather than integrate them, some students used the technology of television to follow lectures at home.

Educational Theorist B.F. Skinner

Burrhus Frederick Skinner (1904–90) was an early innovator, but came relatively late to the field of educational psychology. As a youth, he loved to build machines, but few of them worked. At Hamilton College he majored in English literature. After college, he wanted to become a writer, and moved back into his parents' home. A year later he had only a handful of newspaper articles and a few model ships to show for his labors. He applied to graduate school in psychology, and was accepted to Harvard in 1928.

At Harvard, Skinner was mentored by William Crozier. Crozier was then chair of Harvard's department of physiology, and his field of research was animal behavior. Skinner was interested in the connections between experimental conditions and animal behavior, so he found Crozier's work of great interest. Skinner won a fellowship and studied behavior patterns in rats, discovering a concept he called operant behavior. The rats' behavior was determined not by anything that happened before their action, but by its consequences. For example, the rats would press a bar in their cages faster if the bar press resulted in food. Skinner studied the consequences of varying behavior and reward patterns and described the successful patterns of behavior reinforcement he found as operant conditioning. In simple terms, operant conditioning arranges reinforcement patterns to produce a desired behavior.

Skinner's work enabled him to begin a faculty career. He taught in Minnesota and Indiana, married, and fathered two daughters before returning to Harvard in 1948. That year, he published a utopian vision of society, Walden Two. In 1953 he published Science and Human Behavior, a textbook often used in undergraduate psychology courses. By 1956 Skinner's research into controlling human behavior led him to develop the framework of programmed instruction. In observing his daughter's fourth grade classroom, he noticed that rote learning of mathematics did not provide the immediate feedback that many students needed. A student could complete an entire sheet of problems, and then have to wait for feedback until the next math class.

Skinner designed a teaching machine that broke down skills into small steps, and then corrected students as they worked on the machines, either repeating concepts as necessary, or progressing on to further steps. Because he was working over 30 years before the introduction of the personal computer, his machines fell out of fashion quickly. However, his educational theories and methods were influential into the early 1970s, and they have been revisited in the computer age.

In 1956 Skinner founded a prestigious academic journal, the Journal of the Experimental Analysis of Behavior. In 1957 his book Verbal Behavior sought to explain why humans communicate in the ways that they do. One of his most lasting contributions to educational psychology is the idea that positive reinforcement, or rewarding performance of a desired behavior, is more effective in shaping human behavior than punishment.

included music, fine arts, journalism, vocational classes, and foreign languages. These elective classes were not available everywhere, but were most
often offered in wealthier or larger school districts due to the availability of
teachers and funding for facilities and materials.

SPUTNIK, AND MATH AND SCIENCE EDUCATION

On October 4, 1957, the Soviet Union launched the first successful unmanned
satellite, Sputnik, into space. The United States reacted first with alarm, and
then with massive national investments into space science research and development. During the time of the Cold War, when fear of Communism was at
its height, the United States believed that a successful national defense rested
on having weapons and intelligence capabilities superior to the Soviet Union.
Widespread dissatisfaction with American schools spread, as politicians and
educators alike began to worry that U.S. students would not be able to compete with the students of the Soviet Union.

In 1958 President Eisenhower signed the National Defense Education Act
(NDEA). This act pumped over $100 million into math, science, and engineer-
ing education programs from elementary schools through higher education.
The federal government demonstrated that centralized funding could directly
affect public school curriculums nationwide, also making the nation's defense
priorities clear educational priorities. The result was a "back-to-basics" education movement that quickly brought an end to the progressive era of student-
directed learning in the majority of public school classrooms. By the early 1960s
classroom teaching was under greater scrutiny than it had been in decades.

The federal agency charged with overseeing reforms in science and math
curricula was the National Science Foundation (NSF). Founded in 1950, the
NSF funded science and engineering research as well as educational initiatives
such as the NDEA. After the launch of Sputnik, the NSF took a two-pronged
approach to improving science and math education nationwide.

First, it created programs meant to improve the knowledge base of math
and science teachers. By encouraging and funding teachers in these subject
areas to earn M.A.s, the NSF meant to increase the number of highly qualified
teachers in public school classrooms. This program led to an overall increase
in well-trained teachers across the country, but a side effect was that a number of teachers who earned such degrees left teaching for higher-paid jobs in
industry and administration.

Second, NSF sought to improve the teaching materials used in classrooms
by convening panels of experts to develop K–12 math and science materials.
This part of the initiative was ultimately unsuccessful because the materials
developed were often unsuited to actual classroom situations. Teachers did
not understand the abstractions of the "new math" curriculum well enough
to teach successfully. Parents found the concepts too difficult to help their
children with homework. Both were suspicious of a federal curriculum that

limited application of math concepts that they considered basic skills such as division, fractions, percentages, and geometry. By the 1970s, there was a public backlash against the NSF curricular materials, and most of the NSF educational programs ceased.

CONCLUSION

Tension between federal and local controls of public school curricula continued into later decades, but *Brown v. Board of Education* and desegregation remain the hallmarks of educational progress in the 1950s and 1960s. Desegregation efforts would extend for years and would soon provoke new violence during the controversy over busing in Boston in the early 1970s.

HEATHER A. BEASLEY

Further Readings

Beals, Melba Pattillo. *Warriors Don't Cry: A Searing Memoir of the Battle to Integrate Little Rock's Central High*. New York: Washington Square Press, 1995.

Brown v. Board of Education. 347 U.S. 483 (1954). Available online: http://www.findlaw.com. Accessed April 2008.

Cuban, Larry. *How Teachers Taught: Consistency and Change in American Classrooms 1880–1990*. New York: Teachers College Press, 1993.

Eisenhower, Dwight D. Eisenhower Archives. Available online: http://www.eisenhower.archives.gov. Accessed October 2008.

Gibboney, Richard A. *The Stone Trumpet: A Story of Practical School Reform, 1960–1990*. Albany, NY: SUNY Press, 1994.

Lappan, Glenda T. "Lessons from the Sputnik Era in Mathematics Education." Available online: http://www.nationalacademies.org/sputnik/lappan1.htm. Accessed April 2008.

Mondale, Sarah, and Sheila Curran Bernard. *School: The Story of American Public Education*. Boston, MA: Beacon Press, 2001.

Nichols, David A. *A Matter of Justice: Eisenhower and the Beginning of the Civil Rights Revolution*. New York: Simon and Schuster, 2007.

Rotherham, Andrew J., and Jane Hannaway, eds. *Collective Bargaining in Education*. Cambridge, MA: Harvard Education Publishing, 2006.

Skinner, B.F. *A Brief Autobiography*. Available online: http://ww2.lafayette.edu/~allanr/autobio.html. Accessed April 2008.

Tyack, David B. and Larry Cuban. *Tinkering Toward Utopia: A Century of Public School Reform*. Cambridge, MA: Harvard U. Press, 1995.

Urban, Wayne and Jennings Wagoner. *American Education: A History*. Boston, MA: McGraw Hill, 2000.

Chapter 9

Science and Technology

"It will not be one man going to the moon . . .
it will be an entire nation. For all of us must work to put him there."
—President John F. Kennedy

BY 1950 SCIENCE and technology were intertwined with the military and, more broadly, with concerns about national security. Science and technology had rallied to the national defense in World War II. Computers, radar, and the atomic bomb were fruits of the close relationship between science, technology, and military planners. Consensus had formed that science and technology were vital to the defense of the United States. The postwar world was full of threats that only science and technology could counter.

THE COLD WAR

Rather than peace, the end of World War II brought an uneasy coexistence between the United States and the Soviet Union. The emerging Cold War caused both the United States and the Soviet Union to invest heavily in weapons developed by scientists and engineers. Security concerns escalated in 1949 when the Soviet Union detonated an atomic bomb, increasing the prospect that the two nations might annihilate one another with nuclear weapons.

The fall of China to Communism in 1949 underscored the fact that Communist regimes could field larger armies than the United States. To counter the Communist threat, the United States would need to leverage science and technology in lieu of manpower. The Korean War seemed to validate the premise that Communist governments were inherently expansionistic. To

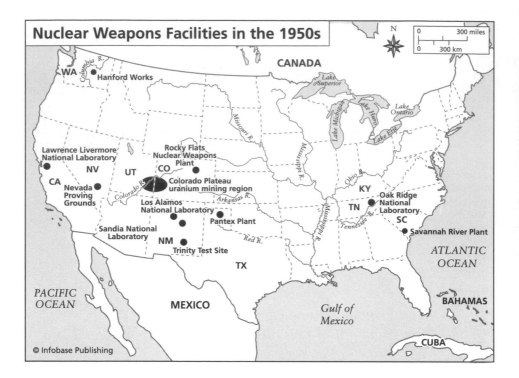

Nuclear Weapons Facilities in the 1950s

meet the Communist threat the Defense Department spent money on science and technology. In 1950, the year that the Korean War began, the Department of Defense spent $700 million on research and development. The next year the amount rose to $1.3 billion, and in 1952 to $1.6 billion. By 1952 the Defense Department and the Atomic Energy Commission funded 40 percent of research in industry and academe.

The Department of Defense and the Atomic Energy Commission were not alone in funding science and technology. The Army, Navy, Air Force, and several federal agencies all funded research. In 1950 Congress created the National Science Foundation to fund research in science and engineering. Unlike the Defense Department and the military, the National Science Foundation was not beholden to fund military research, but had a broad mandate to fund basic and applied science and engineering.

The division of science into "basic" and "applied" predates the formation of the United States. Basic science aims to advance knowledge without regard to utility, whereas applied science seeks only useful knowledge. By the time the National Science Foundation was founded, basic science had come to rival applied science in the funding of research. Scientists had done well to link basic science and technology, envisioning a pipeline in which government funded basic science at one end to reap technology at the other end. This coupling of basic science and technology, while popular, is not accurate. Basic science generates knowledge, not technology. The link is closer among applied science, engineering, and technology. Computers, for example, were the product of the alliance between applied science, engineering, and technology. In its early years the National Science Foundation did not have the money to fund research on a grand scale. The National Science Foundation's budget was only $151,000 in 1951. From this modest beginning the budget rose to $3.5 million the next year, $130 million in 1959, and nearly $500 million in 1968.

In the 1950s scientists and engineers conducted research at universities, foundations, and government agencies. They communicated the results of their research in peer review journals and at scientific and engineering conferences. Scientific and engineering associations sponsored these journals and conferences. Because of growing specialization, most of the scientific and engineering associations limited their membership to the practitioners of a single discipline. Entomology, electrical engineering, and innumerable other disciplines each had its own association. The fragmentation of science and engineering into subfields made it difficult, perhaps impossible, for anyone to be knowledgeable in every subfield. The specialist had replaced the generalist to the benefit of the discovery of specialized knowledge, and to the detriment of the synthesis of several subfields into a meaningful whole.

Science, engineering, and technology had formed a close alliance with mathematics. Physics and chemistry had a long history of employing mathematics to express knowledge, and by the 1950s even biologists, population geneticists in particular, were using mathematics to express their research findings. Fragmented though they were, science, engineering, and technology could agree on mathematics as a universal language. A few sciences resisted the drift toward mathematics. Botany and entomology, for example, remained descriptive rather than quantitative, especially when they did not use genetics. The land-grant colleges, where many scientists and engineers taught and conducted research, much of it applied, were in the midst of a transition from colleges with several thousand faculty and students, to universities with tens of thousands of faculty and students. At these universities the agricultural sciences and engineering were the leading areas of research. In the postwar era, scientists and engineers, wherever they worked, commanded greater prestige than at any time in the past.

THE HYDROGEN BOMB

The Cold War had its own logic in which the United States and Soviet Union each used science, engineering, and technology to develop ever more lethal weapons before the enemy. The Soviet detonation of a uranium bomb in 1949 split American physicists into two camps. Former Manhattan Project leader J. Robert Oppenheimer and Albert Einstein led one camp of physicists in opposing the building of the hydrogen bomb. Oppenheimer asserted that a hydrogen bomb would have no military value. An arsenal of uranium and plutonium bombs would give the military more than enough destructive capability. A hydrogen bomb would have value only against cities, with their hundreds of thousands of civilians. Such carnage would only heighten the savagery of war. Joining Oppenheimer, Einstein opposed the building of a hydrogen bomb on ethical grounds. The radioactive fallout from the detonation of a hydrogen bomb, Einstein feared, would be great enough to poison all life, thereby extinguishing life on earth. Einstein and Oppenheimer won support from the Atomic Energy Commission. Oppenheimer used his position as head of its General Advisory Committee to gain a recommendation against building a hydrogen bomb. The Atomic Energy Commission, as was its responsibility, reported its recommendation to President Harry S Truman.

In contrast to Einstein and Oppenheimer, former Manhattan Project physicist Edward Teller led the camp of physicists in support of building a hydrogen bomb. As early as 1942 Teller had advocated that the United States build a hydrogen bomb. A realist, Teller understood that the Soviet Union would build a hydrogen bomb if the United States delayed or did nothing. In an arms race the United States could not afford to finish second without imperiling its security. Truman shared Teller's view and, shunting aside the Atomic Energy Commission recommendation, directed the commission on January 31, 1950, to build a hydrogen bomb.

In contrast to uranium and plutonium bombs, a hydrogen bomb was a fusion rather than a fission weapon. A fusion bomb unifies two atoms into a single atom. Teller proposed to fuse together two hydrogen atoms to make a helium atom. One helium atom weighs slightly less than two hydrogen atoms because a fraction of its mass converts to energy in accord with Einstein's famous equation $E=mc^2$. Because the speed of light squared equals 90 million billion meters per second squared, a tiny amount of matter converts to enormous energy. Simple in conception, the development of a hydrogen bomb was not without an obstacle. In order to fuse two hydrogen atoms, physicists must infuse the atoms with tremendous energy. But where could physicists find this energy? The solution, Teller

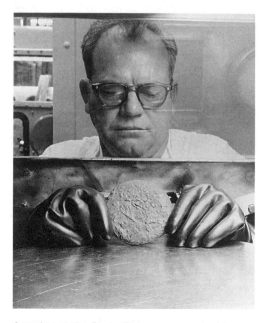

A worker at the Rocky Flats weapons plant in Colorado handling plutonium inside a glove box.

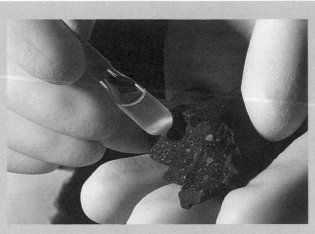

A piece of the Murchison meteorite beside a tube holding particles found in the meteorite.

Toward the Origin of Life

One of science's great mysteries is how life originated. Some think life arose elsewhere in the solar system and landed on earth as the passengers on a meteorite. This life would have been primitive, no more complex than bacteria. Nobel laureate Harold Urey thought life had originated on earth, not elsewhere. He proposed that his graduate student at the University of Chicago, Stanley Miller, undertake an experiment in 1953. Urey assumed that earth's early atmosphere was similar to that of Jupiter, containing ammonia, methane, and hydrogen. Urey suggested that Miller pump these gases into a chamber partially filled with water to simulate the primordial ocean. Miller generated electric sparks in the mixture to simulate lightning. In only a few weeks Miller derived amino acids, the precursors of protein. Although amino acids are not alive, they are found in all life, implying that the first life was made of amino acids.

Urey and Miller found evidence for their view that life had arisen spontaneously in a reducing atmosphere in the Murchison meteorite, a meteorite that fell to earth in 1969. The meteorite contained the same amino acids and in the same proportion that Miller had generated. Yet how life arose on earth remains a mystery. No one yet knows how the amino acids combined to form life, or how they replicated. In contrast to amino acids, DNA can replicate itself. But DNA is far more complex than amino acids. No one has yet shown whether or how amino acids assembled into DNA or another self-replicating molecule. For all his efforts Miller did not demonstrate how life originated. He showed only that amino acids could arise rapidly in a reducing atmosphere. Given billions of years (earth is 4.5 billion years old) these amino acids, combining and recombining innumerable times, may have assembled into a self-replicating molecule. Perhaps life arose from such humble beginnings.

The 70,000-ton hydrogen bomb exploding over Enewetak Atoll on November 1, 1952.

understood, lay in detonating a fission bomb to energize the hydrogen atoms. A hydrogen bomb thus had two components: a conventional uranium or plutonium bomb, and a mass of hydrogen atoms. Mathematician Stanislaw Ulam calculated that the radiation from a fission bomb would compress the hydrogen atoms into a tiny volume, and then excite them to the high energy necessary for them to fuse into helium atoms. Teller, Ulam, and a team of physicists and engineers gathered at Los Alamos, New Mexico. Developing and testing a small prototype first, Teller's group was ready to detonate a hydrogen bomb in late 1952. Fearful of criticism from the media, Truman insisted on the greatest secrecy. On November 1, 1952, Teller and his colleagues detonated a hydrogen bomb in the Marshall Islands. The blast was 450 times more powerful than the plutonium bomb dropped on Nagasaki, Japan, yielding 10.4 megatons of energy. At 20 feet tall and 70,000 tons, the bomb was too large to have been delivered by airplane. Its military value was therefore scant. By February 1954, Teller's group had miniaturized the bomb, achieving a weapon small enough to be carried by airplane to its target. Despite being smaller than the first hydrogen bomb, "Shrimp" yielded 15 megatons of energy, one-third more than the first hydrogen bomb. By then the Army had nuclear warheads capable of being fired like artillery. Nuclear missiles followed, launched either from the ground or from a submarine. The Soviets developed their own nuclear arsenal, and the United States found itself in the midst of a lethal and expensive arms race. Some physicists and journalists, taking their cue from Einstein, wondered whether humanity could survive a nuclear war. For all its achievements, science could not guarantee a positive outcome.

NUCLEAR POWER

Radioactive atoms were useful for more than making bombs. These atoms could generate electricity by a similar process as that used to detonate a fission bomb. The physicist who wished to generate electricity from fission shot neutrons at radioactive atoms, though never as fast or as many as was necessary to create an explosion. The radioactive atoms, upon impact by a neutron, split, releasing energy in the form of heat. In many nuclear reactors the heat from fission boiled water. The boiling water rose as steam, which entered a chamber. There the steam spun a turbine which, acting as a dynamo, generated electricity. The Truman administration favored the funding of solar energy over nuclear power. In contrast, President Eisenhower gave the speech "Atoms for Peace" in December 1953. Eisenhower urged the federal government to fund the building of nuclear reactors for generating electricity. Optimistic about the potential of nuclear energy, Lewis Strauss, chairman of the Atomic Energy Commission, predicted in 1954 that electricity would become so plentiful that it would be too cheap to sell. In this Utopian vision, public utilities, awash in electricity, would give it away.

Events unfolded rapidly. In 1949 the Atomic Energy Commission empowered the National Reactor Testing Station (today the Idaho National Laboratory) in Arco, Idaho, to build a nuclear reactor. In 1950 the National Reactor Testing Station began construction on Experimental Breeder Reactor-1, generating electricity from it on December 20, 1951. The reactor yielded 100 kilowatts of electricity per hour. The station also built the Boiling Water Reactor Experimental Facilities, the first nuclear power plant to generate electricity from steam. On July 17, 1955, the Boiling Water Reactor lit Arco's streets, buildings, and homes. The success of the Arco reactors led other cities in the United States to build nuclear power plants. The Santa Susana Field Laboratory in Los Angeles built a nuclear reactor in April 1957, and Westinghouse built a reactor in Shippingport, Pennsylvania, that December.

The Shippingport Atomic Power Station, which began operating in December 1957, was the country's first large-scale central station nuclear power plant.

In addition to civilian use of nuclear energy, the U.S. Navy moved quickly to power its ships by nuclear reactors. Admiral Hyman G. Rickover led the Navy into the era of nuclear power. The USS *Nautilus* was in 1955 the first submarine to be powered by a nuclear reactor. Because a nuclear reactor can operate for years, the *Nautilus* could stay submerged far longer than a conventional submarine. Underwater for long durations and away from Soviet submarines, the *Nautilus* threatened the Soviet Union by patrolling the ocean undetected. In 1960 the Navy launched the USS *Enterprise*, the first nuclear powered aircraft carrier. Like the *Nautilus*, the *Enterprise* could patrol the ocean much longer than a conventional aircraft carrier.

COMPUTERS

In 1950 computers were large and slow by today's standards. In 1951 J. Presper Eckert and John Mauchly, inventors of the Electrical Numerical Integrator and Computer, designed the Universal Automatic Computer (UNIVAC). Weighing nearly 15 tons, UNIVAC had 5,200 vacuum tubes and used 125 kilowatts of electricity per hour. Curiously UNIVAC used vacuum tubes rather than transistors, which Bell Laboratory's William Shockley, John Bardeen, and Walter Brattain had invented in 1948. The result of using vacuum tubes rather than transistors was a computer the size of a room. Able to calculate 2,000 addition or subtraction problems a second and 450 multiplication problems a second, UNIVAC could store 1,000 words or numbers in its memory, each up to 12 letters or numbers long. On March 31, 1951, Eckert and Mauchly sold the first UNIVAC to the Census Bureau, which used it in 1952 to predict the outcome of the presidential election between Dwight D. Eisenhower and Adlai Stevenson. On election night UNIVAC analyzed three million votes (7 percent of the total), forecasting that Eisenhower would win with 438 electoral votes. When the polls closed, Eisenhower won with 442 electoral votes, underscoring the accuracy of UNIVAC. Between 1951 and 1958 Eckert and Mauchly sold 50 UNIVACs, most of them to government

An early electronic computer, this EDVAC (Electronic Discrete Variable Automatic Computer) was used by the U.S. Army from 1951 to 1961.

Since it was built in 1963, the Arecibo Radio Telescope in Puerto Rico has had many functions, including work in the search for intelligent life in the universe, as well as interstellar research and military uses.

agencies, the military, and large corporations. In addition to these sales, Eckert and Mauchly gave a UNIVAC each to Harvard University, the University of Pennsylvania, and Case Institute of Technology.

In the 1950s computer scientists began building computers with transistors, rather than vacuum tubes, to reduce their size. The integrated circuit hastened the trend toward miniaturization. In 1952 radar technician Geoffrey Dummer conceived the idea of an integrated circuit, but failed to build it. In 1959 Texas Instruments scientist Jack Kilby built an integrated circuit using the element germanium. Because germanium is rare and expensive (only 131 pounds were mined worldwide in 1950), Fairchild Semiconductor scientist Robert Noyce built an integrated circuit in 1961 with the more plentiful and cheaper silicon. An integrated circuit was so small that it fit on a one-inch square chip. Thanks to the integrated circuit, the space program of the 1960s used a computer small enough to fit aboard a rocket, and the Minuteman missile used a computer small enough to fit aboard the missile. Computers that in 1950 were the size of a room, had by the late 1960s shrunk to the size of a television.

Still too expensive for the average American, computers spread in the 1950s and 1960s to businesses. No longer the preserve of physicists and mathematicians, the computer courted a wide audience of business people, many of

Pratt and Whitney JT3D turbofan jet engines on a British Caledonian Boeing 707 passenger plane.

Boeing 707

Using the Boeing 367-80 as a prototype, Boeing found the Air Force eager to use it in refueling its combat planes. The commercial prospects of the 367-80 were modest. The fuselage was wide enough for only four passengers in a row, once space was allotted for the stewardesses. The fuselage expanded to accommodate six passengers in each row, the 707 made its first flight in December 1955. Pan American, which had ordered twenty 707s from Boeing in 1955, made the 707's first commercial flight from New York City to Paris in 1958. Boeing revamped the 707 several times, changing sizes and engines to suit buyers. The most popular engine on the 707 was the Pratt and Whitney JT3D, a turbofan jet engine with high thrust and modest fuel consumption. The first variant of the 707 was the 707-120, a small, fast jet. The 707-138 had a short body. The 707-320 had long wings and the powerful JT4A turbofan jet engine. The 707-420 was identical to the 320, except that the 420 used Rolls-Royce Conway turbofan jet engines, a change Boeing made to attract British carriers. The 707-320C had a large door to accommodate cargo, rather than passengers.

The 707 was part of a revolution in air travel. During its lifetime the 707 went from servicing a small clientele of business people, to hosting large numbers of business travelers and vacationers. In the 1950s and 1960s air travel became a mass phenomenon. Airport terminals grew, the number of runways multiplied and their length increased, and the number of jobs grew for baggage handlers, stewardesses, and attendants to make passenger reservations. The 707 succumbed to its success. By the 1970s it was no longer large enough to accommodate all of the people who wanted to fly. Other aircraft manufacturers, notably Douglas, competed with Boeing by designing bigger planes. Boeing upgraded too, designing the 747. In 1983 the 707 flew its last flight in the United States, though Iran and Argentina still use the 707.

whom had no advanced training in science and mathematics. They needed a simpler programming language than the languages academics had invented. In 1953 International Business Machines (IBM) scientist John W. Backus began work on a simple programming language that would in 1954 become the Mathematical Formula Translating System (FORTRAN). In 1959 the Pentagon's Short Range Committee wrote the Common Business Oriented Language (COBOL). In 1960 Dartmouth College mathematician John Kemeny and Dartmouth's Kiewit Computer Center director Thomas Kurtz wrote Beginner's All-Purpose Symbolic Instructional Code (BASIC), the simplest of the three languages. It had only 14 commands, compared to the hundreds of earlier programming languages.

AUTOMOBILE AND AIRPLANE

The heady days of the 1950s and 1960s (before the oil embargo of the 1970s) witnessed the production of fast cars and big engines. In 1955 Chevrolet introduced its first eight-cylinder engine into several of its models, including the sporty Corvette. The V8 with a two-barrel carburetor rated 165 horsepower, one with a four-barrel carburetor registered 185 horsepower, and a third version tallied 195 horsepower, attracting teen boys who wanted to impress girls. In 1955 Ford tried to match Chevy by putting a V8 in its Thunderbird, though it reached only 120 horsepower. In 1957 Chevy upgraded its V8 so that the third of its three versions topped out at 270 horsepower. In 1957 Chevy was the first to use fuel injection in its engines. Fuel injection was standard, for example, in the 1957 Corvette and Bel Air. Hoping to compete with Chevrolet, Buick put a V8 in several of its models in 1957. In 1965 the Ford Mustang rated 225 horsepower and in 1967 320 horsepower. Eager to compete with Chevrolet and Ford, the Plymouth Barracuda registered 235 horsepower, and the Pontiac Firebird came with one of three eight-cylinder engines in 1967, the third topping out at 325 horsepower.

The automobile was more than fast and powerful. New technology made the experience of driving more comfortable and led to other improvements. In 1960 the Chevy Valiant was the first car to have an alternator, rather than a generator to produce alternating current for the headlights and other electrical accessories. During the 1960s the alternator became standard on American cars. In 1961 power steering and power brakes were standard on the Ford Thunderbird. The Thunderbird came with an added touch: the steering wheel pivoted 18 inches to the right, easing the driver's entrance and exit from the car. In 1963 Studebaker was the first American automaker to equip its cars with disc brakes. In 1965 both the Corvette and American Motors Corporation's Rambler Marlin had four-wheel disc brakes. In 1965 power windows and power seats were standard on the Cadillac DeVille. In 1966 the Oldsmobile Toronado was the first car with front wheel drive since Auburn Automobile Company's Cord in 1937.

Like the automobile, the airplane became faster and more powerful, adopting the jet engine to overpower its predecessor, propeller driven aircraft. The Navy and Air Force used jet fighters and bombers in the Korean War. In 1951 Boeing designed the B-47, and in 1952 the B-52, both jet bombers, though neither saw action in Korea. The B-52, pounding targets, was a symbol of American power in the Vietnam War. Not simply a military supplier, Boeing designed jet planes for commercial use. In 1954 Boeing designed the 367-80, a prototype of the more popular 707, with a cruising speed of 592 miles per hour. In 1955 Pan American Airways bought 30 707s. Intent on competing with Boeing, Douglas designed its first jet, the DC-8, in 1955. In 1955 Pan American bought 20 DC-8s and United bought 30, using them for its nonstop transatlantic flights.

DEOXYRIBONUCLEIC ACID (DNA)

In 1944 a team of biologists led by Oswald Avery identified DNA as the molecule of heredity. Further work revealed that DNA contributed nothing to a cell's metabolism. Rather than participate in biochemical reactions, DNA was a set of instructions that directed the chemical reactions in a cell. To learn how DNA performed this function, biologists needed to know the structure of DNA. At Kings College in London, Rosalind Franklin bombarded DNA with X-rays, which rebounded to photographic plates. Using the pattern of X-rays on the photographic plates, Franklin demonstrated in 1951 that DNA has a helical structure.

Without Franklin's knowledge, her supervisor Maurice Wilkins gave the photographic plates to American zoologist James Watson and British graduate student Francis Crick. In 1953 Watson and Crick announced that DNA forms a double helix. The helix forms a spiral "staircase" with two nucleotide bases at each step. There are four nucleotide bases and they bond only in pairs. Adenine bonds only with thymine and guanine bonds only with cytosine.

The discovery of the now famous double helix illuminated several aspects of biology. First, the fact that sequences of nucleotide bases code for genes confirmed that genes are arrayed in a line on chromosomes. Second, the double helix revealed how DNA replicates. DNA unzips along the staircase leaving a sequence of unbonded nucleotide bases. Consider the pairs AT, GC, and TA. When they split apart along the axis of the staircase, one trio of unbonded bases will be A, G, and T. Because A bonds only with T, the first nucleotide base in the sequence will pair AT. Because G bonds only with C, the second nucleotide base in the sequence will pair GC, and the third will pair TA, an exact copy of the pairs before they unzipped. This mechanism explains how DNA doubles itself during mitosis. Third, the structure of DNA at last made clear the definition of a mutation. A mutation is a chemical change in any nucleotide bases or any group of bases. In replicat-

John Glenn reviewing artwork in February 1962. "Friendship 7" was his nickname for the capsule in which he orbited earth.

John Glenn

The first American to orbit earth, John Herschel Glenn, Jr., was born on July 18, 1921, in Cambridge, Ohio. He attended school in New Concord, Ohio, and received a B.S. in engineering from Muskingum College in New Concord. He received a pilot's license in 1941 and entered the Naval Aviation Cadet Program in March 1942. The U.S. Marine Corps commissioned Glenn a second lieutenant upon his completion of the cadet program in 1943. He was a fighter pilot during World War II, flying 59 missions. Flying over the Marshall Islands, he attacked antiaircraft guns and by war's end had risen to captain. During the Korean War he flew 63 missions. On July 16, 1957, Glenn made the first transcontinental flight in a supersonic jet. At more than the speed of sound, Glenn flew from California to New York in three hours, 23 minutes.

In April 1959, NASA selected Glenn to be an astronaut. Upon returning to earth after his historic flight Glenn was a hero, cheered by the throngs of Americans who came to his parade. In 1964, Glenn, eager to enter politics, resigned from the space program, though his initial bids for office were unsuccessful. In 1965 he retired from the Marines a colonel to manage Royal Crown Cola. In 1974, after losing four years earlier, Glenn won election to the U.S. Senate, where he served until 1999. In 1976 he hoped to be Jimmy Carter's vice presidential candidate, but Carter bypassed him for Walter Mondale. In 1984 Glenn ran to be the Democratic nominee for president, but again lost to Mondale. In 1998 Glenn was once more an astronaut in a program to monitor the effects of space flight on the elderly. He won numerous awards, among them the Distinguished Flying Cross, the NASA Distinguished Service Medal, and the Congressional Space Medal of Honor.

This Gemini capsule from the second U.S. manned space program was used 1964–66. The Gemini program flew 12 flights that tested human endurance in space, and worked to improve maneuvering and reentry, all skills that would later help with the moon landing.

ing itself, a strand of DNA may mutate, for example, by coding for an extra cytosine-guanine pair.

Finally, the structure of DNA made clear the function of ribonucleic acid (RNA). RNA is similar to DNA except that it has the nucleotide base uracil, rather than thymine; that it exists in both the nucleus of a cell, where DNA resides, and in the cytoplasm of a cell, where DNA is not found; and that it is often single, rather than double stranded. When DNA unzips it may make a copy of RNA, rather than of itself. Once RNA has assembled from a strand of DNA it leaves the nucleus and directs the chemical reactions in a cell from the cytoplasm. A sequence of three nucleotide bases direct the assembly of an enzyme and sequences of varying lengths code for a gene, which directs the assembly of proteins. DNA and RNA are the blueprint by which a cell assembles itself.

THE SPACE PROGRAM
In 1957 the Soviet Union launched Sputnik, the first satellite to revolve around earth. Worried that Sputnik revealed a gap in rocket technology with the Soviets in the lead, in 1958 Congress created the National Aeronautics and Space Administration (NASA) to pursue a space program. NASA was to improve

rocket technology so that the United States would overtake the Soviet Union. Results were not encouraging at first. The Soviet Union launched the first man into space in April 1961. Less than a month later, on May 5, 1961, NASA launched Navy Commander Alan Shepard, Jr. into space. On February 20, 1962, Marine Lieutenant Colonel John Glenn, Jr. became the first American to orbit earth. In June 1965, NASA built a new command center in Houston, Texas, and that month Air Force Major Edward White became the first American to walk in space.

Impressive as these achievements were, catastrophe struck on January 27, 1967, when fire engulfed a spacecraft while on the ground, killing the three astronauts on board. An investigation revealed that an electric wire, covered by a cracked piece of insulation, generated a spark. In the spacecraft, the atmosphere of pure oxygen stoked the spark into a fire that reached 1,000 degrees Fahrenheit. The astronauts could not open the hatch because NASA had bolted it shut as a precaution against its opening when the spacecraft landed in the ocean. By the time technicians opened the door, the three men were dead. Ironically one of the three, Virgil "Gus" Grissom, had warned NASA for months that the spacecraft was poorly designed. Beset by criticism from Congress and the public, NASA suspended the space program for 21 months, time it used to build spacecraft to new standards of safety.

The Mission Control Center for the 1962 Mercury mission and other early missions. NASA later built a new command center in Houston, Texas, that became the Johnson Space Center.

Neil A. Armstrong took this photograph of Air Force Colonel Edwin "Buzz" Aldrin on the moon as they explored their landing area on the Sea of Tranquility.

On October 11, 1968, NASA resumed space flights, and on December 24, 1968, Air Force Colonel Frank Borman, Major William Anders, and Navy Captain James Lovell, Jr. became the first to orbit the moon, coming within 70 miles of its surface. On May 18, 1969, Apollo 10 launched its lunar module within nine miles of the moon, and on July 20, 1969, civilian Neil Armstrong and Air Force Colonel Edwin "Buzz" Aldrin landed on the moon. By one estimate one-third of the world's population watched the moon landing on television. On November 14, 1969, Navy commanders Charles Conrad and Alan Bean made a second landing, discovering bacteria on the unmanned Surveyor 3. The microorganisms must have originated on earth. Remarkably they had survived not only the voyage into space, but had also lived on the moon more than two years.

CONCLUSION

While the space race that resulted in the moon landings is one of the most visible achievements of the era, other developments with roots in Cold War competition left lasting legacies. Nuclear power has provided energy, pro-

"We Walked on the Moon"

On July 16, 1969, the Apollo 11 mission blasted off in fulfillment of President Kennedy's vow in 1961 that the United States would land a man on the moon before the end of the decade. Four days after the launch of Apollo 11, the lunar module Eagle landed on the surface of the moon. On September 16 the three astronauts of Apollo 11 appeared before a joint session of Congress to describe their experiences. Excerpted below is the testimony of Colonel Edwin E. Aldrin from the congressional record.

Distinguished ladies and gentlemen, it is with a great sense of pride as an American and with humility as a human being that I say to you today what no men have been privileged to say before: "We walked on the moon." But the footprints at Tranquility base belong to more than the crew of Apollo 11. They were put there by hundreds of thousands of people across this country, people in government, industry and universities, the teams and crews that preceded us, all who strived throughout the years with Mercury, Gemini and Apollo.

Those footprints belong to the American people and you, their representatives, who accept it and support it, the inevitable challenge of the moon. And, since we came in peace for all mankind those footprints belong also to all people of the world. As the moon shines impartially on all those looking up from our spinning earth so do we hope the benefits of space exploration will be spread equally with a harmonizing influence to all mankind...

Our steps in space have been a symbol of this country's way of life as we open our doors and windows to the world to view our successes and failures and as we share with all nations our discovery. The Saturn, Columbia, and Eagle and the Extravehicular Mobility Unit have proved to Neil, Mike and me that this nation can produce equipment of the highest quality and dependability. This should give all of us hope and inspiration to overcome some of the more difficult problems here on earth. The Apollo lesson is that national goals can be met where there is a strong enough will to do so.

duced waste that will remain dangerous for years, and added a new level of fear for residents living near plants. The spread of computers has changed daily life for Americans in innumerable ways. One less visible development, however, was the increase in funding of the National Science Foundation in the 1950s and 1960s; this funding has had a significant impact on the American scientific community, especially in universities.

CHRISTOPHER CUMO

Further Readings

Aldrin, Buzz. *Reaching for the Moon*. New York: HarperCollins, 2005.

Bilstein, Roger. *Flight in America, 1903–1983: From the Wrights to the Astronauts*. Baltimore, MD: Johns Hopkins University Press, 1984.

Bonsall, Thomas E. *The Cadillac Story: The Postwar Years*. Stanford, CA: Stanford University Press, 2004.

Brack, Andre. *The Molecular Origins of Life: Assembling Pieces of the Puzzle*. Cambridge: Cambridge University Press, 1998.

Donnelly, Judy. *Moonwalk: The First Trip to the Moon*. New York: Random House, 1989.

Ericson, Eric. *The Boeing 707*. New York: Princeton Architectural Press, 2003.

Kevles, Daniel. *The Physicists: The History of a Scientific Community in Modern America*. Cambridge, MA: Harvard University Press, 1987.

Kramer, Barbara. *John Glenn: A Space Biography*. Springfield, NJ: Enslow Publishers, 1998.

Mayr, Ernst. *The Growth of Biological Thought: Diversity, Evolution, and Inheritance*. Cambridge, MA: Harvard University Press, 1982.

Newton, David E. *Nuclear Power*. New York: Facts on File, 2006.

Phelan, Glen. *Double Helix: The Quest to Uncover the Structure of DNA*. Washington, D.C.: National Geographic, 2006.

Rhodes, Richard. *Dark Sun: The Making of the Hydrogen Bomb*. New York: Simon & Schuster, 1995.

Sears, Stephen W. *The American Heritage History of the Automobile in America*. New York: American Heritage Publishing Company, 1977.

Sorensen, Lorin. *Famous Ford V8s*. St. Helena, CA: Silverado Pub., 2002.

Spencer, Donald D. *The Timetable of Computers: A Chronology of the Most Important People and Events in the History of Computers*. Ormand Beach, FL: Camelot Publishing Company, 1999.

Chapter 10

Entertainment and Sports

*"I find television very educating.
Every time somebody turns on the set,
I go into the other room and read a book."*
—Groucho Marx

WHEN MEN AND women returned home after serving in World War II, they began marrying and having children in large numbers, producing the generation that became known as the Baby Boomers. The Great Depression had ended with the advent of World War II, and the economy was booming. Americans had more leisure time and more money to spend than at any time in history. By the mid-1950s, the first postwar babies had begun reaching their teens and early adulthood, and they were searching for an identity that was distinctly their own, an identity that encompassed the clean-cut California beach look and the long-haired counterculture—and everything in between. Children of the postwar era grew up when phenomena such as the Cold War, McCarthyism, the Civil Rights and women's movements, and the Vietnam War were pervading influences. Rock and roll music first appeared in the mid-1950s, when the Civil Rights movement and the blending of black and white music produced the most diverse generation in American history up to that point. Baby Boomers not only influenced music, but also American culture, society, and politics.

Teenagers had money to spend in the postwar era. In 1956 alone, 13 million teenagers spent $7 billion on entertainment, food, clothing, and personal items. Rock culture developed its own language, rituals, foods, and fads. Some crazes, like the Davy Crockett hat and the poodle skirt, were short-lived, but

Developments in Recording and Sound

Several developments in the delivery of sound influenced life in postwar America. Although the transistor had been invented in 1947, its impact would be felt in the 1950s and 1960s. Replacing vacuum tubes, the transistor accelerated the miniaturization of technology in a way that would make it more accessible to the masses. The transistor radio not only allowed the portability of listening to music or sports on radio, it inspired composers such as John Cage to create music that utilized the new appliance, such as his *Imaginary Landscape no. 4*, aleatoric music for 12 radios.

Research into binaural or stereophonic sound began in the 19th century. But commercial recording using stereo was initiated in 1954 by the Radio Corporation of America (RCA), in a recording of the Boston Symphony. But these did not appear on long-playing discs until a few years later. In 1955, EMI presented its "stereosonic" records. By 1958, the first stereo discs were marketed in the United States. On the album *Stereo Action Unlimited* (RCA Victor, 1961), Marty Gold and his orchestra performed "Did You Ever See a Dream Walking." Here the sound switched between the speakers in a demonstration of stereophonic sound.

Another evolutionary step in creating more accessible recordings was the development of the long-playing vinyl record, often called the LP. Although these had been developed during the Great Depression and World War II, they became a staple in the musical world in the 1950s and 1960s. While RCA had developed the 45 rpm disc, Columbia introduced its 12-inch 33 1/3-rpm disc in 1948. This increased the playing time for one side of the record from a few short minutes to about 20 minutes.

In 1963 Philips, a Dutch firm, introduced cassettes, self-contained twin hub cartridges, to assist dictation machine technology. Norelco first sold these in the United States in 1964. By 1968, the Philips-Norelco system became the industry standard, using 1/8 inch wide (3.18 mm) tape. Cassette players like these allowed people to record sound, unlike vinyl records, and proved particularly useful for compiling oral histories.

A portable transistor radio from the 1960s.

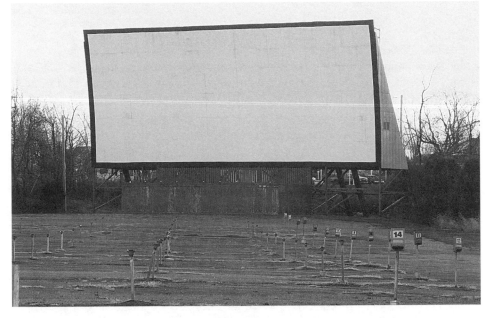

Symbols of the convergence of prosperity, leisure, and the automobile in postwar America, drive-in theaters were popular hangouts for teenagers, reaching a peak of popularity around 1958.

rock music continued to influence society long after it had ceased to be the dominant force in American music. In the postwar period, radio disc jockeys had a good deal of influence on teenagers, who were highly susceptible to promotions of particular artists and music-related products, and images of rock stars appeared on a range of "must-have" products. At afterschool hangouts around the country, teenagers gathered to eat and listen to music. Hamburgers and pizzas became their top culinary choices. Modern generations were later given a glimpse of that world with the movie *American Graffiti* (1973) and a similar-themed television show, *Happy Days* (1974–84), both of which starred Ron Howard, who had grown up before the public playing Opie Taylor on the popular *Andy Griffith Show*.

POPULAR MUSIC OF THE 1950S
At a time when westerns were mainstays of television and movies, cowboy songs were popular with many Americans. Hank Williams was the dominant figure of country/western music. Hits such as "Your Cheatin' Heart" and "Jambalaya" made Williams a household name. His "I'm So Lonesome I Could Cry" became a country music classic, and was later covered by artists as diverse as Elvis Presley and Garth Brooks. Television played a major role in promoting popular musicians. Crooner Perry Como and bandleader Tommy Dorsey had their own shows, and Nat "King" Cole became the first African-American

To Kill a Mockingbird

In 1960 Alabama author Harper Lee published her only novel, *To Kill a Mockingbird*. The book, which won a Pulitzer Prize for Literature in 1961, related the story of Jean Louise "Scout" Finch and her brother Jem, who were growing up in the Depression South at a time when the races were strictly segregated. Their father Atticus Finch, who is based on Harper Lee's own lawyer father, is asked to take on the case of Tom Robinson, a black man who is accused of raping a white woman. Ignoring their father's orders to stay away, Scout, Jem, and their friend Dill watch the trial from the balcony where African-American spectators are required to sit. As the trial progresses, it becomes clear to Scout and to the reader that the alleged rape was only in the mind of Tom Ewell, the apparent victim's father, who could find no other way to reconcile the fact that he had found his daughter trying to kiss a black man.

Atticus explains to his children that, "The one place where a man ought to get a square deal is in a courtroom, be he any color of the rainbow, but people have a way of carrying their resentments right into a jury box." The events that follow the trial go a long way in helping the Finch children learn about racism and hatred. When Scout finally meets the legendary "Boo" Radley who lives next door, she also learns about compassion and understanding. Although Jem gripes because Atticus tells him he's too old to play baseball, Scout recognizes the true worth of her father's character, remarking that "It was times like these when I thought my father, who hated guns and had never been to any wars, was the bravest man who ever lived."

The book became a movie in 1962, with Gregory Peck starring as Atticus Finch. Mary Badham played Scout, and Phillip Alford appeared as Jem. The film won an Academy Award for Best Picture, and Peck and Badham won Oscars for Best Actor and Best Supporting Actress, respectively. Robert Mulligan also carried home an Oscar for Best Direction. *To Kill a Mockingbird* has become an American classic, and regularly appears on lists of the most influential books of the 20th century. In 2007 Harper Lee was presented with a Presidential Medal of Freedom by President George W. Bush.

singer to host his own television program. Urban folk music, which had begun in rural areas during the Great Depression, was also popular. The Weavers, led by political activist Pete Seeger, won national acclaim with "Goodnight Irene," which rose to number one on the pop charts. Many people saw folk artists as un-American, and three of the Weavers, including Seeger, were accused of being Communists. They were cleared when their accuser admitted he had fabricated the charges.

The American music scene changed forever in 1954 with the emergence of Elvis Presley and the birth of rock and roll. While young people quickly claimed the new genre as their own, parents and other adults were quick to condemn, believing that it undermined the authority of family, church, and state. Psychiatrist Francis Braceland called rock and roll a "communicable disease." Most adults objected to the fact that rock concerts produced screaming, jumping, and sometimes fainting crowds that appeared totally out of control. After violence broke out at an Alan Freed show, officials in Boston and New Haven banned rock concerts from all public venues. A 1958 Ronnie Haig hit sang of being "banned in Boston, condemned in Cleveland, and banished from Baltimore." In Atlanta, officials banned all young people under the age of 18 from attending public dances unless they were accompanied by a parent or guardian or carrying written permission from a parent or guardian.

As might be expected, some of the most severe criticisms of rock and roll came from former music idols. Frank Sinatra said that rock and roll was "sung, played, and written for the most part by cretinous goons." *Time* magazine quoted a therapist as stating that rock and roll grew out of a "deep-seated abnormal need to belong." Some adults were sure that rock was a tool employed by communists to bring down American society from within. Clean-cut Pat Boone was seen as a viable alternative to other rock singers of the late 1950s. Boone, who was frank about being a born-again Christian, was married to the daughter of country legend Red Foley and was the father of two daughters.

Over the next several years, Jerry Lee Lewis, Roy Orbison, Carl Perkins, Johnny Cash, Chuck Berry, Fats Domino, and Little Richard joined Presley and Boone as top recording artists of the day.

In 1955 rhythm and blues (R&B) became a national phenomenon. This African-American genre was a blend of several other forms of music. It tended to be softer and more plaintive than earlier forms of African-American music, as evidenced by Frankie Lymon's "Why Do Fools Fall in Love," and Little Anthony and the Imperials' "Tears on My Pillow." When record producers told R&B singer Ray Charles to sing like he did in church, his efforts gave birth to soul music, also known as the "secular form of gospel music." Soul allowed African-American musicians to retain a distinct identify after other styles had been co-opted by the white community.

Jukeboxes became popular in the 1950s, and remain one of the icons of the era.

Many of the dance crazes that swept America in the 1950s and 1960s were first introduced on *American Bandstand,* a daily show on which a group of teenagers danced to hit records and enthusiastically applauded popular artists introduced by host Dick Clark. The twist craze began on *American Bandstand* with Chubby Checker's song, "The Twist." Checker announced that the correct way to do the twist was to "imagine you've just stepped out of the shower and you're drying your back with a big towel. At the same time, you're stubbing out a cigarette with your foot." The twist craze was popular with adults as well as teenagers, and soon there were other twisting songs such as "The Peppermint Twist" and "Twist and Shout." In addition to the twist, Americans gyrated to the watusi, the pony, the hully gully, the fug, the shake, the jerk, and the lurch. Such dances were preferred by some adults over traditional slow dancing that placed couples in close proximity.

In its early years, rock and roll was seen as a male genre. When asked to sing the new music in 1958, Philadelphia native Connie Francis replied that it was "too savage" for girl singers. Despite her scruples, Francis became a top female singer with hits such as "Lipstick on Your Collar" and "Who's Sorry Now." The other top female artist of the period was Brenda Lee, who had been singing on the radio since she was five years old. Girl groups such as the Supremes, which featured Diana Ross, also became extremely successful. Covering a range of styles, popular male singers of the early rock and roll era included Johnny Cash, Buddy Holly, Ricky Nelson, Frankie Avalon, Chuck Berry, Nat "King" Cole, Neil Sedaka, Perry Como, Little Richard, Fats Domino, Sam Cooke, Fabian, and James Brown. The rock world was shaken on January 22, 1959, when a plane crash took the lives of Buddy Holly, Richie Valens, and the Big Bopper. Four months later, Eddie Cochran was killed in another plane crash.

Chuck Berry deserves a lot of the credit for creating rock and roll, and his songs often became symbols of the era. In "Roll over Beethoven," Berry articulated the excitement that many young Americans felt for rock music:

You know, my temperature's risin'
And the jukebox blows a fuse
My heart's beatin' rhythm
And my soul keeps singing the blues.
Roll over Beethoven and tell Tchaikovsky the news.

TELEVISION AND FILM OF THE 1950s

In September 1951, the final section of coaxial cable was laid, connecting the East and West coasts of the United States so that nationwide television programming became available for the first time. NBC ruled the airwaves with hits such as *The Milton Berle Show, Kraft Television Theater, Your Show of Shows,* and *Dragnet.* By mid-decade, CBS had taken the lead with hits such

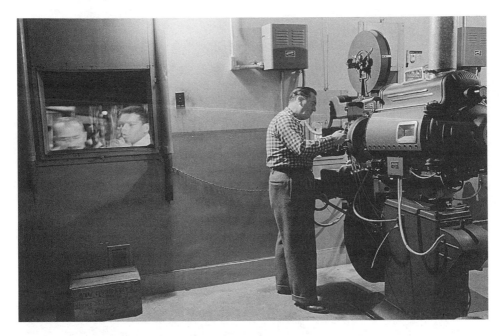

A projectionist working in a movie theater in February 1958. Despite their popularity in the late 1950s, drive-in theaters could not compete In the winter, and their average attendance dropped to 500,000 a week, while indoor theaters averaged 34.2 million weekly viewers.

as *I Love Lucy*, *The Ed Sullivan Show*, *Arthur Godfrey's Talent Show*, and *The Jack Benny Show*. Programs of the 1950s ranged from variety shows that owed their origin to vaudeville to adult westerns in which the good guys were always successful in defeating the bad guys to situation comedies that extolled the American nuclear family.

Walt Disney was one of the most significant influences on entertainment in the postwar period. With *The Mickey Mouse Club* (1955–59), Disney presented a cadre of young stars who had been carefully vetted to represent wholesomeness, affability, and respect for authority. In a regular Sunday night series that was alternately called *Disneyland* and *Wonderful World of Disney* (1954–90), the Disney studio brought a plethora of movies and television series to American families. Disney offerings, like most shows of the 1950s, sent a clear message that democracy and the American way of life were the keys to happiness. Minorities were virtually absent from television and the movies in the 1950s, except in stereotypical roles that ranged from domestics to criminals. Except for a few situation comedies, women were generally relegated to subsidiary roles.

Movie audiences were drawn to musicals, biblical features, and comedies in the 1950s, and the top-selling movies of the decade were *The Ten Commandments*, *Ben Hur*, *Around the World in 80 Days*, *The Robe*, and *South Pacific*. Top critics' choices were more varied, including the Gene

The Beatles greeting fans as they arrive at New York's Kennedy Airport on February 7, 1964. Their success in the United States brought significant change to American music.

The Beatles and the British Invasion

Rock and roll spread to England, and British musicians were heavily influenced by the new sound. In 1957, Liverpool teenager John Lennon began putting a band together. He formed a friendship with Paul McCartney and invited him to join the band. Lennon was an avid fan of Elvis Presley, Jerry Lee Lewis, Buddy Holly, and the Coasters. In 1960, the band became the Beatles, and George Harrison joined the group. Two years later, Ringo Starr replaced drummer Pete Best. That same year, the Beatles experienced their first success with "Love Me Do." Beatlemania spread to the United States, and, like Elvis Presley before them, the group appeared on the popular *Ed Sullivan Show*. Early Beatles fare included light romantic songs such as "I Wanna Hold Your Hand."

The Beatles had become involved with drugs by the mid-1960s, and some songs were written in drug-induced highs. The death of their manager Brian Epstein in 1967 contributed to mounting tensions, and the group decided to follow individual careers, playing their last concert on January 30, 1969. Despite great encouragement, they never reformed as a group.

In the United States, the success of the Beatles ushered in the musical period known as the British invasion. British imports included The Rolling Stones, The Who, The Byrds, Herman's Hermits, The Dave Clark Five, and The Hollies. Their songs ranged from the sexually explicit to the admittedly silly. Ironically, British imports killed the careers of many of the rock and roll idols who had influenced the British sounds.

Kelley/Debbie Reynolds musical *Singin' in the Rain*, the courtroom drama *12 Angry Men*, the Jimmy Stewart thriller *Rear Window*, and the war drama, *Bridge on the River Kwai*. Teenage movies of the 1950s ranged from the squeaky clean *Gidget*, starring Sandra Dee, to odes to teenage rebellion that included *Rebel without a Cause* and *The Wild One*. Science fiction was also popular with American audiences, and a young Michael Landon starred in *I Was a Teenage Werewolf*. By the end of the decade, sex among teenagers was receiving more attention in American film. In 1959 Sandra Dee and Troy Donahue starred in the film version of Sloan Wilson's novel, *A Summer Place*. Dee and Donahue play two teenagers who find both physical and emotional comfort in one another when their worlds are turned upside down by divorce and scandal.

POPULAR MUSIC OF THE 1960s

The 1960s did not begin well for rock and roll. Rock music had been assailed on all sides at the end of the previous decade. Disc jockeys had been censured for accepting money to play particular records in the "payola scandal." Many radio stations switched from rock to other genres. Elvis Presley was in the Army, Buddy Holly had been killed, Jerry Lee Lewis was in disgrace, Little Richard had become a minister, and Chuck Berry was in jail. Important events were taking place, however. In 1960 at the suggestion of Smoky Robinson, Berry Gordy established Motown Records and began developing the Motown sound. Interwoven with the growing Civil Rights movement, soul music became the voice of Black Power for many recording artists. Over the course of the decade, Detroit native Aretha Franklin earned the title "The Queen of Soul" with hits such as "Respect." James Brown, who like Franklin, had begun his career in R&B, became known as the "Godfather of Soul." While many 1950s singers continued to rule the charts until 1963, American music was set to experience a second rock revolution, which came to be known as the British invasion. That invasion was precipitated by the arrival of the Beatles in the United States in 1964.

As rock music matured, so did its fans, and rock enthusiasts covered the gamut from teenagers in bobby sox and rolled-up blue jeans to clean-cut college students to long-haired members of the counterculture. In San Francisco's Haight-Ashbury, a cadre of Baby Boomers established a "hippie" community, where "make love not war" was the ruling mentality, and rock music and drugs were a part of daily life. Television introduced middle-class teenagers to the hippie scene of Haight-Ashbury, and many teenagers were fascinated by the fringed vests without shirts, long skirts, and stringy hair. Marijuana, amphetamines, and LSD became a major part of the rock scene for those who had endorsed the psychedelic era. The Beatles's "Sgt. Pepper's Lonely Hearts Club Band" has been called the "ultimate psychedelic pop culture statement." On August 22, 1966, Beatle John Lennon announced, "Christianity will go. It will vanish and shrink. We're more popular than Jesus Christ right now." The resulting uproar was overwhelming, and Lennon was forced to apologize. He defended himself by saying that he had failed to realize that his impromptu analogy would be turned into international news.

As the death toll mounted in Vietnam, Americans engaged in accelerating antiwar protests. One of the first openly antiwar songs was Barry McGuire's "Eve of Destruction," written by P.F. Sloan in 1965.

> *The eastern world, it is exploding*
> *Violence flarin', bullets loadin'*
> *You're old enough to kill, but not for votin'*
> *You don't believe in war, but what's that gun you're totin'*

The song, like many other protest songs of the period, was highly critical of the practice of sending Americans into war, then rotating them out once they learned survival skills. New recruits were vulnerable and more likely to be killed.

Folk music became a national phenomenon in the 1960s and was often viewed as the voice of the people. Folk was frequently about protest, and the 1960s produced many folk songs by artists such as Janis Joplin; Joan Baez; Peter, Paul, and Mary; and the Kingston Trio. The most influential voice in folk music was Bob Dylan, who later became a major influence on rock music. Dylan began his career as a rock musician, but was absorbed into folk while living in Greenwich Village. The success of the Beatles lured Dylan back to rock, and he released the album *Bringin' It all Back Home* in 1965. His "Blowin' in the Wind" became an anthem of the war protest movement.

> *How many roads must a man walk down*
> *Before you call him a man?*
> *Yes, 'n' how many seas must a white dove sail*
> *Before she sleeps in the sand?*
> *Yes, 'n' how many times must the cannon balls fly*
> *Before they're forever banned?*
> *The answer, my friend, is blowin' in the wind,*
> *The answer is blowin' in the wind.*

Although used by the war protestors in the 1960s to point out the evils of war, Pete Seeger's "Where Have All the Flowers Gone" was written in 1956 in response to McCarthyism and the anti-Communist witch hunt of the House Un-American Activities Committee. The song bemoans the fact that there are no flowers because they have all gone to young girls, who in turn have all gone to soldiers. The soldiers have gone to their graves, on which the flowers have since been placed. Antiwar protests had become a national phenomenon by

Elvis Presley and the Birth of Rock and Roll

It has been argued that without Elvis Presley's contributions, the rock revolution may never have happened. John Lennon once said, "Before Elvis, there was nothing." The year Presley released his first record, "That's All Right, Mama"/"Blue Moon of Kentucky" (1954) is considered the birth year of rock and roll. Presley did not invent the genre; it evolved from a number of musical trends that came together in the 1950s, most notably the music of African Americans. In 1952, white teenagers began buying the records of African-American artists, and a record store owner in Cleveland, Ohio, convinced disc jockey Alan Freed to play black music on his radio show.

In Memphis, record producer Sam Phillips, who was closely watching the new trend, had been looking for a white boy who could "sing like a black." Phillips found that person in Elvis Presley, a child of the South who loved music of all kinds, and who had been exposed to African-American music from an early age. When Presley appeared on Dewey Phillips's radio show to promote his record, Phillips was careful to mention that Elvis went to Humes High, a white school in Memphis. More than 7,000 orders for the record were received following the show. By June 12, Sam Phillips had signed Presley to a recording contract. When Bill Haley and the Comet's "Rock around the Clock" made the top 10, the fate of rock and roll was sealed.

By 1956, Elvis Presley had hits with "Blue Suede Shoes" and "Heartbreak Hotel," and was selling 75,000 records a day. During the 1950s, he had 11 top 40 hits, and four of them rose to number one. Presley was able to lose himself in music to the extent that his movements mirrored his emotional reactions. Those movements created enormous controversy because they were seen as lewd and suggestive, providing critics with ammunition to contend that rock and roll was dangerous to American youth. In locations as diverse as Birmingham, Alabama, and Portland, Oregon, Presley records— even "White Christmas"—were banned. Bruce Springsteen best summed up Elvis Presley's impact on music, "There have been a lot of tough guys. There have been pretenders. And there have been contenders. But there is only one king."

Elvis Presley in the Jailhouse Rock film in 1957.

the late 1960s, and 50,000 protestors marched on Washington, D.C., in 1967, resulting in 600 arrests. Dr. Martin Luther King, Jr. announced the following year, "I oppose the war in Vietnam because I love America." Other clergymen joined the protest. After the Tet offensive of January 1968, the number of Americans supporting the war in Vietnam declined sharply.

Rhodes Scholar Kris Kristofferson established a career as a country singer, but his sympathies were often more in line with folk music than with traditional country. Although country music had spread outside the south during the Depression and World War II as southerners migrated into other parts of the country, the heart of country music remained in the southeast and the cowboy country of the southwest. During the postwar period, Kristofferson and other artists such as Johnny Cash, Ray Charles, Conway Twitty, and Kenny Rogers helped to blur the lines between rock and country.

The top-selling artists for the 1960s were all rock musicians. The top three were the Beatles, Elvis Presley, and Ray Charles. For the first time, female musicians were also in that group, represented by Brenda Lee and the Supremes. The top five hits of the decade were the Beatles's "Hey Jude," Percy Faith's "Theme from a Summer Place," Bobby Lewis's "Tossin' and Turnin'," the Beatles's "I Want to Hold Your Hand," and the Monkees "I'm a Believer." While Elvis Presley's influence on the medium had declined somewhat, his "Are You Lonesome Tonight" and "It's Now or Never" were numbers eight and 10, respectively. The other top 10 hits of the decade were Marvin Gaye's "I Heard It through the Grapevine," the Fifth Dimension's "Aquarius/Let the Sunshine In," and Zager and Evans' "In the Year 2525."

TELEVISION AND FILM OF THE 1960s

In 1960, 88 percent of American homes owned at least one television. Over the course of the following year 1.2 percent of American households purchased color televisions, and 7 percent of televisions obtained the capability of receiving UHF channels, which gave viewers choices beyond the three broadcast channels. "Rural television" was hugely popular in the 1960s, and shows such as *The Andy Griffith Show*, *The Beverly Hillbillies*, *Green Acres*, *Petticoat Junction*, and *Gomer Pyle, USMC* consistently received high Nielsen ratings. At the end of the decade, CBS abruptly yanked several top-rated rural shows and announced it was headed in a new direction. Female actors headlined shows in increasing numbers in programs such as *Bewitched*, *I Dream of Jeannie*, *The Flying Nun*, *The Donna Reed Show*, and *The Doris Day Show*. In 1968, singer/actress Diahann Carroll made history by becoming the first African-American woman to headline her own show, starring as the single mother of a young son. Other shows also broke down barriers for women. *The Mary Tyler Moore Show* depicted a young woman living on her own in Minneapolis, and *That Girl*, starring Marlo Thomas, featured a young actress pursuing a career in New York City.

A number of 1960s television shows specifically targeted the teenage audience. *The Patty Duke Show* portrayed two identical cousins, both played by Duke, who mirrored the two sides of teenage girls. One (Patty) was the typical sloppy and irresponsible teen, and the other (Cathy) was neat and eager to please the adults in her life. In *Gidget*, Californian Sally Field played a surfing enthusiast who went from one scrape to another. There were also musical shows for teenagers, including *Hullabaloo* and *Shindig*. The *Monkees*, which was about a struggling rock group, turned its four stars into overnight rock sensations. By the late 1960s, teen-oriented shows had begun to mirror the more socially conscious and politically involved teen scene. *The Mod Squad*, for instance, featured an integrated cast of three teen detectives who helped the police solve crimes.

In 1960 the average movie fare was $.69, and audiences flocked to movie theaters to see a variety of films. The top films of the decade were *The Sound of Music*, *The Graduate*, *Doctor Zhivago*, *Butch Cassidy and the Sundance Kid*, and *Mary Poppins*. The Academy of Motion Pictures awarded Best Picture honors to a variety of films, ranging from musicals to historical sagas to stark dramas. Oscars went to *The Apartment*, *West Side Story*, *Lawrence of Arabia*, *Tom Jones*, *My Fair Lady*, *The Sound of Music*, *A Man for All Seasons*, *In the Heat of the Night*, *Oliver*, and *Midnight Cowboy*.

The First Super Bowls

Vince Lombardi (1913–70) won the first two Super Bowls as head coach of the Green Bay Packers. At the conclusion of the 1966 football season, the Packers defeated the Kansas City Chiefs 35 to 10, on January 15, 1967, in the first Super Bowl game. Held at the Los Angeles Memorial Coliseum, it was broadcast by both CBS and NBC.

The cost for a 30-second commercial was $42,000. Attendance, not sold out, was 61,946. The second Super Bowl game, after the 1967 season, was held at the Orange Bowl, in Miami, Florida. The Green Bay Packers defeated the Oakland Raiders 33-14 on January 15, 1968. In both of these games, Packer quarterback Bart Starr was selected the most valuable player.

Following the 1968 season, the third such game was called the Super Bowl for the first time. On January 12, 1969, also played at the Orange Bowl, Quarterback Joe Namath and the New York Jets debunked the pundits that had predicted a victory for the Baltimore Colts, led by quarterbacks Johnny Unitas and Earl Morrall. Since then, this game has evolved into one of the most watched television events of the year and garners some of the highest advertising revenue on television.

As with television, a number of movies targeted teenage audiences. In the 1950s, Elvis Presley pursued a film career in dramas such as *Love Me Tender* and *Loving You*. After he was released from the army, Presley resumed his film career with formalistic romances, singing his way into the hearts of young girls. The most memorable of those films was *Viva Las Vegas* (1964) with Swedish-born siren Ann-Margret. The Beatles turned songs into movies: *A Hard Day's Night* (1964) and *Help!* (1965). A series of *Beach Party* movies targeted the teenage audience. The series starred Annette Funicello, who had been the object of many young boys' fantasies while appearing on Walt Disney's original *Mickey Mouse Club*. Still under contract to Disney, Funicello was forbidden to wear bikinis in the series. Teen heartthrob Frankie Avalon played her love interest, but sex was generally a matter of inference. Appeals to the rock generation were also evident in more dramatic films such as *Splendor in the Grass* (1961), the title of which was taken from the poem of the same name by William Wordsworth. The tale of star-crossed lovers dealt with what "good girls" were not allowed to do in the 1960s and starred Natalie Wood and Warren Beatty.

Another popular movie of the period with wide teenage appeal was *Bonnie and Clyde* (1967), the story of adventure-loving Bonnie Parker (Faye Dunaway) and Clyde Barrow (Warren Beatty), who robbed banks from Oklahoma to Texas during the Depression. The film was classified as an allegory of cultural and social decadence. One of the best-loved and most successful films of the decade was *The Graduate* (1967), starring Dustin Hoffman and Anne Bancroft. In the film, Ben Braddock, who has been cast adrift by his recent college graduation, has a brief affair with Mrs. Robinson, a friend of his parents. Paul Simon and Art Garfunkel captured the affair for perpetuity in "Mrs. Robinson," which Paul Simon wrote for the film:

> *Hide it in the hiding place where no one ever goes.*
> *Put it in your pantry with your cupcakes.*
> *It's a little secret just the Robinsons' affair.*
> *Most of all you've got to hide it from the kids.*

SPORTS IN THE 1950s AND 1960s

In the postwar period, sports continued to constitute a major pastime for Americans, who found themselves with an unprecedented amount of leisure time. Baseball was the chief form of entertainment for many males, who could relate all details of particular games at the drop of a hat. A favorite tale was of the 1956 World Series in which Don Larsen of the New York Yankees pitched a perfect game, not allowing a single Brooklyn Dodger to reach first base. The Yankees ruled baseball in the 1950s, winning eight American League pennants and laying claim to the series title six times. Among National League teams, the Brooklyn Dodgers carried home four pennants and claimed one other after their move to Los Angeles. The Philadelphia Phillies, the New York Giants, and the Milwaukee Braves also won pennants during the 1950s.

By the 1960s, baseball was losing ground to football as America's favorite spectator sport. After becoming coach of the floundering Green Bay Packers in 1959, Vince Lombardi led the team to NFL Championships in 1961, 1962, and 1965. The Packers won the Super Bowl in 1966 and 1967, the first two years the event was held. The following year, quarterbacks John Unitas and Earl Morrall were expected to propel the Baltimore Colts to victory, but an upset by the New York Jets under the leadership of quarterback Joe Namath proved them wrong. Over time, the Super Bowl became the most highly anticipated event of professional football, and sponsors were willing to lay out large sums of money to purchase commercials.

CONCLUSION

Of all the transformative events in entertainment in the postwar years, the Woodstock Music and Art Fair, held August 16–18, 1969, in Bethel, New York, became a defining moment for the popular entertainment and culture of the era. At Woodstock, over 400,000 spectators took part in the largest open-air music festival of the decade. Themes raised were peace, a back-to-the-land movement, drug use, and the new multicultural music, including that of sitarist Ravi Shankar of India. An era that had begun in fear with McCarthyism ended with an exhibit of collective awareness and freedom that has left a lasting impression on American culture.

ELIZABETH R. PURDY
RALPH HARTSOCK

Further Readings

Altshuler, Glenn C. *All Shook Up: How Rock 'n' Roll Changed America*. New York: Oxford University Press, 2003.

Ashby, LeRoy. *With Amusement for All: A History of American Pop Culture since 1830*. Lexington, KY: University of Kentucky Press, 2006.

Bodroghkozy, Aniko. *Groove Tube: Sixties Television and the Youth Rebellion*. Durham, NC: Duke University Press, 2001.

Brooks, Tom and Earle Marsh. *The Complete Directory to Prime Time Network TV Shows 1946–Present*. New York: Ballantine Books, 1988.

Campbell, Michael. *And the Beat Goes On: An Introduction to Popular Music in America, 1840 to Today*. New York: Schirmer, 1996.

Caruth, Gorton. *The Encyclopedia of American Facts and Dates*. New York: Harper Collins, 1993.

Christenson, Peter G. and Donald F. Roberts. *It's Not Only Rock 'n' Roll.*
    Creskill, NJ: Hampton, 1998.
Crawford, Richard. *America's Musical Life.* New York: W.W. Norton, 2001.
du Noyer, Paul. *The Story of Rock 'n' Roll: The Year-by-Year Illustrated
    Chronicle.* New York: Schrimer, 1995.
Farber, David and Beth Bailey. *The Columbia Guide to America in the 1960s.*
    New York: Columbia University Press, 2001.
Garofalo, Reebee, *Rockin' Out: Popular Music in the USA.* Boston, MA: Allyn
    and Bacon, 1997.
Geller, Larry and Joel Specter. *If I Can Dream: Elvis' Own Story.* New York:
    Simon and Schuster, 1989.
Goffman, Ken and Dan Joy. *Counterculture through the Ages: From Abraham
    to Acid House.* New York: Villard, 2004.
Gregory, Ross. *Cold War America 1946–1990.* New York: Facts on File,
    2003.
Griffith, Robert. *The Politics of Fear: Joseph McCarthy and the Senate.*
    Amherst, MA: University of Massachusetts Press, 1987.
Hendler, Herb. *Year by Year in the Rock Era: Events and Conditions Shaping
    the Rock Generations That Reshaped America.* Westport, CT: Green-
    wood, 1983.
Jackson, John A. *American Bandstand: Dick Clark and the Making of a Rock
    'n' Roll Empire.* New York: Oxford University Press, 1997.
Levy, Peter B., ed. *America in the Sixties—Right, Left, and Center.* Westport,
    CT: Praeger, 1998.
Marcus, Greil. *Mystery Train: Images of America in Rock 'n' Roll Music.* New
    York: Plume Books, 1997.
Pichaske, David. *A Generation in Music: Popular Music and Culture in the
    Sixties.* New York: Schrimer Books, 1979.
Redd, Lawrence N. *Rock Is Rhythm and Blues (The Impact of Mass Media).*
    East Lansing, MI: Michigan State University Press, 1974.
Rollins, Peter C., ed. *The Columbia Companion to American History on Film.*
    New York: Columbia University Press, 2003.
Rubin, Rachel and Jeffrey Melnick, eds. *American Popular Music: New
    Approaches to the Twentieth Century.* Amherst, MA: University of Mas-
    sachusetts Press, 2001.
Starr, Larry and Christopher Waterman. *American Popular Music from Min-
    strelsy to MTV.* New York: Oxford University Press, 2002.
Tawa, Nicolas. *Supremely American: Popular Song in the Twentieth Century:
    Styles and Singers and What They Said about America.* Lanham, MD:
    Scarecrow Press, 2005.
Tyler, Don. *Music of the Postwar Era.* Westport, CT: Greenwood, 2008.

Chapter 11

Crime and Violence

*"Criminal: A person with predatory instincts who
has not sufficient capital to form a corporation."*
—Howard Scott

THE 1950s STARTED out as a time of prosperity for America—false prosperity, some might say. With the war over and behind them, Americans looked forward to having more peaceful lives. Unfortunately, hidden tensions in society would begin to catalyze feelings of uneasiness and distrust in government that materialized in the late 1960s. The 1950s also began with another war, the Korean War, and ended at the height of the Vietnam War.

The wide distribution of television also brought change to society. Early TV shows were filled with images of the ideal democratic society. These shows promoted a consumerist lifestyle and America-centric social values, as well as anti-Communist views. But underneath the wholesome and prosperous image of the United States lay the rising tensions of the Cold War. After the Korean War, people had relaxed in the new consumerist society, but were still fearful of the Communist Soviet Union and of possible nuclear war. These fears were reinforced by Joseph McCarthy, a congressman who claimed there were Communist spies within U.S. institutions. Thus, the fear of Communism became a nationwide paranoia.

The TV also allowed the public to see grisly details of world events, including local crimes. When Americans turned on their TVs, images of murders and robberies were broadcast into their homes, making them increasingly fearful. In addition, social turbulence had begun to reach the breaking point, calling for societal change. In 1954, the *Brown v. Board of Education* decision to desegregate schools resulted in mounting racial tensions, and aggressive campaigns to assert minority and civil rights.

Aside from racial tensions and Cold War fears, new aspects of crime appeared in the United States. Near the end of the 1950s the serial killer emerged with the crimes of Ed Gein and Harvey Glatman. The Mafia at this time had become entrenched as a powerful and feared crime organization that intimidated even the Federal Bureau of Investigation (FBI). Few laws had been established to address the underhanded methods used by organized crime.

THE FBI

The FBI is known as the top law enforcement agency in the United States. But catching criminals is not an easy task. In fact, the FBI went through a great deal of turmoil before becoming the law enforcement giant it is today. Sometimes the FBI lacked the backing of law needed to arrest felons, and had to resort to illegal methods to gain leads on criminals.

On March 14, 1950, the FBI began its Ten Most Wanted Fugitives list, a practice it has continued. Each month, the FBI would name 10 suspects as most wanted, and offer a reward for information on their whereabouts and assistance in apprehension. This was similar to how bounties were posted in the old West, but the apprehension was to be done by law enforcement agencies. Among the first fugitives named were famous murderers like William Nesbit and bank robbers like Willie Sutton.

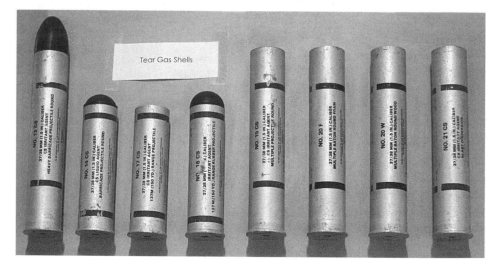

Tear gas shells similar to those used by police in the 1960s, when race riots occurred in numerous cities across the United States. There were also riots in 125 U.S. cities after the April 4, 1968, assassination of the Reverend Martin Luther King, Jr.

Frank Costello, one of the most powerful mafia figures of the 1950s and 1960s, testifying in 1951 at the Senate Special Committee to Investigate Organized Crime in Interstate Commerce, also known as the Kefauver Committee for its chairman, Senator Estes Kefauver.

The FBI conducted anti-Soviet activities during the Cold War. J. Edgar Hoover, the head of the FBI at the time, was a staunch anti-Communist and made it a priority to search for spies and pro-Soviet elements in the United States. During this time, the FBI arrested many violators of the Smith Act and subsequent security-related laws. Aside from Cold War operations, the FBI actively investigated local crimes. In 1955, a passenger plane exploded in midair and the FBI handled the investigation. Some of their methods, such as reassembling the plane, are still used today by the National Transportation Safety Board.

In addition, as civil rights became a growing issue, laws were passed that criminalized civil rights violations. Gambling and racketeering were also criminalized during this period, allowing the FBI to apprehend operators of gambling outfits. Some of the main operators were from the Mafia, an organization that would become the FBI's main focus.

RISE OF THE MAFIA
In the 1950s and 1960s, the Mafia, also known as *La Cosa Nostra*, gained notoriety as the biggest crime group in U.S. history. After establishing its connections

and bases of power during the Depression, the Mafia was the top crime organization in many major cities, and its influence spread into business and local crime operations like gambling and racketeering. The Mafia worked around federal and state laws and was able to maintain operations without consequences. But due to the increasing activities and reach of the FBI, Mafia activities were met with public disapproval.

The first real mob boss after Prohibition was Carlo Gambino, a Sicilian by birth who had come to America to join his relatives, the Castellano crime family. Gambino worked as an associate of mob leader Lucky Luciano and took over the New York mob. It is possible that his rise to power came from having the old mob boss, Albert Anastasia, murdered in 1957. Anastasia had been a member of the Depression-era gang dubbed Murder, Inc. by the media. By the time Gambino took power, the FBI was fully aware that organized crime leaders were forming alliances to strengthen their organizations. Key to arresting these criminals was an insider named Joseph Valachi. Valachi informed the FBI on the details of the American Mafia. New legislation also helped to empower the FBI to pin down the activities of the Mafia and apprehend its members.

Another significant personality of the 1950s was Jimmy Hoffa. A food service worker who later became an organizer of the infamous Teamsters Union, Hoffa took over in 1957 when former president Dave Beck was jailed. Hoffa made use of criminal connections, especially with the Mafia, and sometimes encouraged unlawful means to coerce employers to give in to their demands. This gave the Mafia a foothold in business and industry.

Despite his achievement of making the Teamsters into a powerful organization, Hoffa ran afoul of the Mafia, who are believed to have caused his disappearance and presumed death in 1975. How Hoffa died, and whether his body could still be found remains a source of fascination for the American public, and Hoffa is still remembered as a legendary American labor leader.

KENNEDY AND KING ASSASSINATIONS

One of the most memorable crimes of the 1960s was the assassination of President John F. Kennedy on November 22, 1963. While the president was riding in a motorcade on his way to a speech in Dallas, Texas, an unseen assailant fired shots, one of which fatally struck Kennedy in the head. Investigations by the police later led to the arrest of Lee Harvey Oswald, a worker at the Texas Depository, from where the shots were allegedly fired. But before Oswald could be brought to trial, he was shot dead by nightclub owner Jack Ruby, ending once and for all any possibility of learning Oswald's motivation for assassinating the president.

A post-mortem investigation body, the Warren Commission, led by Chief Justice Earl Warren, was subsequently formed to investigate the facts about the assassination. The conclusion was that Oswald assassinated Kennedy. At

Crime in Popular Culture

The 1950s, often dubbed the Golden Age of movies, also saw great interest in crime films, particularly with the increased popularity of film noir. This style of film used high-contrast light and shadow, and emphasized moral ambiguity and crime-related plots. The main characters would be morally ambivalent, the women usually deceivingly dangerous. Examples of such movies are *The Maltese Falcon* and *Casablanca*. Depression-era gangsterism and other crime themes of the past were heavy influences on the era's popular culture.

While the film noir genre had its start earlier, it peaked in the 1940s and 1950s. The 1950s was marked by movies with distinctive styles such as *Kiss Me Deadly* (1955), *The Big Combo* (1955), and *Touch of Evil* (1966). *The Asphalt Jungle* (1950) can be considered a crossover movie into the new decade, as can *Sunset Boulevard*. In these movies, the world of crime is shown very bleakly, and often leads to unhappy endings.

Another landmark film that influenced public views of crime was Alfred Hitchcock's *Psycho* (1960). This movie is credited with having started the "slasher flick" genre, using elements of horror and suspense to draw an excited audience into the antagonist's dark world of murder. *Psycho*'s antagonist Norman Bates was loosely based on real-life serial killer Ed Gein.

On television, viewers would get more entertainment not just from mean-faced detectives like Philip Marlowe, but also a fantasy element with crime stopped by superheroes like Superman and Batman. Film noir also saw some 1960s incarnations with *Cape Fear*, *The Manchurian Candidate*, *Mickey One*, and *Point Blank*.

Not only were the crime fighters superheroes, but also detectives and real people such as *Martin Kane, Private Eye*. Elliott Ness was known in a 1960s TV series before *The Untouchables* became a film in the 1980s. The 1960s would also have more unusual protagonists in shows like *The Fugitive*, *Mission Impossible*, *The Mod Squad*, and *Ironside*. The longest-running crime drama until the 1980s, *Hawaii Five-O*, debuted in 1968.

Crime fiction would also see a lot of print and comic book treatment. Before World War II, comic book heroes caught criminals, and even settled domestic problems such as abandoned children and abuse. After the war, they would go after Chicago Mob–style gangster crooks. Most of the villains of Batman, for example, came from organized crime. The setting of Gotham was originally fashioned after the bleak streets of gangster-era cities, although the tone was lightened for the campy 1960s series starring Adam West.

The printed word was also very important; in fact, many great crime movies were novels or short stories before being made into movie scripts. This includes Patricia Highsmith's *The Talented Mr. Ripley*, *Our Man in Havana* by Graham Greene, and *The Real Cool Killers* by Chester Himes. J.D. Salinger's *Catcher in the Rye* would influence the shooting of John Lennon in 1980. Movies and other adaptations would often start from prose literature.

the time, there was no federal law that made the killing of the U.S. president a federal crime. It was treated as a local homicide. The law was modified by Congress afterward, making the killing of the president a federal offense.

Even today, some believe that Oswald was not the true assassin, or was not acting alone. Conspiracy theories about the Kennedy assassination included Mafia involvement, alleging that the Mafia hired a hit man to assassinate Kennedy and used Oswald as a scapegoat. The alleged reason for the assassination was that Kennedy knew mob secrets that endangered them in relation to Cuba. Future investigations would reveal that CIA agents had been in talks with the Mafia about the possibility of using them to topple Cuban leader Fidel Castro.

Another famous assassination occurred on April 4, 1968. Civil rights leader Martin Luther King, Jr. was just leaving his room at the Lorraine Motel in Memphis, Tennessee, when a shot rang out and he fell to the floor. James Earl Ray was later apprehended in London and charged with the assassination. King's murder contributed to a rash of unrest that was already plaguing the country. As with Kennedy, King's murder was the subject of conspiracy theories, placing the blame most often with the U.S. government, which was seen as a white-dominated regime intent on keeping black people subservient. King's assassination is among the events that reflect the racial tensions

President John F. Kennedy and First Lady Jackie Kennedy with the Governor and First Lady of Texas not long before the assassination on November 22, 1963.

of the time, as well as the distrust that people were developing toward the government.

MISSISSIPPI BURNING AND RACIAL CRIMES

High profile people like John F. Kennedy and Martin Luther King were not the only socially relevant murder victims. On June 21, 1964, three civil rights workers, one black, James Chaney, and two Jewish men, Andrew Goodman and Michael Schwerner, disappeared. The men were on a drive to Meridian, Mississippi, during which they were briefly jailed by a local deputy. Searches later revealed their bodies in Olen Burrage's Old Jolly Farm near Philadelphia. A trial was held for 18 suspects, including the deputy and connected officials, although Edgar Ray Killen, a local minister, was acquitted. Seven men were declared guilty for conspiring to murder in the famous Mississippi Burning trial.

The window on the sixth floor of the Texas School Book Depository is open, showing the spot where the Kennedy assassin took his shots.

Nearly 40 years passed before any further action on the case was taken. Three movies were later made about the event, but real progress came when journalist Jerry Mitchell uncovered more evidence, and was joined by three high school students who made their own investigation as part of a school project. Mitchell also discovered an informant for the FBI during the earlier investigation, who was later determined to be patrol officer Maynard King. All information led to the conviction of Edgar Ray Killen, a former member of the Ku Klux Klan.

These racially-motivated killings exemplify the racial tensions of the 1960s, including the existence of extremist groups that propagated racism. The killings also demonstrate how much racism was an accepted part of social institutions, and how some people in the government believed that security was more important than civil rights.

DRUG USE AND ABUSE

One of the lasting crime legacies of the 1960s was the illegal drug trade. Recreational drugs have been used for millennia, with poppy seeds being used in Egypt and opium having been popular in the 19th century until the time of prohibition. Marijuana was banned in the 1930s in a brief hearing that some today consider farcical. In the 1950s, the Beat Generation starting using drugs with the pioneering example of Timothy Leary, a professor who was kicked out of Harvard for enjoining students in testing and using LSD.

A springboard came in the form of the 1960s counterculture. When the first "flower children" gathered at Berkeley Campus and other places in 1967, and later in the first Woodstock concert in 1969, some of them already carried narcotic substances such as marijuana and opium. LSD, known by its street name acid, was purportedly immortalized in The Beatles' song "Lucy in the Sky with Diamonds." These drugs were not yet illegal, and were therefore freely distributed. Most drug prohibitions came as a result of this vast increase in the use of drugs for recreation.

When the 1960s ended, a culture of drug use had been established. This culture, according to the FBI, started a vast network of drug dealers and traffickers. The creation of drug cartels became a serious national issue. Thus, in the 1970s the Drug Enforcement Administration was founded to address the problem.

TERRORISM
Before September 11, 2001, terrorism was already a part of life in America. Before the Islamic and Arab fundamentalists gained precedence, the terrorists

In the aftermath of a bomb explosion at the home of NAACP attorney Arthur Shores in Birmingham, Alabama, onlookers stopped to see the damage on September 5, 1963.

of the 1950s were Puerto Ricans who sought independence from American control. In 1950, an attack was mounted against the U.S. government when some Puerto Ricans tried to attack the residence of President Harry Truman in order to assassinate him.

In 1954, four Puerto Rican nationalists opened fire on the Capitol Building. They did not kill any politicians and they were apprehended. On May 1, 1961, Puerto Rican-born Antulio Ramirez Ortiz hijacked a National Airlines plane and forced it to fly to Cuba. After this, no other significant terrorist attacks were made by Puerto Ricans.

Domestic terrorism was also felt during the civil unrest against the Vietnam War, especially after the Tet Offensive and the revelation of the My Lai Massacre. The Weathermen were a group of leftist students who used violence, mostly bombings of government offices, as a form of protest against the U.S. government. Their ultimate goal was to overthrow the U.S. government and replace it with a socialist regime. The Weathermen disbanded soon after the Vietnam War ended.

SERIAL MURDER

Despite the focus on the Cold War, local crime never received a reprieve from national attention. Among the more sensational topics featured in news was murder. In fact, television coverage unveiled a horrifying new world that many people had not seen before, the world of serial killers. A serial killer is defined as one who kills repeatedly, usually following a pattern or a practice. The concept of the serial killer is well known today, but in the 1950s, American society was only beginning to recognize the serial killer, even if such a type of killer had existed throughout many periods in history.

Ed Gein is perhaps one of the most memorable killers from the 1950s because of his bizarre practices. The trail to Gein started when store employee Bernice Worden was declared missing on November 16, 1957. Investigators went to the Gein farm on the outskirts of Plainfield, Wisconsin. When police went inside, they found the skins of women hanging from the ceiling, and body parts kept in pots and pans. Aside from Bernice Worden, Gein was also tried for the murders of two other women. He was found legally insane and spent the rest of his life in a mental hospital. The once mild-mannered Gein became known as a monster in the media, and inspired several movie characters.

Another notorious killer was Harvey Glatman. He is considered the first signature killer, meaning he followed an identifiable pattern that marked his method of killing. Glatman would pose as a photographer of nude models and call women to set up assignments. Once there, he would restrain his victims, rape them, and kill them. He was caught while trying to catch his last potential victim, Lorraine Vigil. He was executed at San Quentin in 1959.

Television as well as print media often ran stories of high-profile killings. What would catch the public's fascination was the psychology behind the

Cold War Espionage

Nothing, perhaps, marks the tensions of the 1950s more than the Cold War. While it was an international affair, the warnings of Joseph McCarthy made the government certain that there were Soviet-aligned spies within the United States. And such fears were not unfounded; the FBI confirmed that secrets were being leaked to the Soviet Union. As early as 1945, copies of secret documents were found in the possession of a magazine concerned with Russian-American relations. In 1946, Soviet leader Joseph Stalin declared that capitalism must be overcome by Communism.

Even before the McCarthy era, the Alien Registration Act or Smith Act of 1940 outlawed teaching ideas about overthrowing the American government. Given the nature of Communism, American Communists were implicated. The McCarran Security Act, introduced in 1950, required all Communist organizations to register with the Attorney General. Then came the Immigration and Nationality Act of 1952. The act called for the deportation of subversive individuals in the country, and the barring of known subversive individuals from entering. Finally, the Communist Control Act of 1954 outlawed all Communist activity in the United States. Communism became criminalized. Nevertheless, a Communist Party of the United States, founded in 1919, continued to exist throughout the Cold War and up until today. During the Cold War, their ties with the Soviet Union and other Communist countries marked them as a threat to national security. They had to operate from hiding most of the time.

One of the biggest concerns from the Communist threat was the possibility of nuclear war. In 1949, the Soviet Union exploded its first nuclear bomb. Some American officials believed that local knowledge on bomb-making was leaked to the Soviets. Thus, the public was ingrained with the fear of Soviet spies, a fear that continued to the end of the Cold War.

In 1950, husband and wife Julius and Ethel Rosenberg were arrested for spying for the Soviet Union. It started with the arrest of Klaus Fuchs, a scientist who worked at Los Alamos who confessed to have given information on the Manhattan Project (the atomic bomb creation project) to the Soviets. The line of informants soon led to Julius Rosenberg, who was known to have Communist leanings. In 1951, the Rosenbergs were put on trial. The case for Julius Rosenberg had evidence, but Ethel was detained as a hostage to make Julius talk. The main evidence against the Rosenbergs was the testimony of other espionage suspects.

In addition, both Rosenbergs were members of the U.S. Communist Party. They protested their innocence to the end. When the Rosenbergs were declared guilty, their sons Robert and Michael and friends campaigned to free them. But only four Supreme Court justices voted to overturn the verdict, and it was not enough. The Rosenbergs were executed in Sing Sing Prison in New York on June 19, 1953, via electrocution.

The Ku Klux Klan, the bane of the 1920s, was still active in the 1960s and is seen here facing opposition while marching in support of Barry Goldwater's presidential nomination at the Republican National Convention in San Francisco, California, in July 1964.

killer's criminal behavior. After Gein, Glatman, and other similar killers, most serial killer profiles would reveal disturbed and abused people whose killings were the product of their psychological problems.

KITTY GENOVESE MURDER

One night in 1964, a woman was stabbed and murdered in New York City. Kitty Genovese had parked her car in a Long Island Railroad lot, in a building adjacent to her residence. Waiting for her in a car nearby was a man named William Moseley. Hidden in the shadows, he had watched her as she parked. When Genovese spotted him and ran, Moseley chased her and stabbed her in the back. A neighbor yelled from a window, and Moseley temporarily moved away. Meanwhile, Genovese got up and tried to get inside the building, but Moseley found her and stabbed her again. He then raped her and stole some of her belongings. An apartment door opened and some voices were heard, but no one interfered. Moseley left Genovese and even exchanged glances with a milkman before going into his car and driving off. One of the neighbors called the police, but Genovese had already died before she could be brought to the hospital. Moseley committed more crimes and was caught while holding a mother and daughter hostage in their house. The FBI was contacted and apprehended Moseley later on. He was sentenced to life in Great Meadow Correctional Facility in upstate New York.

The Kitty Genovese murder was appalling due to the inaction of many witnesses. Over 30 people were reported to have witnessed Genovese's murder. It left the impression in the public that people were starting to become apathetic and uncaring, perhaps due to the changing attitudes in society and the growing isolation of a person in a big city. It implied that people no longer cared if a crime was being committed on their doorstep, just as long as it was another person suffering. It also implied that if you lived in a big city, there was a greater chance of being a crime victim without anyone coming to help. It gave the name to the Genovese Syndrome or Bystander Effect, the phenomenon of witnesses failing to report when a crime is committed.

CHARLES MANSON

In the middle of 1969, one of the most gruesome crimes to date happened in California. In the house of director Roman Polanski, household help found actress Sharon Tate, friend Jay Sebring, and others brutally murdered. The perpetrators of the crime were led by Charles Manson, a cult leader who had a string of juvenile offenses and a prison record.

In 1967, Manson, a recently released convict, set up a group called the Family with several young runaways and teens influenced by the hippie culture that was popular at the time. A large proportion of the Family was composed of women. The Family took up residence at a Death Valley ranch. In July 1969, Manson and some followers tried to extort money from Gary Hinman. Hinman refused because he had no money, and he was killed by Manson and his followers.

In August, Manson directed five members to break into the house of movie director Roman Polanski and kill everyone in it. Polanski was in Europe at the time, and thus the victims were Tate, her friends, Jay Sebring, Wojciech Frykowski, Abigail Folger, and driver Steven Parent. The next night, the Family killed Leno and Rosemary Labianca in their home. Members of the Family would be caught on other charges, but a dorm mate of Susan Atkins would inform the Los Angeles Police of the Family's activities. The Manson Family members are in still in jail today. Manson's group was one of the early cults to commit gruesome crimes, and would foreshadow other cults such as Jim Jones's People's Temple, Heaven's Gate, and the Aum Shinkyo groups.

BANK ROBBERY AND THEFT

The 1950s started with one of the most well-known bank heists of the decade—the Brinks Robbery of 1950 in Boston. It was one of the most well-planned bank robberies, wherein the perpetrators studied the layout of the Brinks building and the movements of the people. Once the bank robbers were familiar with the building's activities, they performed dry runs of the robbery. Then they hit the bank on the evening of January 17.

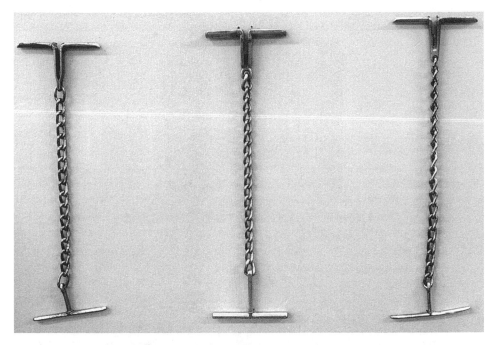

Police officers used these "nippers," also known as "come-alongs," like handcuffs to restrain arrested suspects.

The robbers came in wearing peacoats, Halloween masks, gloves, and crepe-soled shoes. They walked in, threatened and tied up employees, and walked away with $3 million in cash and checks. The men would soon fall to a series of investigations and leads, although the example of this "perfect bank robbery" has continued to fascinate people ever since. Perhaps inspired by this, bank robberies would continue to be common. They would become a staple in TV programs, and banks and financial institutions would be forced to hire stronger security for protection.

ACCESS TO LAW ENFORCEMENT

The witnesses to the Kitty Genovese murder did not have the convenience of dialing 911. The 911 emergency number would be introduced in the late 1960s. Police and other emergency agencies were contacted through their local station numbers, and through normal telephone operators. England had been the first country to institute a three-digit number for calling the police, which is 999, in 1937. New Zealand followed with their 111 number in 1958.

It was clear that the United States was behind in this aspect, so a fire chief and President Lyndon Johnson's Commission on Law Enforcement and Administration of Justice in 1967 both recommended having this three-digit

A 1960s Motorola police radio. The first call ever placed to the nation's new 911 system came in on February 16, 1968, in Haleyville, Alabama.

emergency number. AT&T had press announcements sent out that the service would be started in 1968. However, Alabama Telephone Company president Bob Gallagher beat them to the punch and hosted the first ever 911 call on February 16, 1968, in Haleyville, Alabama.

The 911 system was gradually implemented all over the country, and would become nationwide in 1973 as the result of a government ruling. Canada changed its former 999 system to 911 in 1972. Since then, the 911 number has become the standard emergency calling system for the whole of the United States and Canada.

CRIMINAL JUSTICE IN THE 1950s AND 1960s

The criminal justice system at this time was undergoing rapid transformations. This is due in large part to the appointment of Earl Warren, considered one of the most liberal chief justices to take office. Warren oversaw many changes to the justice system, including the granting of more rights to suspects and offenders to offset abuses committed by penal authorities and law enforcement agencies. Some of the landmark cases that established police procedures on suspect rights occurred in the 1960s.

In 1961, the police in Cleveland, Ohio were tipped that a bomber was hiding in the house of Dollree Mapp. They went to her house and demanded entrance, but Mapp refused to let them in, arguing that they did not have a warrant. The police left, then returned several hours later and forced their way in the house, with a phony piece of paper they claimed to be the warrant. Mapp was arrested for having some pornographic material in her house. She appealed to the Supreme Court and it ruled in the *Mapp v. Ohio* case that the Cleveland police violated the Fourth Amendment because they broke into a citizen's house without a warrant. Evidence acquired in such a manner broke the Fourth Amendment and was consequently invalidated.

Also in 1961, a Florida defendant named Clarence Earl Gideon was declared guilty of burglary in court without the benefit of legal counsel. He later wrote to the Supreme Court, arguing that the Sixth Amendment allowed him to be provided with a lawyer if he could not hire one himself. The court ruled in his favor. Thus, in *Gideon v. Wainright*, the Supreme Court ruled that defendants do have the right to counsel in all cases, and if unable to provide it for themselves, can be provided with such at government expense.

Police detectives investigating a burned-out car after a riot in Brooklyn, New York, in 1964. Police procedures and investigative techniques continued to improve in the 1950s and 1960s.

In 1966, *Miranda v. Arizona* set the procedure for police to inform suspects of their rights. Ernesto Arturo Miranda was arrested in 1963 for rape. He was brought into a room and coerced into confessing. Because the confession was the only evidence that could be used to incriminate him, Miranda's lawyer, Alvin Moore, appealed to the Supreme Court. Justice Warren ruled that the confession was obtained in violation of Fifth Amendment rights and made it mandatory for police officers to inform suspects of their rights. This act of reading to the suspect his rights prior to questioning is called "Mirandizing" by police officers.

The national attitude of concern for civil rights dominated the judicial as well as political atmosphere. The Cold War had made the U.S. government paranoid and overprotective to the point of violating human rights in the process. The majority of Americans were indifferent to such violations because the Soviet Union and Communism were thought of as a greater threat than civil rights violations.

CONCLUSION

The postwar years started with relative peace, although the shadow of the Cold War loomed. Local crime issues that were previously overshadowed by the events of World War II suddenly came to the forefront. Racial issues, civil unrest, and televised crime turned a period of relative peace into turmoil and unrest, and were further spurred by the onset and eventual escalation of the unpopular Vietnam War. Changes in the justice system were also made, resulting in practices that form the basis for contemporary law enforcement procedures.

The increase in crime in America was caused by many factors, including internal tensions and radical societal changes. This period is marked by societal reforms and changes in the crime world. The organized crime world of the Mafia was revealed, and new concepts in criminology would be practiced, such as the scientific examination of psychological motivations for killing. The 1950s and 1960s heralded a time when American society would find crime an inevitable part of life.

CHINO FERNANDEZ

Further Readings

Bureau of Justice Statistics, U.S. Department of Justice. Available online: http://www.ojp.usdoj.gov/bjs/welcome.html. Accessed April 2008.

Dispatch Monthly Magazine, "History of 911." Available online: http://www.911dispatch.com/911/history. Accessed February 2008.

Drug Enforcement Agency Museum. "Illegal Drugs in America: A Modern History." Available online: http://www.deamuseum.org. Accessed February 2008.

Dwyer, Kevin and Jure Florillo. *True Stories of Law & Order*. New York: Berkley, 2006.

Federal Bureau of Investigation, "History of the FBI—Postwar America: 1945–1960s." Available online: http://www.fbi.gov/libref/historic/history/postwar.htm. Accessed February 2008.

Kaiser, David. *The Road to Dallas: The Assassination of John F. Kennedy*. Cambridge, MA: Belknap Press, 2008.

Linder, Douglas O. "The Mississippi Burning Trial." *Famous Trials*. Available online: http://www.law.umkc.edu/faculty/projects/ftrials/price&bowers/Account.html. Accessed February 2008.

McCann, Joseph T. *Terrorism on American Soil: A Concise History of Plots and Perpetrators from the Famous to the Forgotten*. Boulder, CO: Sentient, 2006.

Radosh, Ronald and Joyce Milton. *The Rosenberg File*, 2nd ed. New Haven, CT: Yale University Press, 1997.

Ripley, Tim, "CDISS Terrorism Programme," *Center for Defense and International Security Studies*. Available online: http://www.timripley.co.uk/terrorism/index.html. Accessed February 2008.

Schmalleger, F. *Criminal Justice: A Brief Introduction*. Upper Saddle River, NJ: Prentice Hall, 2007.

Sutherland, Jon and Diane Canwell. *True Crime*. London: The Foundry, 2003.

Chapter 12

Labor and Employment

"The fight is never about grapes or lettuce. It is about people."
—Cesar Chavez

BY 1949 AMERICANS realized that the Great Depression was over. Despite the fears expressed by pundits as World War II closed, victory over Germany and Japan did not lead to a resumption of the desperate poverty and violence of the 1930s. Instead, the next two decades brought prosperity and higher living standards for many Americans. There were new opportunities for both men and women, and a movement toward decreasing workplace discrimination. At the same time, the economy was transforming in ways that would eventually change the nature of work for many people. Much change in the era also stemmed from union activity, but without the violence of previous decades.

DEMOBILIZATION

When the war ended, there had been some difficulties with demobilization and converting a wartime economy back to peace, but for the most part, it had been seamless. Soldiers came back from Asia and Europe and took over the jobs held by women during the war. Women left the factories and returned home to raise their children. The factories switched from producing B-17 bombers to airliners, from military radios to civilian radios and later televisions, and from tanks to refrigerators.

More importantly, the generation that reached adulthood before and during the war moved out of the "old neighborhood," rapidly filling up the new suburbs

175

that Abe Levitt and so many other developers were creating, buying dream homes with G.I. loans and new cars with money saved from wartime salaries and allotments, and pursuing college degrees and a higher quality of life.

By 1949 men of this generation were accepting university degrees and moving up in their chosen fields, often becoming supervisors, union shop stewards, or junior executives. They understood organization and teamwork, had broad perspective, and saw the necessity of maintaining both a strong national defense and a strong economy. At the same time, having endured so much suffering and bloodshed, they sought the financial and personal rewards of these struggles; they might not want to rock the boat, but they wanted their share of the profits. American workers were no longer masses of serfs, but rather skilled, capable, team players.

These social factors heavily impacted the American worker and the American workplace. By 1949, William H. Whyte, Jr., a former Marine officer turned staff writer for *Fortune* magazine, studied these men, in their snap-brim hats and double-breasted (later three-button) suits, who believed in punctuality, a stitch in time, and plenty of elbow grease. He called them Organization Men, who sought to ensure that their organizations ran smoothly, favoring compromise and cooperation over conflict.

This attitude played into the labor-management field. With unions now legitimized by law, strikes were simply an annoying but legitimate piece of negotiations. Strikebreakers were no longer hired to attack workers. Machine-guns, company scrip, and barbed wire were gone from factories and coal mines. Police officers were no longer the tool by which companies broke strikes—they merely stood guard at picket lines to ensure that traffic flowed on the street, and insults between strikers and onlookers did not turn into fistfights.

TRUMAN AND THE TAFT-HARTLEY ACT
Union-management battles were now fought in conference rooms and arbitration meetings, and the terms of the struggle were mundane: hours, wages, grievance procedures, health and vacation benefits, and seniority rights. Business leaders no longer denounced unions as Communist fronts. They did not have to: unions were often as anti-Communist as the bosses, if not more so.

Nevertheless, union-management disputes could still shut down businesses and create headlines. In March 1952 the steel companies refused to abide by a wage mediation board that offered a 26-cent-an-hour wage hike to workers without the $12-per-ton rise in steel prices the companies sought. The board only offered the mills a $4.50 price hike per ton. The mills were producing record tonnage, but workers had not seen a raise since 1950.

President Harry S Truman, worried that a strike would impede the flow of military supplies to NATO and the troops in Korea, ordered his Secretary of Commerce, Charles Sawyer, to seize the mills and run them as government property, signing Executive Order No. 10340 to do so on April 8, 1952.

The Suburbs and the Organization Man

The end of World War II saw the rise of the corporation—or "organization," as in sociologist William Whyte's 1956 bestseller *Organization Man*, drawn from interviews with corporate chief executive officers. Corporations attracted and bred a certain type of person, a certain psychology, someone who was comfortable conforming to existing standards and who did not rock the boat. Meanwhile, Whyte pointed out, enrollment in academic courses like the sciences and humanities was on the decline, while enrollment rose in practical career-oriented courses like engineering and business. Whyte attacked the suburbs as the domestic version of the corporate workplace and the popularity of personality testing for providing molds for these conservative corporation types to fit into.

The spread of the suburbs meant more and more social activity was constrained to the local neighborhood, in the form of dinner clubs, bridge parties, and cocktail parties, all held in peoples' homes, often on a rotating basis. Because of this, Whyte perceived that there was an enforced need to be "outgoing," to sacrifice some portion of privacy and consider your home an extension of the neighborhood, leaving few truly private spaces—not to do so meant fewer social outlets. More and more, Whyte said, the corporate man was tolerant of other lifestyles, but unable to empathize with them; if not xenophobic, at least incapable of understanding the desire to be anyone else, to live any other way.

Texan sociologist C. Wright Mills was even more outspoken than Whyte about the changing American society of the 1950s. In the wake of World War II, he saw the role of the sociologist as not a simple cataloguer of social trends, but also a captain in the culture wars, fighting negative and harmful change where he found it.

The minimum duty of the sociologist in Mills's view was to let the common man know what was going on, and what the consequences could be—rather than stepping back and acting as a neutral observer. He called himself an academic outlaw because so many of his colleagues thought he was crossing a line.

In books like 1956's *Power Elite* and 1959's *Sociological Imagination*, Mills talked about the effects of the suburbs, and of the automobile on making the suburbs possible. The housewife, he said, was as much a specialist as the doctor or the lawyer, a specialist in purchasing and nurturing. He described the class of white collar workers as the new working class, and was the first to discuss celebrities as a group unto themselves, independent of financial class.

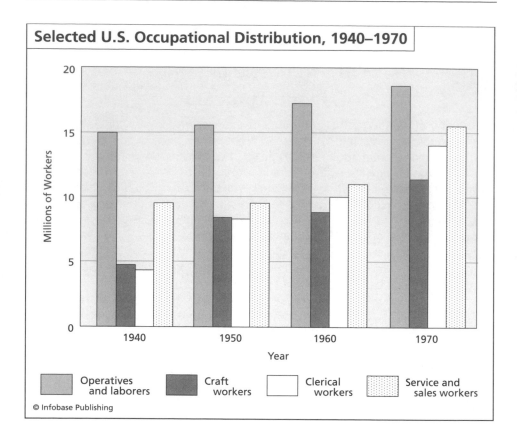

Selected U.S. Occupational Distribution, 1940–1970

Millions of Workers

Year

Operatives and laborers · Craft workers · Clerical workers · Service and sales workers

© Infobase Publishing

The next morning, 88 steel mills were open for business, with the same men working and same managers supervising. The only difference was the American flags that flew over the mills instead of corporate banners. Truman's move seemed a success, like his threat to draft the railroad workers, but both steel owners and the media recoiled. Newspapers tartly pointed out that if a president could seize steel mills under his "inherent powers," the press would be next. Federal Judge David A. Pine agreed, and in a blistering 4,500-word opinion, said the threatened strike would be "less injurious to the public than the injury which would flow from a timorous judicial recognition that there is some basis for this claim to unlimited and unrestrained Executive power."

Depressed and upset, Truman promised to abide by the court's decision, but appealed to the Supreme Court, which ruled against the president by a 6-3 majority on June 2, with five liberal judges in the majority. "We cannot with faithfulness to our constitutional system hold that the Commander in Chief of the Armed Forces has the ultimate power as such to take possession of private property in order to keep labor disputes from stopping production. This is a job for the nation's lawmakers, not for its military authorities," said Judge Hugo L. Black, delivering the majority opinion. That evening, to show there were no hard feelings, Black invited Truman and the other justice to a party at his home in Alexandria.

The next day, the steelworkers went out on strike in what would become the longest and most costly steel strike in the nation's history—a seven-week period that saw huge losses on both sides: 21 million tons of steel and $400 million in wages, and two million workers idle. The military output for 1952 was cut by a third. In July, Truman summoned Phil Murray, head of the Congress of Industrial Organizations (CIO), and Benjamin Fairless, the head of U.S. Steel, to his office and demanded a settlement. He got one: a $.21 an hour raise for the workers and a steel price increase of $5.20 a ton, about the same as the $4.50 originally offered.

It was a major defeat for Truman and a political battle for both labor and management, but two points were obvious: no violence had resulted from the strike, and nobody had used the Taft-Hartley Labor-Management Act of 1947. The Taft-Hartley Act reversed some of the force of the Wagner Act of 10 years before, by enabling a federal mediator or judge to slap on an 80-day "cooling-off" period to prevent a strike. In theory, the 80-day period would be used for negotiations, but unions objected, saying such a cooling-off time only benefited management.

Worse, the Taft-Hartley Act contained a "States Rights" section that allowed individual states to override provisions of national labor law. The result was that 21 states passed "right-to-work" laws that outlawed closed shops and prevented unions from disciplining or discharging members who did not pay their dues. That crippled unions in Southern states still trying to organize textile mill workers, where most "right-to-work" laws existed.

LABOR AND RED-BAITING

The growth of unions in America had made them dizzy with success. Some unions and locals were petty dictatorships, increasingly dominated in some cases by organized crime. Unions were raiding each other's members in jurisdictional disputes, ignoring democratic procedure, discriminating against blacks and Latinos. Signing union leaders would on occasion make "sweetheart" deals with bosses, maintaining labor peace in return for payoffs or at the behest of mobsters seeking to maintain order. Activities like these caused a backlash that led to the Taft-Hartley Act.

But the law itself was also part of a postwar reactionary trend in American politics, which saw a brief return to isolationism, the dismantling of many New Deal reforms, followed by increasingly harsh anti-Communist rhetoric and "red-hunting" activities in both the private and public sectors.

Organized labor was soon a victim of the red-baiting, as it had been before the war. The CIO was hard-hit by the allegations and accusations, as it had left-wingers like the Reuther brothers and Sidney Hillman among its leadership, and had enjoyed Communist support before, during, and after the war.

The CIO did move on its own suspected Reds, with the National Maritime Union's George Curran and the Transport Workers' Union's colorful Michael J. Quill, both New York-based unions, taking the lead in 1947. Phil Murray replaced fellow-traveler Lee Pressman with future Supreme Court Justice Arthur J. Goldberg as CIO attorney. In its 1949 national convention, the CIO made the pursuit of Reds in its ranks a major issue when Murray himself said, "There is enough room within the CIO movement to differ about many subjects, many ideas, questions of reform within the CIO, economics, social, and trade-union policy—yes, plenty of room, plenty of room, but there is no room within CIO for communism." With that, the CIO booted out the United Electrical Workers as a Red-run front, replacing it with the International Union of Electrical, Radio, and Machine Workers. The Farm Equipment Workers union was also ousted, its role given to the United Auto Workers. Ten other unions also faced charges, and nine of them were expelled as Communist-dominated. Among them were the West Coast Longshoremen, Marine Cooks, Food and Tobacco, and the Fur and Leather Workers. At the same time, the CIO chartered its first white-collar union, the 250,000-member Communications Workers of America.

THE FADING BLUE COLLAR

The creation of that union marked the beginning of a massive change in the American workplace and homes as the Eisenhower era took over in 1953. The blue collar was being bleached. In 1953, 60 percent of all American families reported wages in the middle-class brackets. Detroit assembly line workers drove the expensive new cars they built, and could buy stock in their companies. Eighteen million American industrialized workers were unionized by 1954, and thanks to union contracts, health plans, dental plans, and pension plans, those workers could enjoy a middle-class quality of life. Guaranteed wage increases, cost-of-living wage increases, productivity negotiations, overtime pay, formal grievance procedures, seniority rights, strict safety policies, credit unions, and even union bowling leagues gave workers a

A fishmonger weighing fish at the Fulton Fish Market in New York City in 1963.

quality of life their parents had not enjoyed. Many of the subjects that had been the center of labor's most violent episodes were now sorted out peacefully through grievance procedures and binding arbitration.

By 1956 the number of blue-collar workers was surpassed by the number of white-collar workers. Corporate welfarism was now entrenched as good business practice. Profit-sharing plans, employee input on company decisions, and training and apprenticeship programs replaced the machine-guns and company stores of the past. The stores themselves were no longer implements of owner oppression, but perks and benefits for employees, offering their workers the business's goods at a discount. Corporate wel-

Construction workers on a dam project around 1950. By 1956 there were more white-collar than blue collar workers in the United States.

farism appeared in other ways. RCA issued company neckties. Ritchfield Oil built model homes, and IBM erected country clubs, landscaped its factories, and offered its workers subsidized health-care, paid holidays, and sick leave. Reynolds Tobacco engaged company chaplains, while Eastman Kodak and Du Pont brought in staff psychiatrists. There were increasing federal benefits as well. By 1951 about 75 percent of America's workers were paying in to Social Security, adding to their retirement benefits.

With America becoming a white-collar nation of team-oriented businesses, its two major labor organizations began seeking ways to cooperate as well. The CIO and American Federation of Labor (AFL) had sided together against the Soviet-led World Federation of Trade Unions in the international sphere. In November 1952, Phil Murray of the CIO and William Green of the AFL died within a few days of each other. George Meany, the former secretary-treasurer of the AFL, took over as that organization's president. Walter Reuther had already succeeded Murray as boss of the CIO at their 1952 convention. With the old order's two representatives and jurisdictional wars gone from the scene, the new leaders were ready to reconcile.

There were other major reasons for unification. With President Eisenhower in office, the nation's continued rightward shift was moving against unions, and with that, decisions by the National Labor Relations Board. The two major unions had their own weaknesses: the AFL could not act efficiently against racket-dominated locals, while the CIO's leadership had just enough Communists to appear dangerous to middle-class voters. Unification would enable the combined leadership to address both problems and present management with a stronger front.

On December 5, 1955, the American Federation of Labor and Congress of Industrial Organizations was founded, putting 16 million workers, more than 85 percent of all union members in a single "House of Labor," with George Meany as president, William F. Schnitzler as secretary-treasurer, and Walter P. Reuther as head of the newly created Industrial Union Department and vice-president of the AFL-CIO.

Meany was a good symbol for the AFL-CIO. A burly, ham-fisted Bronx-born plumber, he had left high school after one year to gain his apprenticeship, and been a plumber ever since, supporting his widowed mother and family. He rose steadily through the AFL plumbing ranks, rising to become president of the New York State Federation of Labor. He held the secretary-treasurer post of the AFL for 13 years before becoming its president. Armed with a large head, snub-nosed Irish face, and a thick cigar, Meany made the perfect symbol for American unions. He needed to be tough. As the AFL and CIO moved towards amalgamation, they faced a grave issue that was a major embarrassment for labor: the International Longshoreman's Association, made infamous by Elia Kazan's movie *On the Waterfront*.

THE REAL *ON THE WATERFRONT*

The movie itself had a factual basis. In 1949, reporter Malcolm Johnson won a Pulitzer Prize for the *New York Sun*, in the category of local reporting, with a series entitled "Crime on the Waterfront." His series exposed the labor racketeering, extortion, and corruption on the Brooklyn and Manhattan piers, and inspired Hollywood.

Reality was grim. The International Longshoreman's Association (ILA) was a major political and economic force on the East coast, the New York docks particularly. Dominated for decades by "Lifetime President" Joseph Ryan, the union moved vast quantities of goods through the docks, and controlled hiring through the daily "shape-up" on the piers, which often meant that union members worked only one day a week, and owed their jobs to local bosses and gangsters.

In 1951, following a 25-day strike and a questionable ILA election, New York Governor Thomas E. Dewey, who had gained national fame as Brooklyn's "racket-busting D.A.," ordered the docks investigated by State Industrial Commissioner Edward Corsi. His team examined witnesses, and the revelations were a news sensation. In 1953, the New York Waterfront Commission was created to oversee the docks and eliminate the mobsters. The AFL, outraged, suspended the ILA in August 1953, and created the International Longshore-man's Brotherhood (ILB) as a replacement. Ryan resigned as head of the ILA.

The National Labor Relations Board conducted an election in December to see who would represent the longshoremen, and the ILA won. Dewey, how-ever, was unimpressed, and launched a campaign to overturn the vote. Tension between the two rival unions simmered and exploded in March 1954, when Teamster Union boss Dave Beck refused to cross an ILB picket line, and ILA men refused to touch Teamster-driven trucks and went on wildcat strikes. Other unions supported the ILA, defying the AFL's order, and violence erupted as adherents of the two unions slugged it out. The National Labor Relations Board ordered everyone back to work and held new elections, which the ILA won. The ILB crumbled and ultimately joined the ILA, which continued to control New York's docks, with Anthony Scotto ultimately in charge of Brooklyn's powerful Local 1814 by 1963.

While the longshoremen battled on the docks, labor in general faced massive reorganization. As the 1950s ended and the 1960s began, the three most pressing labor issues were technology, imports, and race.

An assembly room inside the International Longshoremen's and Warehousemen's Union Hall in Port Hueneme, California. The hall was built by the U.S. Navy during World War II to help attract skilled longshoremen to the area.

Women sorting tomatoes at the Iris Fruit Corporation in the Brooklyn Terminal Market in Brooklyn, New York, in 1962.

Technology came first. With the development of the transistor, the computer, and miniaturization, industry found that many tasks could now be done by electronic robots far more cheaply and safely than human workers or oil-powered machinery. Many craft unions, like the Horseshoers, Coopers, and Broom and Whisk Makers' Union, found their numbers spiraling downward. Satellite-powered telephones and direct-distance dialing put the Commercial Telegraphers' Union out of work as well.

Industrial unions were affected, too, as steel, automobile manufacturing, and other assembly-line businesses turned to automated production. By 1963, automation was eliminating 200,000 factory jobs annually. Worse, many of the workers eliminated were senior men, who could not easily switch jobs late in their productive lives.

Unions and companies approached these changes in many different ways. After the 1959 steel strike, for example, the United Steelworkers (USW) and the steel companies established committees to figure out what to do with workers rendered redundant by technology. Kaiser Steel and USW in December 1962 came up with a plan to retrain workers made redundant by automation. Armour Company and its unions created a similar plan.

Nevertheless, as the 1960s went on, it was clear that America's unions were no longer leading great charges to organize workers in factories, but instead engaged in holding actions to protect jobs for slowly dwindling numbers. Industry increasingly moved to Southern states, where "right-to-work" laws made unionization difficult. As American domestic industries like steel, cars, and coal gave way to foreign competitors (steel and cars), or new technology (coal), union membership numbers began to drop.

THE TRIUMPH OF THE TRANSIT WORKERS

Ironically, as the blue-collar workers lost union power, white-collar and non-industrial workers became unionized and more powerful. Retail clerks, communication workers, service employees, and schoolteachers all became unionized and became increasingly powerful. Even athletes unionized—in 1966 major league baseball players fired the management-appointed head of their union, Judge Robert Cannon. They replaced him and the union's only assets (two filing cabinets) with United Steelworkers economist, negotiator, and Brooklyn Dodgers fan Marvin Miller. He promptly forced the game's owners to raise minimum salaries from $7,000 to $10,000 a year. At the time, half of all America's self-employed workers were earning $15,000, so the 500 top major league baseball players felt they had a considerable grievance. Willie Mays was the highest paid ballplayer at the time, earning $105,000 after 15 years in the majors, while football's Joe Namath was offered a $400,000 contract before putting on a professional uniform.

That same year, New York's newly-elected Mayor John V. Lindsay was greeted with a transit strike on his first day in office, when Michael J. Quill, the leader of the Transit Workers' Union (TWU), took his subway train operators out of the tunnels. Quill was a fiery Irish-born former Communist who had risen to lead the Transit Workers' Union during the 1930s. In 1948, he broke with his Red allies when they opposed a subway fare hike that Quill thought was necessary to win his men a raise. Quill then purged his union of Communists, but continued to hurl harsh rhetoric at union rallies, his Irish brogue getting thicker as he spoke. Quill opposed the TWU's CIO-led merger with the AFL, accusing the AFL as being a union of "racketeering, racism, and raids." He also fired abuse at his sometime ally, Mayor Robert Wagner, during heated contract negotiations during the 1950s, threatening strikes. Each time, however, Wagner and Quill were able to avert a job action through quiet negotiations.

A paymaster machine from the 1950s.

Not so in 1966, when the aristocratic liberal Republican John Lindsay took office on January 1, 1966, at midnight. Precisely five hours later, Quill took his 34,000 workers off their jobs, demanding a four-day workweek and 30 percent pay hike. Lindsay publicly denounced the union, and had Quill jailed for contempt of court in ordering the strike. From behind bars, Quill called "Mayor Lindsley" a "pipsqueak" and "a boy in short pants." Asked if he would apologize to the court, Quill shouted, "The judge can drop dead in his black robes!" Nonetheless, New York City's population and economy ground to a halt for 12 days in mid-winter. More than 1.5 million workers stayed home, crippling business, while others turned to car pools, hitchhiking, bicycling, or even walking. Even so, Lindsay was forced to give in on terms more generous than the TWU originally sought. Three days after emerging from jail and signing the contract, Quill died of a heart attack. In a supreme irony, the Teamsters union local that drove New York's hearses was staging its own strike, and no drivers were available. The union authorized drivers to work the Quill funeral.

The Transit Workers' triumph empowered New York's other municipal workers. In quick succession, doctors, nurses, sanitation men, and social

Eugene Smallwood, who worked for the Curatolo Banana Corporation in Brooklyn, New York, weighing bananas.

workers staged their own job actions. The garbage men went out in February 1968, and the teachers followed that fall, in a battle not over money, but over a decentralization program that fired 14 white teachers in a mostly black school district. Angered over the potential job loss, the mostly Jewish teachers' union refused to work until the city-wide Board of Education stripped the district of its power. Lindsay refused to take sides, and the strike dragged on for three months, forcing the district to hire substitutes and embittering relations between New York's Jews and blacks.

LABOR AND CIVIL RIGHTS

African-American workers in general struggled to make gains after the war, as the Civil Rights movement reached across the nation. During the 1940s, some 26 AFL affiliates specifically barred blacks from membership. In 1963, the Brotherhood of Locomotive Firemen and Enginemen became the last such union to drop the Jim Crow clauses from its constitution. Nevertheless, the Brotherhood of Sleeping Car Porters was the only union where black labor leaders could flex their muscle, and as the passenger rail industry declined in postwar America, that strength weakened.

The 1960s Civil Rights movement brought attention to the racism of workplaces, particularly the construction industry. In New York, blacks staged sit-ins at construction sites to protest the lack of hiring and training programs for African Americans. One such protest was planned for the opening of the 1964 World's Fair, to denounce that exhibition's failure to hire black workers. It was to consist of protestors stalling their cars on highways leading to the fair, but poor organization and a strong police presence stopped the plan before it began. Construction unions, however, facing pressure from protesters and politicians alike, began to get the point, and began setting up training and antidiscrimination programs. As more blacks entered and moved up in the workforce, African Americans began to take increasing leadership roles in locals and entire unions.

Latino workers also faced struggles, and their battles took the national stage when Mexican-American farmworker Cesar Chavez formed the National Farm Workers Association (later the United Farm Workers [UFW]) in an abandoned Fresno movie theater in 1962, to fight for the often cruelly exploited migrant farm workers of California, whose grinding poverty was graphically depicted by CBS reporter Edward R. Murrow in his documentary *Harvest of Shame.*

In 1965, the UFW in Delano, California, voted to strike against the grape growers, and that decision turned into a five-year battle punctuated by Chavez going on highly celebrated fasts, a 340-mile march from Delano to Sacramento, and a national boycott of California grapes that was honored by as many as 17 million Americans. The UFW's struggles resembled the 1930s union battles, with Texas Rangers fighting strikers, and attempts by grape growers

In the 1940s, as many as 26 AFL union affiliates had barred blacks from membership. This crowd of protestors demanded fair housing, education, and employment at the "March on Washington for Jobs and Freedom" in 1963.

to sign "sweetheart" deals with the Teamsters Union to create a compliant workforce. Chavez's struggles would continue into the 1970s and 1980s, as did the grape boycott.

JIMMY HOFFA

The presence of the Teamsters Union as an employer strikebuster in the California grape fields was just one example of that union's grim history in the postwar era, a history whose human symbol was James Riddle Hoffa. Born in Brazil, Indiana, in 1913, Hoffa grew up in Detroit, where he dropped out of school in the ninth grade due to the Great Depression. He began working at Kroger's Food, loading and unloading trucks, working 12-hour shifts that began at 4:30 P.M. He and his coworkers were paid only for when they actually shifted cargo, but were required to sit around the warehouse, without pay, for the entire shift. Pay was two-thirds company scrip redeemable for Kroger's food products and one-third cash, and the foreman was vicious and abusive, hiring and firing workers on a whim. Hoffa and his coworkers were infuriated and began to quietly organize. When two workers were fired for going at midnight to a food cart, 18-year-old Hoffa took his coworkers off the job, refusing to unload perishable strawberries. Faced with a massive loss of goods, the Kroger bosses agreed to meet with Hoffa in the morning if he and the other men unloaded the trucks immediately.

After several days of negotiations, Hoffa won his union a 13-cent-an-hour wage increase, a guaranteed half-day's pay, an insurance plan, and union recognition. Hoffa quickly filed his chapter with the AFL. A year later, Hoffa was fired for fighting with a plant foreman, but he quickly became an organizer for the International Brotherhood of Teamsters, taking the Kroger union into it with him. As Hoffa rose through the Teamster organization, so did the man he would replace, Dave Beck, who became the union's first executive vice president in 1947. The following year, when the AFL's machinists' union went on strike at Boeing, Beck announced he would organize the workers at Boeing, to raid the AFL machinists. The Teamsters Union then signed a secret deal with the aircraft manufacturer to work as strikebreakers. The AFL machinists saw one-third of their members join the Teamster local, and the AFL strike was broken. The AFL leadership was furious and denounced Beck.

The Teamsters' nominal president, Daniel J. Tobin, sought to remove Beck via the AFL's executive council, but Beck allied with his rival, Hoffa, to ensure there were enough votes on the council to override any action Tobin would take. Beck and Hoffa forced the council to approve the Teamster raid on the Machinists. Beck then re-organized the Teamster Union from its four divisions into 16 divisions, without Tobin even being present at the reorganization meeting. A president without power, Tobin tried to strip Beck of his power at the 1952 Teamster convention. Beck forestalled this move, and maneuvered Tobin out of his job. At the convention, Tobin nominated Beck for president, and he was elected by acclamation.

With Beck and Hoffa in charge, the Teamsters Union's practices became unsavory at best, and illegal at worst. It was a union that organized a wide range of industries, from Hollywood animal wranglers to truck drivers to garbage men. As the 1950s went on, Teamster locals and leadership

James "Jimmy" R. Hoffa with his son James P. Hoffa at a dinner in 1965.

became increasingly connected with organized crime elements, creating "paper locals," no-show jobs, "sweetheart" contracts, skimming dues, and extortion. In New York, mobsters controlled both the garbage carting company and its union local.

These developments resulted in Beck being convicted for tax evasion and misuse of union funds, and his replacement by Hoffa in 1957. The same year, the AFL-CIO expelled the Teamsters and its 1.5 million members, but under Hoffa's skillful leadership, the union continued. Using selective strikes and boycotts, Hoffa made massive gains for his workers. At the same time, he channeled the union's vast pension funds to mob-backed projects, including Las Vegas hotels.

These activities drew the fire of Senate hearings and investigations by Attorney General Robert F. Kennedy, which led to federal legislation to attack organized crime, and Hoffa's conviction for witness tampering in 1964. His replacement, Frank Fitzsimmons, took over, and proved more pliant than Hoffa in supporting organized crime. Under Fitzsimmons, the Teamsters increasingly became seen by the public as being an arm of organized crime, its rank and file being muscle for mobster leadership, and in turn, so was organized labor. It was a major debacle for unions, and a staggering irony: as they became more accepted and a greater part of the American social, political, and economic fabric, they went from being seen as crusaders for the nation's often oppressed laborers, to being ruthless criminal barons.

CONCLUSION

This image would bode poorly for unions and labor as the 1960s ended. As the American economy was beginning its gradual shift toward postindustrialization, the abuses that forced the creation of unions in the first place were mostly eliminated and replaced by new abuses: criminal behavior by labor and management leaders, environmental threats to worker health, and continued discrimination in promotions and hiring against minorities and women. At the same time major gains were made: American workers enjoyed higher living standards than their predecessors; health, training, education, and pension plans undreamed of by previous generations; protections against abuses and better futures.

DAVID H. LIPPMAN

Further Readings

Bender, Thomas. ed. *Rethinking American History in a Global Age*. Los Angeles, CA: University of California Press, 2002.

Brooks, Thomas W. *Toil and Trouble: A History of American Labor*. New York: Dell, 1965.

Chafe, William H. *The Road to Equality*. *American Women Since 1962*. New York: Oxford University Press, 1994.

Gordon, Jennifer. *Suburban Sweatshops: The Fight for Immigrant Rights*. Cambridge, MA: Belknap Press, 2005.

Hahn, Peter L. *Crisis and Crossfire: The United States and the Middle East Since 1945*. Washington, D.C.: Potomac Press, 2005.

Hickman, Paul W. and Thomas P. Curtis, eds. *Immigration Crisis: Issues, Policies, and Consequences*. New York: Nova Science, 2008.

Karas, Jennifer. *Bridges and Barriers: Earnings and Occupational Attainment among Immigrants*. New York: LFB Scholarly Publishing LLC, 2002.

Kelley, Robin D.G. *Into the Fire: African-Americans Since 1970*. New York: Oxford University Press, 1996.

LaFeber, Walter, Richard Polensbury, and Nancy Woloch. *The American Century: A History of the United States Since 1941*. Armonk, NY: M.E. Sharpe, 2008.

Patterson, James T. *Grand Expectations: The United States, 1945–1974*. New York: Oxford University Press, 1996.

Manchester, William. *The Glory and the Dream: A Narrative History of America, 1932–1972*. Boston, MA: Little, Brown, and Company, 1974.

Montgomery, David. "Molting Pot: A Small Immigrant Town Simmers in the Wake of a Brutal Murder." *Washington Post* (September 2, 2008).

Morty, Myron A. *Daily Life in the United States, 1960–1990: Decades of Discord*. Westport, CT: Greenwood, 1997.

West, Elliott. *Growing Up in Twentieth Century America: A History Reference Guide*. Westport, CT: Greenwood, 1996.

Chapter 13

Military and Wars

*"How many deaths will it take till he knows
that too many people have died?"*
—Bob Dylan

ALTHOUGH AMERICANS WERE only four years removed from winning World War II, 1949 was not an optimistic year. Having the benefit of plans stolen from Americans, the Soviet Union exploded its own atomic bomb a good decade before analysts thought it would. And, after a period of civil war that World War II had interrupted, China became a Communist country. The next two decades would bring international conflicts with roots in the fear of the spread of Communist power. The legacy of Hiroshima and the ongoing Cold War meant that the specter of nuclear war became a lasting part of the American consciousness in this era. By the end of the 1960s, the drive to contain Communism had left the nation mired in war in Vietnam, and bitterly divided at home.

KOREA

Cold War fighting came in Asia, not Europe, in a little-known place called Korea. The United States and the Soviet Union had split Korea at the 38th parallel at the end of World War II, so that they could disarm Japanese troops occupying the area. However, just as they had in Eastern Europe, the Communists extended control over North Korea and refused to relinquish it. In the summer of 1950, a U.S. State Department report outlining its intent to defend the Pacific Rim from Communism seemed to ignore Korea, and, with

An American military newspaper announcing the Communist advance in 1950. By 1953, two million American troops had served in Korea.

the backing of the Soviet Union and Communist China, North Korea invaded South Korea in July, attempting to unite the two halves of the country.

The initial Communist drive worked, pushing South Korean troops south to the city of Pusan. Alarmed and determined, U.S. President Harry Truman ordered American troops stationed in Japan to go to Korea and stem the apparent rout. They did, giving Truman time to get permission from the newly formed United Nations for the United States to lead a coalition to push back the Communists. With the United States providing the bulk of the force and material for the Korean War, American General Douglas MacArthur devised an invasion of South Korea's Inchon Harbor in September 1950. This put U.N. troops behind the Communist lines, forcing them to pull out of the south and back north of the 38th parallel.

Then, Truman allowed MacArthur to go beyond the realm of containment, push into North Korea, and attempt to unite the country under a democratic system. At first, MacArthur's advance was successful and rapid, but when he reached the North Korean border with China, thousands of Red Chinese troops poured across the border and began driving the Americans back. Their retreat was as rapid as their advance, and by Christmas 1950, the war had stalemated roughly along the 38th parallel.

MacArthur and Truman feuded over the conduct of the war, with the general advocating expanding the war into China. Unwilling to escalate the conflict into World War III, Truman declined, but when MacArthur publicly denounced the president, Truman fired him. MacArthur returned home to adoring crowds—he had, after all, won World War II in the Pacific, and, like them, did not understand the new concept of limited war. He delivered a famous speech to Congress in which he said, "Old soldiers never die . . . they just fade away." He also studied a run for the presidency. Because Truman's popularity had plummeted, he decided not to run for reelection in 1952.

The first concern of the army during the Korean War was manpower. The World War II draft had continued essentially without interruption, but with smaller requirements than during the war. The military met its needs by drafting 585,000 men and calling to active duty National Guardsmen and 806,000 reservists. The call-up was controversial. Many of the reservists, some of

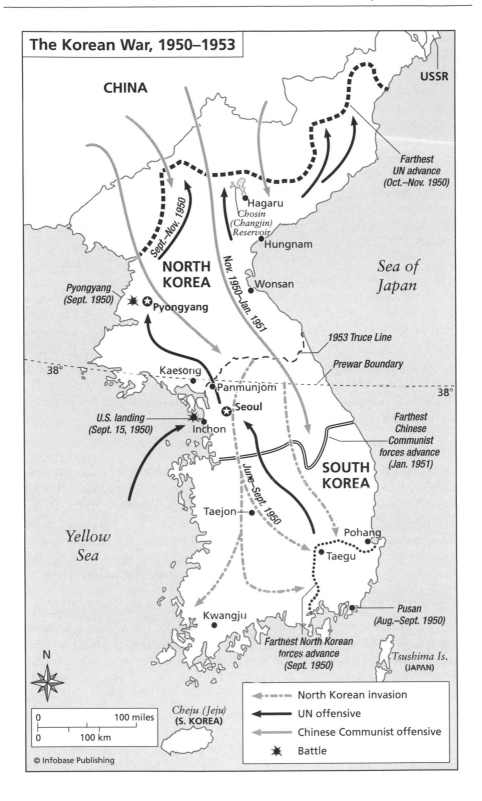

The Korean War, 1950–1953

CHINA

USSR

Farthest
UN advance
(Oct.–Nov. 1950)

Sept.–Nov. 1950

Hagaru
Chosin
(Changjin)
Reservoir
Hungnam

Nov. 1950–Jan. 1951

NORTH
KOREA

Sea of
Japan

Pyongyang
(Sept. 1950)

Pyongyang

Wonsan

1953 Truce Line

38°

Kaesong

Prewar Boundary

Panmunjom

38°

Seoul

U.S. landing
(Sept. 15, 1950)

Inchon

Farthest
Chinese
Communist
forces advance
(Jan. 1951)

SOUTH
KOREA

June–Sept. 1950

Yellow
Sea

Taejon

Pohang

Taegu

Kwangju

Pusan
(Aug.–Sept. 1950)

Farthest North Korean
forces advance
(Sept. 1950)

Tsushima Is.
(JAPAN)

N

Cheju (Jeju)
(S. KOREA)

◄·–·–·	North Korean invasion
◄━━━	UN offensive
◄━━━	Chinese Communist offensive
✸	Battle

0   100 miles
0   100 km

© Infobase Publishing

whom had seen combat in World War II and hoped to never see another battlefield, had had little training since the end of the war. The government was also not asking the public or industry to mobilize as it had in 1941 and 1942, and civilians could muster little enthusiasm for a war in which the goal was not to achieve victory as in World War II, but to maintain an arbitrary line of containment.

The Department of Defense began rotating men out of the combat zone after one year. The policy tended to comfort the public, but it increased manpower and training demands and forced more reliance on the draft. In 1951, Congress passed the Universal Military Training and Service Act, but it really did not create universal American military service. Men 18 years and older were subject to a draft, but college, health, and job deferments were liberally interpreted. Truman also sought to allocate $7 billion for defense spending between 1950 and 1953, and the Defense Production Act of 1950 gave him the power to direct war production if necessary.

The battlefield remained stalemated until July 1953. A negotiated settlement saw the country remain divided, as if no war had occurred. For that, the United States had sent more than two million soldiers to Korea, where some 54,000 of them died. The end of the war had none of the patriotic jubilation that accompanied the end of World War II. Returning Korean veterans could expect to take advantage of the same G.I. Bill of Rights that World War II vets had. The G.I. Bill guaranteed veterans college opportunities, home and farm loans, insurance, and other benefits.

IKE YEARS

With Dwight D. Eisenhower's election to the presidency in 1952, the American military took on a new look. Rather than committing American forces to brushfire wars around the globe, Ike would let American allies do it, but with long-range assistance from American air forces. He would also build up American nuclear reserves while cutting military manpower, reducing draft requirements, and cutting conventional military spending.

Eisenhower's New Look military focused on nuclear power, long-range bombers, missiles, and nuclear-powered naval vessels. Nuclear testing, above and below ground and at sea, continued throughout the 1950s. At the Bikini Atoll in the Marshall Islands in the Pacific, the military conducted the first successful test of a hydrogen bomb in 1952. Bikini Atoll had already found its way into popular culture in 1946 when it lent its name to a style of swimsuit that debuted a few days after a nuclear test. In 1954, it found fame again with the release of the Japanese monster film *Godzilla*. In the movie, nuclear testing at Bikini was responsible for releasing the monster from a block of ice.

In 1954, the Strategic Air Command, or SAC, had about 1,000 bombers capable of delivering nuclear weapons. By 1960 it had 2,000, many of them

Crew run to a Strategic Air Command B-52 heavy bomber armed with hound dog missiles in an Air Force photo from the 1960s. Half of such crews were on continuous alert and would have rapidly been airborne if signaled by the ballistic missile early warning system.

the modern B-52 Stratofortress. The B-52 quickly earned a reputation as a dependable workhorse bomber. B-52s have seen service in all American wars since the 1950s, from Vietnam through the Iraqi War that began in 2003; they have never, however, fulfilled their original mission: dropping nuclear bombs on an enemy. The B-52 found its way into American pop culture many times. In 1958 the popular teased-up and sprayed women's beehive hairdo became nicknamed the B-52 because it looked similar to the bombers' snout. Actor Slim Pickens gave the 1960s one of its notable screen images when he rode an atomic bomb down from the bomb bay of a B-52 in Stanley Kubrick's *Dr. Strangelove*.

In the mid-1950s, Admiral Hyman Rickover became the father of the nuclear navy as he pushed for nuclear powered submarines. The first, the *Nautilus*, sailed in 1955. Nuclear subs, with their ability to cruise for many months at a time, became excellent nuclear missile launch platforms with the advent of the Navy's Polaris missile in 1960.

The U.S. Army and Air Force dominated American missile and nuclear warhead production in the 1950s. The Air Force produced the intercontinental ballistic missiles (ICBMs) called Atlas, Titan, and Minuteman, while the Army developed intermediate range ballistic missiles (IRBMs) known as Thor and Jupiter. In the 1960s, the Atlas and Titan missiles would be converted for use by the civilian National Aeronautics and Space Administration (NASA) to lift men into space in the Mercury and Gemini programs, respectively. The Soviet Union was working on long-range bombers and ICBMs as well. Fear of what the Soviets were doing led to "bomber gap" and "missile gap" controversies. In reality, any bomber or missile gap was in favor of the United States.

Eisenhower's experience with domestic maneuvers before World War II convinced him that America's internal road system was inadequate to move troops and equipment in time of emergency. His observation of Germany's efficient autobahn system doubly convinced him. Thus he advocated the Interstate Highway Act of 1956. It created the modern American interstate highway system, providing smooth military supply lines east to west. It also subsidized the American trucking industry, spelled the end of railroads as the major form of freight hauling, and put Americans on the road in greater numbers than ever.

NUCLEAR THREAT AND AMERICAN CULTURE

Missiles, nuclear power, the fear of Soviet invasion, or death from the skies permeated the American psyche in the 1950s. Automobiles quickly adopted rocket motifs. Oldsmobile introduced the Rocket 88 V8 engine in 1949, and by the mid-1950s most cars sported grill elements, hood ornaments, or tail lights that resembled nose cones, jets, flying wings, or missiles. Tail fins recalling rocket stabilizers were popular on many cars. What many people call the first true rock and roll song was Ike Turner's "Rocket 88," named for the car engine, in 1952.

Radio dials in those cars all bore tiny Civil Defense symbols on their faces. Fearful that Soviet bombers could hone in on American radio station frequencies

This vintage AM radio dial bears the triangular Conelrad symbol beside the number 65.

the Federal Communications Commission and Civil Defense created a system whereby, in an emergency, key stations would shut down. Others would remain operating, and they were marked by "Conelrad" (short for Control of Electromagnetic Radiation) symbols that told listeners where to tune in case of a national emergency. Between 1953 and 1963, all radios had the Conelrad marks, which were the letters CD inside a triangle.

Civil defense took on added importance in the 1950s. The federal

Fallout Shelter Supplies

Hardly any American community during the Cold War did not have a fallout shelter. Because of the nature of radioactive fallout after a nuclear war, shelters were specifically built underground or in basements in existing structures. The Department of Defense Office of Civil Defense, working with local coordinators, stocked the shelters with emergency supplies, which came in bundles for 50-person allotments. Supplies were only intended to last for a two-week stay in the shelter, leaving people to return outside and face the residual effects of radiation on their own.

Supplies included 17.5-gallon barrels of water; each person could have one quart a day. Food was largely carbohydrate-based crackers, wafers, and candy. People were expected to survive on 700 calories a day. Sanitation kits included toilet paper and cups, and shelters also had first aid kits, but the shelters would have been hard-pressed to deal with any infectious outbreak. Shelters designed to hold more than 50 people also got a Geiger counter to detect radiation. As of 1965, the Department of Defense estimated it had stocked enough supplies to protect about 63 million people at a cost of some $128 million.

Ventilation proved to be problematic in the shelters. Stale air had to be removed, but contaminated, radioactive air could not be allowed in. The Department of Defense created a system where people in the shelters could attach plastic tubes to outside vents. Once those vents were opened, shelter occupants could pump bad air out with a portable ventilation kit (PVK) run by either an electric motor or a two-seater bicycle.

By the mid-1970s, the government had determined that most of the provisions in the shelters had probably gone bad. Inspectors toured shelters and recommended that the cereal foods be thrown out; however, they approved retention of some medicines for future use. Obviously, Americans never used the fallout shelters for emergencies. Like so many other Cold War phenomena, they have become quaint reminders of another time.

Below, a 1957 government photograph titled "How to Build a Fallout Shelter" shows a stocked basement fallout shelter. At left, emergency water in cans like this were provided for public Civil Defense fallout shelters.

A U-2 spy plane in the late 1950s. The United States used a U-2 to obtain photographs of the Soviet missiles in Cuba in October 1962.

government and communities created and outfitted fallout shelters underground, where people could take refuge in case of nuclear attack. Shelters included food and medical supplies and health manuals. Americans with enough money might build their own fallout shelters in their backyards and impose disaster drills on their families. Those shelters became notorious as make-out spots for a generation of American teens. Public schools also practiced civil defense drills. "Duck and cover" became the catchphrase of the era; wherever you were when an air-raid siren sounded, you were to duck down, make yourself as small as possible, and cover the back of your head and neck in case of debris. Obviously, "duck and cover," offered little protection from radioactive fallout.

Movies reflected the national obsession. *The Day the Earth Stood Still* (1951) offered aliens Klaatu and Gort warning humans about the dangers of nuclear war. *Invasion of the Body Snatchers* (1956), which featured "pods" taking over the bodies and lives of everyday Americans, was a metaphor for a Communist takeover of the United States. Countless monster movies, from *Godzilla* (1954) to *The Blob* (1958), offered interpretations on the effects of radiation. That trend continued into the comic books of the 1960s: Spider-man, the Fantastic Four, the Incredible Hulk, and others got their super powers from unchecked radiation.

Eisenhower avoided "hot" wars throughout his presidency. He had ample opportunity, however. France, trying to reassert its imperial hold over Vietnam after World War II, found its troops besieged by Communist Vietnamese under Ho Chi Minh at Dienbienphu. When France asked the United States for help, Eisenhower declined. He also avoided confrontations with China over Taiwan and the Soviet Union over the Suez Canal.

Eisenhower also unashamedly advocated high-tech spying on the Soviet Union. In 1956, the Lockheed aircraft corporation unveiled the U-2, a spyplane that could cruise at 70,000 feet—the edge of space—and take sharp photographs of features on the ground. Eisenhower officially denied such overflights until a Soviet missile downed a U-2 and the Russians captured its pilot, Francis Gary Powers. Powers was returned home and Ike cancelled further missions, but he offered no apology. The U-2, which was joined in Cold War intelligence flights by the SR-71 Blackbird, remains in military service today.

Part of the military stability of the 1950s was due to the steady hand of Eisenhower, a seasoned military man. Part of it was due to the fact that Joseph Stalin had died in 1953, and his successor, Nikita Khrushchev, had moderated some of Stalin's hard-line Cold War stance. But with the election of the young and untested John F. Kennedy to the presidency in 1960, Khrushchev chose to heat up the Cold War. He backed the Communist regime of Fidel Castro in Cuba, 90 miles off the coast of the United States. He gloated when an American-backed invasion of Cuba failed in 1961. The next year he sent missiles to Cuba that could target most of the United States or South America. During the Cuban Missile Crisis of October 1962, Kennedy called Khrushchev's bluff. He put SAC on high alert, the U.S. Army and Navy as well, and quarantined the island to prevent more missile shipments from arriving. Then his administration negotiated the removal of the missiles from Cuba. Khrushchev had lost the showdown, but the Soviet Union maintained its pledge to help Communist revolutions in countries around the globe. Vietnam was such a place.

VIETNAM

Having successfully ousted French colonialists in 1954, Communists under Ho Chi Minh sought to bring all of Vietnam under their rule. But the United States stepped into the vacuum left by France, and challenged the idea that people in southern Vietnam wanted to live under the rule of the northern based Viet Minh, as Ho's followers were called. The United States temporarily divided Vietnam north and south at the 17th parallel, then promised free elections in 1956 to decide on a unified government.

As the election approached, it became clear that Ho's Communists would win, delivering the American policy of containment another blow. The United States cancelled the election, and supported Ngo Dien Diem as leader of a quasi-democracy in South Vietnam. Diem, however, was a holdover of the French regime; a Westernized Catholic among a nation of Buddhists, he was roundly hated. In 1960 the Viet Minh, working with Viet Cong (Communist sympathizers who lived in South Vietnam) began operations against Diem's government.

Kennedy ordered American military "advisors" to Vietnam to help the South Vietnamese army fend off Communist attacks. At first the advisors did just that—advise. But soon they were doing much of the fighting for the South. Kennedy had also authorized the creation of an elite force of army combatants, the Green Berets. Before long those skilled fighters were also in Vietnam.

Diem's popularity continued to fall in South Vietnam, and in 1963 the world was shocked by images of a Buddhist monk setting himself on fire in a Saigon intersection to protest Diem. The question for many Americans was immediate: if Diem is so bad, why is the United States supporting him? The answer was simple but unsatisfactory: he was anti-Communist. In November 1963,

Kennedy authorized an American-backed coup against Diem in an attempt to quiet tensions in South Vietnam. The coup succeeded, but Diem died in it. In an event likely unrelated to Diem's death, Kennedy himself was assassinated two weeks later.

Kennedy's presidential successor, Lyndon B. Johnson, faced an immediate dilemma in Vietnam. He could continue to shore up the South Vietnamese government and army against ever-increasing odds, or he could pull out of Vietnam and run the risk of looking "soft" on Communism.

ESCALATION IN VIETNAM

Johnson chose the former, committing more advisors to the area. As he was running for the presidency in his own right in August 1964, Johnson got word of the Gulf of Tonkin incident. The Gulf of Tonkin lay just east of North Vietnam, and American intelligence ships routinely sailed just beyond the international water line, listening to Communist communications. North Vietnamese gunboats allegedly attacked an American cruiser, touching off a firefight. Days later, another similar incident occurred. It has long been regarded that the second incident did not occur, but was instead the figment of some radar operators' imaginations. (In 2008, new evidence suggested that the first incident may also not have occurred, but was instead fabricated by the Johnson administration.) Regardless, Johnson took word of the Tonkin incident to Congress, invoked the dangers of Communism and Red fascism to the free

U.S. Secretary of Defense Robert McNamara using a map of Vietnam to make a point at a press conference on April 26, 1965, as the war escalated.

world, and secured the Gulf of Tonkin Resolution. It gave Johnson free reign to do whatever he saw fit in Vietnam. This was as close to a declaration of war as the United States ever came in Vietnam; the entirety of the war happened under this congressional act. Political theorists have suggested that, given the danger of nuclear escalation following World War II, American politicians were eager to hand over the job of war making to someone else. If that is the case, then the Gulf of Tonkin Resolution is akin to the Ludlow Amendment in 1937 when Congress nearly legislated away its power to declare war.

Johnson had a free hand, but he also had an election to win, and he styled himself as the peace candidate and painted his opponent, Republican Senator Barry Goldwater, as a warmonger. Johnson's "Daisy" ad was famous in the 1964 campaign. In stark black-and-white, it depicted a girl happily plucking petals from a daisy. Suddenly, a voice began a short countdown, and then an atomic bomb exploded. The commercial ended with a voiceover of Johnson speaking about the dangers of atomic war and concluding "We must either love each other, or we must die." A narrator then concluded, "Vote for President Johnson on November 3—the stakes are too high to stay home."

Johnson secured election. He was inaugurated on January 20, 1965; that same month he began a massive bombing campaign over North Vietnam. Over the next year, Johnson also shifted American soldiers from advisory capacities to actual front-line fighting, and he increased the number of soldiers in Vietnam to more than 500,000.

GUERRILLA WAR

October 1965 saw the first large-scale battle between American and North Vietnamese forces. The Battle of the Ia Drang Valley (as depicted in the Mel Gibson movie *We Were Soldiers*) was an American victory, but it was also a test. The North Vietnamese wanted to see how Americans would react to a conventional campaign. They learned that they could never match the industrial and technological might of the United States, which fielded long-range artillery, carrier-based air support, helicopter transports, and superior communication during the battle. Instead, the North Vietnamese adopted a guerrilla style of fighting for the rest of the war. By staging quick hit-and-run raids, the North Vietnamese could negate the strength and size of the American army. The Communists could instead run it ragged by forcing it to conduct endless and strategically pointless search and destroy missions. The irony of the North Vietnamese plan is that it is the same one that a ragged army under George Washington used to defeat the superior army of Great Britain in the American Revolution.

It worked as well in Vietnam. North Vietnamese troops had free access to a network of trails—known collectively as the Ho Chi Minh Trail—that dropped south through Laos and Cambodia, paralleling the western border of South Vietnam. From the trail, they could enter all points of South Vietnam at

A B-66 Destroyer and Air Force F-105 Thunderchiefs dropping bombs on a military target in North Vietnam on June 14, 1966.

will, strike American and South Vietnamese targets, and then disappear. For fear of escalating the war, the United States refused to attack the trail and shut it down. Thus North Vietnamese tactics dragged the U.S. Army into a "war of post"—troops, operating from fixed bases, responded to NVA attacks with "search and destroy" missions, and then returned to their bases. Americans took and held no territory, nor did they deny NVA troops access to the battle-field or destroy their will to fight. For the United States, the war possessed no clear indicators of victory.

DISSENT AND PROTEST

Historian Robert Leckie has said "War itself may be defined as socially approved armed conflict between hostile groups. Without social approval, war simply cannot be waged." All of America's wars had been marked by dissent of some type, but domestic protest and social upheaval became the hallmark of the Vietnam War. Protests began in 1965 and 1966, largely on college campuses and spearheaded at first by professors. Students, insulated from the war by college deferments, then took up the protest.

The initial protest caused, or at least was part of, a "generation gap." The students were Baby Boomers whose fathers had fought World War II. As

Mattel's M-16

Baby Boom–era boys, like boys before them, enjoyed playing with toy guns. Postwar manufacturing, with its new reliance on plastics, made toy guns realistic and affordable. Domestic life was safer then, before the proliferation of civilian shootings at fast-food places, post offices, and schools, and people thought little of children running through neighborhoods staging mock wars. Replicas of western pistols and rifles were always popular, as were hunting rifles, and a variety of guns concealed in briefcases and cigarette lighters made popular by the era's spy movies. A realistic Thompson submachine gun also made toy stores. By 1966, however, Mattel's plastic version of the U.S. Army's main combat rifle, the M-16, was the toy to have. The Mattel M-16 was nearly life-size and boasted a pull-back cocking mechanism, which allowed backyard commandoes to fire short or long bursts. Most boys still used it to dispatch imaginary Germans rather than adapt their play to Vietnam.

The army had adopted the M-16 in the early 1960s to replace the M-1 Garrand that had seen service in World War II and Korea. The M-16 fired the relatively small .223 round, but relied on light construction and a high rate of fire rather than a heavy projectile. The original Army version of the weapon was made in part of light composite plastics, and was plagued by malfunctions in its first years. That gave rise to an urban legend among combat soldiers that Mattel was actually making their weapons as well. Of course, that was not true. The Army worked the bugs out of the M-16 and still uses descendants of the weapon today.

The toy version, however, did not survive Vietnam. As the war became unpopular, so did the public's taste for war-related toys. Even Hasbro's 12-inch G.I. Joe action figure ceased to be a soldier and became an "adventurer." Mattel stopped making the toy M-16, and by 1969 intact ones were becoming a rarity; the short barrel was highly susceptible to snapping off during play. Thus, they have become collectors' items. Purchased for about $10, one in good condition might bring as much as $250 today.

Mattel based its toy gun on an M-16 similar to this 1960s M-16A1 model used by the U.S. Army.

Peace Sign

The peace sign—a vertical line bisecting a circle with two downward slanting lines on either side of the line—became an emblem of American antiwar protests during the Vietnam War. It replaced iconic doves with olive branches as an easy-to-draw, highly recognizable symbol.

The peace sign had its origins in England, where artist Gerald Holtom created it for nuclear arms protests in 1958. Holtom stylized the design from the positions a flag-waiver would assume when sending the semaphore signals for "N" and "D"; the letters stood for nuclear disarmament. The Peace Sign found its way across the Atlantic, and thousands of American war protesters, and even less radical youth who just wanted to be "cool," adopted it. The symbol showed up on necklaces and bracelets, bumper stickers and decals, clothing and tattoos. American G.I.s in Vietnam also used black markers to draw the sign on the camouflage covers of their helmets.

The peace sign was never copyrighted, and has thus been used by social movements around the world.

From its first use, the peace sign came under attack by conservatives. Some alleged that it was an occult symbol; others charged that it was Communist. Still others said that, while it may not be satanic, it was certainly anti-Christian as it depicted an upside-down cross with its arms broken. Finally, Americans who associated the symbol with draft-dodgers and conscientious objectors called it simply "the footprint of the American chicken."

such, they had trouble reconciling World War II—the "good war" that had supposedly settled global issues—with Korea and now Vietnam. Their fathers, patriotic and homogenous in their war service records, short haircuts, white shirts, and skinny black ties, could not understand how their offspring could question American policy, let alone accept their long hair, music, open drug use, and loose sexual mores.

The summer of 1967, with "hippies" clustering in San Francisco, the Beatles releasing "Sgt. Pepper's Lonely Hearts Club Band," and banners proclaiming "Make Love, Not War," became known as the "Summer of Love." It was as much an attempt by young Americans to break from the uniformity of the last 20 years as it was a war protest, but the latter took center stage. In October about 35,000 protestors marched on Washington, D.C., and the Pentagon.

Because of television, images of the war pervaded the lives of those at home like never before. These U.S. soldiers were being airlifted during a search-and-destroy mission in 1966.

Antiwar protests melded with the Civil Rights movement. Protestors claimed that blacks were being drafted in larger numbers than whites; because of poorer education and living standards, black men were not able to gain draft deferments at the same rate as white men. The age-old cry of "rich man's war, poor man's fight" rose around Vietnam.

Even though the protesting was still limited to American youth, the demonstration caused Johnson and the Department of Defense to begin a new public information campaign to keep Americans in support of the war. Ironically, most mainstream Americans did support the war, some 67 percent according to polls. But the Pentagon, with little other evidence to point to, began releasing "body counts"—the number of Communists killed relative to the number of Americans killed in the war. Television had long since changed the way Americans ate dinner; they now clustered around TV sets instead of a family table. Now the body counts changed dinner conversation. Appearing on the three major networks' dinnertime news shows, the body counts (which the Pentagon always manipulated) attempted to prove an American victory. By late 1967, Westmoreland claimed that victory was imminent, and the war had entered a "mopping up" phase.

Ironically, had the war ended then, the United States could have claimed a victory. It had stalled the Communist advance and beaten the North Vietnamese in every major battle. But in an asymmetrical war, which Vietnam had become, the advantage of time rested with the guerrillas. Johnson and his advisors failed to correctly judge the staying power and determination of the North Vietnamese.

THE TET OFFENSIVE

Then came 1968. Ho Chi Minh's chief military strategist, Vo Nguyen Giap, the man who had orchestrated the siege of Dienbienphu against France, had designed an offensive meant to unsettle Americans both in Vietnam and at home. In January during the Vietnamese new year of Tet (when Americans believed the Communists would definitely not attack), Giap planned a series

"All Hell Broke Loose": Life as a Soldier in Korea and Vietnam

The dropping of the atomic bomb on the Japanese cities of Hiroshima and Nagasaki in 1945 did not mean that the United States would no longer be drawn into battles to preserve democracy in other parts of the world. Bobby Martin of the Company 8th Regiment, First Cavalry Division, arrived in South Korea in November 1950. Martin recalls the permeating cold of Thanksgiving Day when the army went "all out to provide the troops with a really good meal." The problem, according to Martin, was "eating it before it froze." Determined to celebrate Christmas, the men cut shapes from cans and decorated trees.

Private 1st Class Herman G. Nelson was sent to the front lines of Korea in August 1950, where the noise from the big howitzers was so loud "it sounded like every weapon in the Eighth Army was firing at the same time." Nelson also remembers the atrocities discovered after the North Koreans fled Taejon, leaving behind the bodies of 29 Americans who had been dumped in an open well. Three hundred others were discovered in the surrounding hills where they had been left to die with their hands tied behind their backs. The same Thanksgiving that Martin was eating a "frozen" Thanksgiving meal, Nelson notes that "all hell broke loose as the Chinese army attacked in force."

The next generation of young American men also found themselves fighting for democracy, but in Vietnam, where it rained continuously and fresh food and laundry were rare. Marine Jon Johnson wrote to his wife in April 1966, "God doesn't know about the Mekong Delta. He didn't create that hell hole." Incoming shells, he said, sounding like "a freight train coming out of the sky."

Joe Paris, also a Marine, wrote to his mother after the death of a friend, declaring that he would "never be the same." He explained that the Vietcong crossed the American lines and "threw a grenade into where my buddy was sleeping." He admitted that he could not "even smile anymore." Navy Seabee Mark Harms described a battle in 1968, recalling that his buddies were "lying on the floor waiting to be hauled away. I never saw so much blood in all my life, and the smell was something else."

U.S. Marines and South Vietnamese troops working together to defend a position against attack at the Battle of Hamo Village during the Tet Offensive in January 1968.

of peripheral attacks on American bases as feints. They would disguise his major assault, which would emerge from the Ho Chi Minh Trail up and down South Vietnam, and target key American strongholds, including the South Vietnamese capital and American headquarters of Saigon.

The feints began in November and December 1967; they included a long and bloody siege at an American firebase at Khe Sahn. They diverted American attention from the thousands of NVA troops, most dressed as civilians, who slipped into the cities and countryside of South Vietnam, preparing to unleash assaults.

The Tet Offensive began in January and surprised everyone. The Pentagon practiced little news censorship in Vietnam, and Americans at home were privy to almost every blow of the offensive. They saw photographs in newspapers and magazines, and they saw film footage on the evening news. Because of film processing and transmission delays, the footage was not live, but close to it. Most incredibly, Americans watched street fighting in Saigon, and saw insurgents attack the American embassy there, igniting a firefight with Marines in the building's courtyard.

The Tet Offensive permanently changed the war. Even though American troops beat back every assault and regained the tactical advantage, the offensive struck exactly where Giap had wanted—at the will of American civilians to continue the war. Middle-aged Americans began to question the war. If, as the Pentagon and Westmoreland said, we were winning, then how could something like Tet happen? While American parents rarely joined in protests with their children, their doubt had more resonance with Johnson; after all, they could vote.

JOHNSON WITHDRAWS

Higher-profile Americans began to openly question the war as well, most notably news broadcasters. While all three networks had correspondents in Vietnam, it was Walter Cronkite, anchorman of the CBS Evening News and widely regarded as "the most trusted man in America," who carried the most weight. Cronkite traveled to Vietnam and interviewed American soldiers, both the G.I.s and the brass, and South Vietnamese soldiers and civilians. When he returned, Cronkite closed one of his evening news broadcasts with a clearly delineated editorial. He said his trip to Vietnam had left him with the conviction that the United States could not win the war, and could only end it by pulling out.

In the White House, Johnson, who watched all three evening news broadcasts on three TV sets simultaneously, watched Cronkite's report with dejection. When it was over, Johnson said to an aide, "If I've lost Cronkite, I've lost middle America." He was right. Cronkite did not represent the radical fringe of American society. He had the ear of middle-class, middle-aged Americans.

Protests escalated, and the Vietnam War destroyed Lyndon Johnson's presidency. He had scored good marks with his Civil Rights and domestic reform programs, but as he said later, "that bitch of a war" wrecked his reputation. In March 1968, Johnson stunned his advisors and the country when he announced on live TV that he would not run for president again. Having filled Kennedy's unexpired term and been elected only once, he could have run, but Vietnam exhausted him, and a poor showing in Democratic primaries indicated his political fortunes had run out. With Johnson out, the political season became a free-for-all. Robert Kennedy appeared to be Democratic front-runner, but an assassin killed him in June. In August, at the Democratic National Convention in Chicago, war protestors rioted in the street and tempers flared on the nominating floor. Eventually Democrats settled on Vice President Hubert Humphrey, who had the impossible task of trying to support his president, while at the same time distancing himself from the unpopular war.

NIXON

Republicans nominated former Vice President Richard M. Nixon. During the campaign, Nixon foreshadowed later trends of politicians appearing on popular variety and talk shows when he appeared on the immensely popular *Rowan and Martin's Laugh-In*; there he ironically intoned one of the show's catchphrases—"Sock it to me." Nixon promised to draw down American troops in Vietnam, and ultimately withdraw from the country "with honor." With Democrats politically disabled by the war, Nixon captured the presidency. He took office January 20, 1969, and ushered in a policy of Vietnamization—letting South Vietnam begin to shoulder the war.

While American troops had fought well and with relatively steady discipline through 1968, the election of Nixon and the pervasive nature of antiwar protests at home indicated that the United States was finished with Vietnam. It might not be out of the country yet, but it was finished.

The last year of the era, 1969, saw morale in the American army in Vietnam deteriorate. If the country was indeed finished with the war, then who wanted to be the last man to die there? Drug and alcohol use, present in all American armies in all American wars, became prevalent. So did insubordination and even "fragging," the practice of killing overzealous officers in the field before they could lead their platoons into an ambush. Morale plummeted even further as men realized Nixon's policy of Vietnamization would not be quick. American involvement would not end until after Nixon was reelected in 1972.

CONCLUSION

If the end of the war in Korea in 1953 had brought little of the celebration that accompanied the end of World War II, the eventual end of the Vietnam War in 1975 would leave a changed country, and an even less optimistic one. The military conflicts that began in the Cold War in the 1950s and 1960s had a very different effect on the country than World War II. The nation was left with a new sense of pessimism, and further conflicts would long be examined in the light of Vietnam. The experience of that war would bring a new desire for rapid, decisive victories and intensify the search for even more technology to keep troops from engaging in close combat.

R. STEVEN JONES

Further Readings

Adler, Bill. *Letters from Vietnam*. New York: Ballantine Books, 2003.

Chambers, John Whiteclay, II, ed. *The Oxford Companion to American Military History*. Oxford: Oxford University Press, 1999.

Civil Defense Museum. "Shelter Supplies." Available online: http://www.civildefensemuseum.com. Accessed May 2008.

Cronkite, Walter. *A Reporter's Life*. New York: Alfred A. Knopf, 1996.

Docs Populi: Documents for the Public, "Origin of the Peace Symbol." Available online: http://www.docspopuli.org. Accessed May 2008.

Herrin, George C. *America's Longest War: The United States and Vietnam, 1950–1975*. New York: Alfred A. Knopf, 1986.

Horwitz, Dorothy G. ed. *We Will Not Be Strangers: Korean War Letters between a M.A.S.H. Surgeon and His Wife*. Urbana and Chicago, IL: University of Illinois Press, 1992.

Karnow, Stanley. *Vietnam: A History: The First Complete Account of Vietnam at War*. New York: Viking Press, 1983.

"Korean War Photo-Documentary" Available online: http://www.rt66 .com/~korteng/SmallArms/kwphotos.htm. Accessed October 2008.

Leckie, Robert. *The Wars of America, Vol. II From 1900 to 1992*. New York: Harper Collins, 1992.

Lewy, Guenter. *America in Vietnam*. New York: Oxford University Press, 1978.

Millett, Allan R. and Peter Maslowski. *For the Common Defense: A Military History of the United States of America*. New York: The Free Press, 1984.

Richard Peters and Xiaobing Li. *Voices from the Korean War: Personal Stories of American, Korean, and Chinese Soldiers*. Lexington, KY: University of Kentucky Press, 2004.

Chapter 14

Population Trends and Migration

*"We all worry about the population explosion,
but we don't worry about it at the right time."*
—Art Hoppe

THE 1950s AND 1960s were marked first by the Civil Rights movement, and second by the rise of modern youth culture in response to the Vietnam War. These two major events were interrelated in complex ways due to the sheer size of the Baby Boom generation and to the environment in which they lived. However, the experiences of older generations of Americans were also important. If a significant portion of the G.I. generation had not witnessed the horrors of the Holocaust, they might not have been as open to the possibility of change, and the Civil Rights movement might have met sufficient resistance to crush it. Instead, their reluctance to bear down at all levels of society meant that resistance to social change occurred in isolated pockets that could be worked around and ultimately overcome when seen to be ineffective holdouts of an older way of thinking.

The extreme mobility that was afforded by the proliferation of the automobile was also an important factor in reshaping the population of the United States. It became easier than ever to pack up and start over, even for the poor and disadvantaged. In addition, the increase in mobility afforded by the widespread availability of the automobile, and the relative absence of internal barriers to migration such as checkpoints or identity documentation, made it easy for a flood of undocumented immigrants to slip into the country, flouting the rules that were supposed to regulate immigration and keep it in balance with the availability of jobs.

THE RISE OF THE SUBURBS

One of the most important developments of the postwar era was the rise of the tract house subdivision. Although suburbs were not new, they had previously been just outside the cities on which they depended, as their inhabitants had primarily used trolleys to commute to work. The rise of the automobile and the creation of the interstate highway system, combined with postwar prosperity and the return of women to full-time motherhood and homemaking, led to a push for a new kind of suburb. People wanted their own homes, but not just a row house with a tiny patch of grass in back. They wanted real yards with room for their children to play, and a garage beside the house in which to park their big new cars with chrome and tailfins.

In response to this demand for a piece of the American dream after the sacrifices of World War II, builders began to create a new kind of suburb. The first was Levittown, New York, but its success quickly spawned similar developments all over the United States. In order to keep prices low, techniques of mass production were brought to bear upon the building industry for the first time. Instead of each house being individually designed for the family buying it, all houses in the subdivision were built to the same basic plan. Instead of building from individual boards on site, entire subassemblies such as roof trusses were pre-assembled at the factory and shipped to the site, saving both time and money. Appliances, fireplaces, even the television set in the living room were built-in units, enabling buyers to finance them as part of the mortgage. Since many of these first-time homeowners were qualifying for a mortgage only as a result of veterans' programs, having built-ins was the only way they were able to afford these amenities.

The effect of building entire communities to the same plans was a drab sameness that would later be mocked as a breeding ground for the conformity that characterized the 1950s. The people who were buying them were so happy to be able to become homeowners that they had no time to worry that everyone else in the neighborhood had one exactly like theirs. After the privations of the war, uniformity of appearance was just background noise.

These communities would be the homes of a whole generation of children, a generation so numerous they would dominate their society throughout their life cycle. The Baby Boom was a marked contrast to the small size of the generations born during the Depression and World War II. During those uncertain years many families had delayed having children, or forgone them altogether. In the postwar prosperity, with veterans eager to settle down and start families, and women being told it was their patriotic duty to give up their

Between 1945 and 1955 15 million new houses were built in the United States; by 1960, 60 percent of American families owned their own homes, many in new suburbs.

wartime jobs to returning men and settle into a life of domesticity, fertility hit an all-time high. Improvements in healthcare meant that few of these children would fall victim to the childhood illnesses that carried away so many in earlier generations.

The Baby Boom generation was also the first to grow up with television. Although radio had brought the outside world into the homes of the G.I. and Silent generations in ways that would have been unthinkable to the people of the 19th century, the addition of the visual element added a profound influence that radio lacked. One no longer needed the sophistication to weave images from words coming out of a speaker—they were now right there on the screen. Even programming designed for children had an immediacy that drew one in.

Because there were so many of them and they represented the realization of hopes and dreams so long deferred, the children of the Baby Boom were the center of attention to an unprecedented degree. These were not children who would be seen and not heard, not when fortunes were to be made by catering to their needs and wants. Whole industries sprang up to provide such things as special foods aimed just at children.

However, the suburbs were not without some very real dark sides. They were based upon racist assumptions of how a society ought to be organized. Even in Northern cities free from legal segregation, social and economic factors created segregated communities, where many white children never encountered an African American or had an Asian playmate. In fact, many of the people who were moving to the suburbs consciously or unconsciously associated the patchwork of ethnic communities in the city with the poverty and crime they wished to escape. They associated white-bread conformity with wholesomeness in communities as well as diet.

The result of this white flight was the increasing deterioration of inner-city neighborhoods, particularly those occupied by minorities. As financial and intellectual capital left these depressed communities, the children in them had fewer and fewer role models of success to give them hope for change.

NORTH TO PROSPERITY

During the first decades of the 20th century, the vast majority of African Americans were poor sharecroppers in the rural South. A few lived in the north, particularly in the great industrial cities where they had formed communities such as Harlem in New York City. But in many parts of the northern United States a white person could go a lifetime without seeing a person of another race save as a stereotypical portrayal in a motion picture or a theatrical performance.

That began to change in the middle of the 20th century. During World War II, as white men went into the segregated armed forces in great numbers, the factories that made essential war material needed workers to replace them, and as a result employers were willing to set aside their prejudices and hire black workers. In response, large numbers of rural Southern African Americans headed north in hopes of leaving behind the continual petty humiliations of Jim Crow laws.

At the same time as those economic factors were pulling African Americans north, increasing automation in the cotton fields was also pushing them off the farm. Cotton had been the mainstay of the rural economy in much of the South, and it had proven surprisingly difficult to mechanize. As a result, the need for cheap labor to harvest the delicate bolls led white plantation owners to oppose the departure of African Americans even while despising them. In some cases the agents of various planters would go to bus stations and forcibly retrieve former sharecroppers who were said to still owe them money. Given the corrupt nature of the accounting systems used by most of their planters when doing the annual settling of accounts with their sharecroppers, those debts could be created with the stroke of a pen.

But in 1944 International Harvester demonstrated the first practical mechanical cotton picker. A single operator could do the work of 50 sharecroppers picking cotton. Even with the annual depreciation on the picker figured into the equation, the economics were clear—sharecropping was on its way out. Although planters might still hire African Americans on a day-laborer basis to weed during the growing season, the old system by which each family

Children playing outside and adults sitting on the porches of wood frame homes in Birmingham, Alabama, in 1963. These houses were considered average for African-American families in Birmingham at the time.

cultivated its own plot in exchange for a share of the resultant crop had come to an end. Unfair and prone to abuses as it had been, its demise left millions of former sharecroppers without work. Some stayed in the towns near where they had formerly farmed, but there were few jobs, and living in town meant constant contact with whites and an endless stream of little humiliations that rubbed their noses in their inferior status.

Relatives coming back from the Northern cities, particularly Chicago, but also Detroit, New York and the like, told stories of high-paying jobs to be had just for being willing to show up, not to mention housing far better than a sharecropper's cabin, and all kinds of material goods. Even more importantly, there was not the continual demeaning subordination to whites that Jim Crow enforced. There were no segregated public facilities, they could sit wherever they wished on public transportation, and they could even vote.

Many of these returning migrants indulged in a little exaggeration, painting everything a little brighter and prettier than it was. They also tended to gloss over the de facto segregation that continued to exist, particularly the utter unwillingness of whites to share their neighborhoods with African Americans, to the point that they would sell their homes and move out if a single black family moved in. But the picture the migrants painted was so rosy that the stream of northward travelers soon became a raging torrent that strained the ability of the cities to accommodate them.

"Asylum for the Oppressed": Refugees From Communism

In 1959, Communist leader Fidel Castro came to power in Cuba and began redistributing the country's lands and wealth. Scores of upper and middle-class Cubans fled to the United States, and most of them settled in nearby Florida, particularly in the Miami area. Large numbers of Cubans who fled the Castro regime were Jewish, and some of their children left Cuba under Operation Pedro Pan, leaving their parents behind.

The American Jewish Joint Distribution Committee (JDC) played a large part in helping Jewish Cubans to resettle in the United States. When Marek Schindelman traveled to Cuba for JDC, he found the situation "disastrous—the rich have left, some having foreseen the situation have sent part of their disposable funds out of the country, but these are few. Most of them have left real assets, houses, apartments—with all their furniture, objects of all kinds."

By 1962, 215,000 Cubans had come to the United States in whatever vessels they could lay their hands on. Castro announced on September 28, 1965, that any Cubans with relatives in the United States were free to leave as long as they were picked up by relatives. President Lyndon Johnson responded to a surge of drownings by launching a series of "Freedom Flights" to transport Cubans safely.

Other political refugees came to the United States from the Dominican Republic, fleeing the tyranny of Rafael Leonides Trujillo. Even after Trujillo's assassination in 1961, Dominicans came to the United States in large numbers with the full support of President Johnson who was determined to keep the country out of Communist hands.

In 1965 Congress passed the Immigration and Nationality Act, opening up slots for immigrants from outside the Western Hemisphere and abolishing the national quota system. The law established a set of preferences for various immigrant classes, including one for "refugees from either communist (or communist-controlled) countries, or those from the Middle East." Political refugees from right-wing dictatorships in the Western Hemisphere, such as Haitians fleeing the Duvalier regime, were not included in a preferred class.

Johnson saw the new bill as a means of repairing "a very deep and painful flaw in the fabric of American justice," which had virtually banned immigrants from the Eastern Hemisphere. Johnson promised all Cubans who wished to flee Communism that the United States was willing to serve as an "asylum for the oppressed" whenever called upon to do so. The following year, Congress reclassified Cuban refugees, paving the way for additional immigrants.

The arrival of so many former sharecroppers also brought the plight of poor African Americans to the awareness of northern liberals. No longer could they treat the indignities of segregation and Jim Crow as something that happened in a distant part of the country disconnected from themselves. The result was a drive to change those circumstances by going down there and bringing change to a part of the country in which racism was as ubiquitous as air.

GROWTH IN THE SOUTH AND WEST

In the 1950s, those cities that had expanded during World War II with the production of shipping and aircraft continued to expand. Seattle, with the Boeing aircraft factories, and Los Angeles, with a host of aircraft plants, rocket manufacturing facilities, and supporting industries, flourished. Naval bases in Vallejo, California, and Bremerton, Washington, also contributed to the West coast boom. Meanwhile, other facilities scattered across the West and South stimulated local and regional economies. Nuclear facilities at Hanford, Washington; Los Alamos and Albuquerque, New Mexico; Oak Ridge, Tennessee; and Amarillo, Texas, brought highly trained scientists and technicians into those communities. With the development of long-range missiles and the first efforts to develop rockets for space travel, communities flourished around the Redstone Arsenal in Huntsville, Alabama, and around the Houston, Texas, and Cape Canaveral, Florida, centers.

Defense and aerospace spending were not the only contributors to the growth of Southern and Western cities and economies. Although Florida, Arizona, and Southern California had long competed to attract retirees with their mild climates, these regions, which were also known as the Sunbelt, saw burgeoning populations, driven in part by often affluent retirees escaping the harsh winters of the upper Midwest and Northeast. Phoenix, Arizona, for example, grew from a small community of 48,000 in 1940 to a huge and sprawling city of 439,000 by 1960, and to 584,000 by 1970. Miami, Florida, expanded from 172,000 in 1940 to 334,000 by 1970. The Miami-Dade County urban area, later to become one of the largest in the nation, had swollen to over 1.2 million by 1970.

Similar population growth across the South and West brought a host of social and political changes. Gradually at first, and more rapidly as time went on, some of the older patterns of racial discrimination and segregation in the South modified. Those changes were partly the result of the Civil Rights revolution of the 1950s and 1960s, led by the 1954 Supreme Court decision in the *Brown v. Board of Education of Topeka* case that ruled segregation of public schools unconstitutional. With the ruling overturning the long-standing legal precedent that "separate but equal" facilities met the constitutional requirement of equal treatment under law regardless of race, formal and institutionalized segregation broke down in transportation, and after 1964, in a wide range of public facilities. These changes, brought by court decisions, direct action demonstrations, and changes in federal law, were further advanced by

Among the daily injustices of Jim Crow laws in the South were segregated public places; the photo shows an African-American man forced to use a separate entrance to a movie theater in Belzoni, Mississippi.

the migrations of people. Tens of thousands of former residents of the upper Midwest and the Northeast crowded into the states of the Deep South, serving to reinforce the changes already underway.

Through the 1950s and 1960s, political candidates for the presidency from the South and West vied for the top position. Richard Nixon from California, Barry Goldwater from Arizona, and Lyndon Johnson from Texas, while they varied greatly in their ideas and their programs, all heralded the growing power and influence of the South and West.

TUNING IN, TURNING ON, AND DROPPING OUT

During the second half of the 1960s the Boomer generation, growing increasingly dissatisfied with their attempts to resolve the problems of American society through mainstream activism, became increasingly radicalized. The sheer numbers of their generation ensured that their experimentations with alternative lifestyles would be far more visible than such 19th-century idealist groups as the Oneida Colony.

Young people flocked to California, where the mild climate made it possible to live in makeshift housing year-round. San Francisco's Haight-Ashbury district became one of the most notable gathering places for young people who wished to live cheaply and experiment with alternative consciousness through recreational chemistry. They organized various music festivals, generally at no cost, as part of their philosophy of rejecting commercialism and materialist culture.

However, even the laid-back atmosphere of San Francisco, named for St. Francis of Assisi, was too urban and mechanistic for some flower children. Hearing the call of the pioneer spirit, they set out to create communities where they could live out their ideals. They often built log cabins and wigwams with their own hands, eschewing not only store-bought lumber, but also power tools. Some rejected monogamous marriage in favor of various forms of group marriage. Although all these communes started with high hopes, few managed to last more than a year. Some foundered as the

This psychedelic rock poster advertised a concert and "happening" in Los Angeles, California.

members discovered through bitter experience that ideals of unstructured cooperation were no substitute for organization; tasks that were everyone's responsibility often become no one's. Other communes tore themselves apart in feuds and petty bickering over issues of leadership and authority when difficult decisions had to be made. Finally, some were hounded to destruction by hostile neighbors who found them simply too strange for their comfort zone.

By the early 1970s the counterculture was losing its impetus. President Nixon's policy of Vietnamization, which enabled the United States to withdraw from the conflict, removed a rallying-point of opposition that had unified disparate groups against the establishment. The disaster of the Altamont free rock concert, which had been billed as a West coast Woodstock, but instead devolved into violence and the beating death of at least one attendee, was a body blow to the idealism on which the counterculture was based. And finally, many of the hippies were simply tired. After struggling so long, they wanted a respite.

IMMIGRATION FROM MEXICO

The 1960s also marked the beginning of an awareness of just how porous America's borders were, in spite of efforts to limit immigration to only those individuals and groups deemed most desirable. In particular, the border with Mexico proved especially porous, largely because so much of it passed through sparsely inhabited deserts. The situation was further complicated by the fact that much of the region had been a part of Mexico until shortly before the Civil War. As a result, there were already sizeable Mexican-American communities into which the border-crossers could move, where the food and customs would be familiar, and they could quickly plug into secular and religious social support networks.

On the Road with the Beats

Although the popular image of the 1950s is one of settled conformity, it was by no means the universal reality. Even the trying circumstances of the Depression and World War II, followed by postwar prosperity, could not entirely extinguish the restlessness that burned within the American spirit. The young people who answered the call of the open road in the 1950s were known as the Beats. They wanted to experience life to the fullest, and the most obvious way to do it was to see the sights, hopping into a car (often stolen, although this may well have been a bit of mythologizing) and driving from town to town with no particular destination in mind. Some even hitchhiked, carrying all their possessions in a backpack, and trusting the kindness of strangers for their transportation.

They also experimented with drugs, particularly the new synthetic stimulants and depressants such as amphetamines and Benzedrine. To them, such drugs were yet another way to seek an authentic experience, freed of the constraining veils of social conditioning. The writing of Jack Kerouac in particular has the feel of someone working under the influence of "speed." It is often breathless, as though the hand cannot keep up with the racing thoughts of the mind behind it. The use of stream-of-consciousness narrative by the Beats was yet another way of pursuing that unfiltered authentic experience.

Although the Beats belonged for the most part to the tail end of the G.I. Generation, they served in many ways as the harbingers of the hippies and the counterculture of the 1960s. They were the first to grow their hair long and cut loose from the comfortable constraints of suburban life.

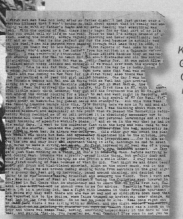

Beat Generation figures Jack Kerouac, Allen Ginsberg, Peter Orlovsky (back row), and Gregory Corso and Lafcadio Orlovsky (front row) on a trip in Mexico. At right, the beginning of Jack Kerouac's On the Road manuscript.

The persistent poverty and rampant corruption in Mexico served as a powerful incentive for illegal immigration. Even doing such poor-paying work as picking vegetables and fruit in the vast truck farms of California's Central Valley could net migrant workers enough money to send ample sums home to relatives remaining in Mexico. Work such as construction or hotel housekeeping paid even better, and the conditions often improved as well.

Aware of this dynamic, the U.S. government ran a program known as the bracero system, in which Mexicans were permitted to enter on temporary visas to do manual labor, particularly agricultural work. The appalling conditions experienced by many of these workers led to the program coming under harsh criticism, such that it was eventually discontinued. However, that policy change did not alter the factors that were driving large numbers of Mexicans to seek opportunities in the North. It merely had the effect of driving it underground, and thus into the hands of the criminal element. Desperate Mexicans would often give their entire life's savings to "coyotes" who promised to guide them across the border. Some proved reliable, but others would lead their trusting victims into the arid Sonora only to abandon them to their own devices with a crude map and little else. The lucky ones were found by the Border Patrol and returned to Mexico after getting medical treatment. For the unlucky, a decent burial for their bleached bones was often the only assistance anyone could offer them.

ILLEGAL IMMIGRATION

Mexicans were not the only nationality crossing America's borders, nor was the Mexican border the only one crossed. Increased border enforcement revealed large numbers of people from a wide variety of countries entering through various ports. The ingenuity applied to the problem of slipping human beings past the vigilance of the Border Patrol was astonishing, if appalling. Almost any vehicle could be equipped with one or more hidden compartments into which a reasonably flexible person could slip. Some were surprisingly sophisticated, but most were makeshift at best, even life-threatening. Hidden compartments under a vehicle's hood exposed the would-be border crosser to the engine's heat, carbon monoxide, and moving parts. Hidden chambers inside shipping containers might trap their occupants for days or weeks should the container be misdirected, leaving the occupants without food, water, or sanitary facilities. Almost every Border Patrol officer had horror stories of finding dying or dead people crammed into such conveyances.

Even after illegal immigrants crossed the borders, their travails were not over. Because they had no recourse to law enforcement, they were easy prey for all manner of abusive practices. Often they would be able to pay only part of their passage up-front, leaving them indebted to the smugglers. Repayment often turned into perpetual debt, since there was no way to keep the smugglers' agents from adding an endless string of "upkeep" expenses to the

Workers from Mexico pulling carrots alongside workers from Texas, Oklahoma, Missouri, and Arkansas in the Coachella Valley in California.

principal, or rigging the wage system so only interest was paid and the principal of the loan never shrank.

Because illegal immigrants worked outside the legal system, their working conditions were subject to no oversight, and were often on a par with the worst of the Gilded Age. Basic safety measures, such as guards over moving parts, were often nonexistent. Injured workers often lacked medical treatment, or had the cost added to the debt they owed their smugglers. Supervisors were free to abuse the workers, taking out personal vendettas on them, or even extracting sexual favors from them. More than a few were outright sex slaves, forced into prostitution or the pornography industry until their youth faded or their health was broken.

However, there was a great deal of controversy about how to deal with the problem. Some people wanted harsh measures, including mass deportations of illegals and stiff jail sentences for those involved in human trafficking. Others felt uncomfortable about the change from what had been a relatively liberal immigration policy in the 19th century, to one so restrictive it seemed to make a mockery of the promise of the Statue of Liberty. As a result, they agitated for a relatively liberal immigration policy, particularly toward refugees and the economically disadvantaged, as well as amnesty programs for those already present in the United States. This controversy over immigration would continue in much the same vein for decades.

CONCLUSION

Because of the size of the Baby Boom generation and the social changes brought about by the Civil Rights movement, the 1950s and 1960s had a profound impact on how and where people live in the United States. Physical changes can still be seen in the large-scale suburban development that continued for decades afterward, in the rise of the cities of the Sunbelt, and in the desegregation of public spaces. On another level, by the end of the 1960s, the process of leveling-out of regional and sectional differences in U.S. culture, which had begun in the 19th century, had sped up. Mores and customs across America were further homogenized by population shifts. Accelerated by transportation networks, communications, national consumer products and national mass media, the cross-state and cross-region migration of populations further melted cultural differences.

LEIGH KIMMEL

Further Readings

Benson, Sonia G., ed. *The Spanish American Almanac: A Reference Work on Hispanics in the United States.* Farmington Hills, MI: Thomson, 2003.

Black, Timuel D., Jr. *Bridges of Memory: Chicago's Second Generation of Black Migration.* Evanston, IL: Northwestern University Press, 2007.

Bontemps, Arna and Jack Conroy. *Anyplace But Here.* New York: Hill and Wang, 1968.

Farley, Reynolds and Walter R. Allen. *The Color Line and the Quality of Life in America.* New York: Russell Sage Foundation, 1987.

Grossman, James R. *Land of Hope: Chicago, Black Southerners, and the Great Migration.* Chicago, IL: University of Chicago Press, 1989.

"Immigration and Naturalization Act of 1965." Available online: http://www.historicaldocuments.com/ImmigrationActof1965.htm. Accessed October 2008.

Jasper, James M. *Restless Nation: Starting over In America.* Chicago, IL: University of Chicago Press, 2000.

Johnson, Lyndon B. "Remarks at the Signing of the Immigration Bill, Liberty Island, New York, 3 October, 1965." Available online: http://www.lbjlib.utexas.edu/johnson/archives.hom/speeches.hom/651003.asp. Accessed October 2008.

Kanellos, Nicolas. *The Hispanic Almanac: From Columbus to Corporate America.* Washington, D.C.: Visible Ink, 1994.

Kaplan, Dana Evan. "Fleeing the Revolution: The Exodus of Cuban Jewry in the Early 1960s." *Cuban Studies* (n.36, 2005).

Lemann, Nicholas. *The Promised Land: The Great Black Migration and How It Changed America*. New York: Alfred A Knopf, 1991.

Le May, Michael. *U.S. Immigration: A Reference Handbook*. Santa Barbara, CA: ABC-CLIO, 2004.

Lieberson, Stanley and Mary C. Waters. *From Many Strands: Ethnic and Racial Groups in Contemporary America*. New York: Russel Sage Foundation, 1990.

Simon, Julian L. *Population Matters: People, Resources, Environment & Immigration*. New Brunswick, NJ: Transaction Publishers, 1990.

Trotter, Joe William, Jr. *The Great Migration: A Historical Perspective*. Bloomington, IN: Indiana University Press, 1991.

Yancey, George. *Who Is White: Latinos, Asians, and the New Black/Nonblack Divide*. Boulder, CO: Lynne Rienner Publishers, 2003.

Chapter 15

Transportation

"Everything in life is somewhere else,
and you get there in a car."
—E.B. White

ALMOST AS SOON as news came of the Japanese surrender in August of 1945, Americans began to look forward to peace. After having endured the privations of war for so long, they wanted to enjoy consumer goods such as new automobiles once again. America's privations were comparatively light, as the mainland never suffered the indignity of an invasion. For the most part, the sacrifices were in the lives of the young men who went overseas and never returned, and in the consumer goods that were foregone while America's industrial might was directed entirely toward the war effort. That industrial might could not be redirected back to civilian production quickly. Factories had to be retooled, and in many cases workers had to be retrained. As a result, it was not until well into 1946 that the first new cars rolled off the assembly lines, and even those were hard to come by. But once the retooling of America's industry was complete, the consumer lifestyle returned with a vengeance.

CHROME AND TAIL FINS
After the privations of the war, Americans wanted concrete rewards for their sacrifices, and Detroit was glad to provide them with cars that matched the new era of postwar prosperity. The new cars were not only roomier, but also had much larger engines that produced far more power than prewar mod-

els. Increasing numbers of cars had V8 engines, which produced a smoother operation than the straight and flat cylinder engines that had powered prewar vehicles. Automatic transmissions, which had previously appeared on only a very few high-end models, became common even on medium-priced models. Although automatic transmission increased manufacturing costs and fuel consumption, the increased ease of handling meant that people who had found the complexity of changing gears overwhelming could drive with ease.

As the automobile became a mature technology and basic features became universal, automakers began to distinguish their offerings through exterior styling. Bumpers and trim were coated in eye-catching chrome. The sheet metal of the body was increasingly styled in sleek shapes that suggested the fighter jets that had become the iconic image of Cold War military power. To further suggest power and speed, manufacturers began to emphasize the lines of the car's rear, beginning with two small bumps flanking the trunk lid in the 1949 Cadillac. These features soon became taller and sharper in successive models, until they developed into distinctive tail fins.

The Beginnings of NASCAR

It is often said that racing improves the breed, and in the earliest days of automobile racing, there was little distinction between race cars and ordinary vehicles. So many automobiles were one-off experimental models that racing was as much a part of the testing process as a sport. But as the 20th century progressed and the auto industry matured, specialized race cars began to develop.

However, the high-powered automobiles Detroit was putting out in the glory days of the late 1940s and 1950s fairly begged to be raced. Particularly in the South, young men often took their street-legal cars to dirt tracks on county fairgrounds and competed against one another. Local merchants might pool to offer a purse of prizes in hopes of getting enough interest to make their investment back in tickets and concessions. However, it was a confused system in which rules were often enforced arbitrarily, and it was uncertain whether an advertised race would actually occur.

Fed up with the chaos, Bill France Sr. formed a sanctioning body for these races, the North American Stock Car Auto Racing or NASCAR league. Although at first he tried to keep the sport to strictly stock, street-legal vehicles, as time went by various modifications became standard, until stock car racing became as specialized as the open-wheel racing (such as Formula 1 and Indy car) leagues to which it had originally provided an alternative.

Improvement in paint technology also made it possible to develop more complex paint schemes. The "tutone" paint job, which involved painting sections of the door and side panels a complimentary or contrasting color to that of the rest of the car, became increasingly popular.

However, by the end of the 1950s the excesses of superficial styling had reached a point at which they began to turn off car buyers. The most famous of these disasters was

This 1959 Cadillac sported elaborate tail fins just when they were about to go out of style.

the Edsel, Ford's attempt to create a midprice car with the flamboyance typically seen in pricier models. However, the body design that was supposed to be forward-looking instead received only ridicule. In particular, the front end had as its dominant feature a vertical grille so tall it split the bumper into two sections and raised the hood line. Critics mocked the Edsel as looking like an Oldsmobile sucking a lemon, while in bars and locker rooms around the nation, more racy anatomical analogies were suggested. The car's failure in the market was so catastrophic that "Edsel" became a synonym for an over-hyped product that fell flat.

The American automotive industry was also coming under fire from another direction. Although so much energy had been poured into making cars faster and more powerful, little attention had been given to safety. For instance, brakes that had been adequate for the cars of the 1920s and 1930s developed a frightening tendency to "fade" with extensive use in the more powerful cars of the 1950s. As they were used, the drums would grow hot and expand just enough that the brake shoes no longer gripped them firmly. Although the effectiveness of the disc brake was demonstrated by Jaguar's race cars in the early 1950s, American manufacturers were slow to adopt them.

Seat belts were also slow to appear in American automobiles. The small company Nash, which produced the Rambler, was one of the first to make them a regular feature in 1952. By 1956 Ford was beginning to offer them as an option. However, less that 20 percent of Ford's cars actually were equipped with seat belts.

But it was the Chevrolet Corvair that came under particular fire. One of the earliest compact cars, it featured an air-cooled engine set in the rear and came in a wide variety of convertibles, coupes, sedans, station wagons, vans, and pickup trucks. The design resulted in several major problems, including contamination of the air in the passenger compartment with oil or carbon monoxide gas if key engine seals were to leak. The Corvair also had steering peculiarities that led to a tendency to roll over in certain situations. In response to these problems, lawyer Ralph Nader wrote a book entitled *Unsafe at Any Speed: The Designed-in Dangers of the American Automobile*. The 1965 book made Nader a target for harassment and launched his reputation as a consumer advocate. More importantly, it increased public awareness of auto safety and led to the 1966 National Traffic and Motor Vehicle Safety Act and the introduction of mandatory seat belts, along with other safety features.

THE INTERSTATE HIGHWAY SYSTEM

The big, fast cars that Detroit was producing and consumers were buying in record numbers needed highways that were built for speed. Even before World War II, Americans had been hearing about the German Autobahn, the network of limited-access divided highways intended to enable Nazi armies to move rapidly throughout the country. Yet the U.S. government was reluctant to invest in such a massive construction project.

When President Dwight D. Eisenhower entered office, he leveraged Cold War fears to press through Congress the legislation that enabled the construction of the Interstate Highway System. As a young lieutenant, Eisenhower had led a convoy of military vehicles across the country over roads that were often grossly inadequate. As a result, he could speak with personal conviction to key Senate and House leaders of the absolute necessity of good roads for the defense of the homeland. His excellent storytelling ability enabled him to give concrete examples in language that would sway not only their reason, but their emotions as well.

On June 29, 1956 Eisenhower signed into law two key pieces of legislation, the Federal Aid Highway Act of 1956 and the Highway Revenue Act of 1956. The latter was remarkable in earmarking federal fuel taxes specifically for highway construction, rather than taking funds from the general budget. The pay-as-you-go arrangement mollified many conservative Republicans who were concerned about the long-term effects of so much government spending in what was nominally a time of peace.

This 1958 highway overpass in Urbandale, Iowa, was the first welded aluminum bridge in the world and remains an engineering landmark.

On November 14 of that same year the first eight-mile stretch of Interstate in Topeka, Kansas was opened with a formal ribbon-cutting ceremony. Although it was only two lanes of the highway and only went to the state line, that first section of I-70 still represented a historical landmark, the beginning of a road that would run almost across the country, going from the East coast to Utah. The site was chosen for symbolic reasons, being the geographic center of the United States, and not far from the birthplace of President Eisenhower.

Wigwam motels, along with other roadside kitsch, spread across the United States in the 1950s as vacationers took to the highways.

Over the next 13 years engineers and road crews toiled to construct what became the most ambitious road-building project in the history of humanity. Along with the Great Wall of China, the Interstate Highway System is visible from orbit. However, even at the beginning of the 21st century the Interstate Highway System remained technically incomplete. The late 1960s marked a period of questioning of industrial progress, leading to the Not in My Backyard or NIMBY movement, which stalled for decades the completion of the last few miles of highway and interchanges. Here and there around the country a "road to nowhere" or "ramp to nowhere" marks the foundering of a grand plan on political realities.

BOOM TIME FOR BUSES

The war had also been hard on bus lines. On one hand, no new buses were being manufactured, and even spare parts were difficult to come by. On the other hand, demand on buses was increased by the large number of soldiers who were traveling by bus, as well as civilians who turned to intercity buses as an alternative to overcrowded trains in a time when gas for civilian travel was almost impossible to come by. As a result, many of the buses on the road by 1946 were in extremely poor condition.

However, high rates of usage during the war had improved the financial position of many of the bus lines, which had been struggling to stay afloat through the lean years of the Depression. With additional funds available for capital expenditures, bus lines began to purchase new buses to replace their aging

Buses and bus transit service improved in the postwar era. Larger transit coaches like this 1961 model had an increased presence on streets and highways, along with large trucks.

fleets. For instance, Greyhound ordered 1,200 new cruiser-style Silversides coaches in 1946.

The new buses that came onto the roads in the decades after the war represented major technical improvements over the buses of the 1920s and 1930s. Not only were they larger and more powerful as diesel engines replaced gasoline ones, but they included more features that gave passengers a comfortable ride. For instance, air conditioning became increasingly common, as did central heating systems that delivered heat throughout the passenger area. Increasing numbers of buses were equipped with lavatory facilities, so passengers no longer had to wait for the next stop.

Furthermore, the intercity bus was not the only form of bus on the roads in increasing numbers. The 1950s also were a boom time for manufacturers of school buses. In earlier decades most children walked to school. On a particularly cold or rainy day they might be able to catch a ride with a friendly neighbor. In cities that boasted mass transportation, schoolchildren might catch a trolley, subway, or city bus. But for the vast majority of schoolchildren, walking to school each day was the norm.

However, after the war, demographic and economic changes led to the elimination of the one-room schoolhouse and the consolidation of schools, resulting in an increase of the distance children would need to commute to school each day. Since those distances were simply not walkable within a reasonable amount of time, and often would involve crossing or following roads on which cars were driving at speeds that made them too dangerous for young children, it became necessary for school districts to provide transportation. Compared to intercity buses, school buses were bare-bones transportation. The rows of bench seats were lightly padded, and there was little in the way

Integrating Mass Transit

America's transportation industry was touched by the sweeping cultural changes of the Civil Rights movement. Particularly in the South, mass transportation systems such as buses and trains were subject to legal restrictions meant to prevent the mixing of the races. Furthermore, they were often implemented and enforced in ways that ensured the routine humiliation of African Americans.

The boycott of the Montgomery transit system sparked by Rosa Parks's action lasted 381 days.

After the landmark *Brown v. Board of Education* decision declared school segregation unconstitutional, leaders in the black community began to hope it could be extended to other forms of segregation as well. However, to challenge it, they needed a test case, a person who was both willing to carry out a court fight rather than merely pay the fine, and whose character was impeccable, able to stand up to the most determined scrutiny.

They found their champion in Rosa Parks, a seamstress who lived quietly with her family and had no awkward secrets in her past. When she was arrested for refusing to give up her seat to a white person on December 1, 1955, the African-American community decided to stage a boycott to show the city of Montgomery, Alabama, just how much the bus system depended on their ridership.

When the city and the bus company met their very modest demands with scorn and ridicule, the original one-day boycott stretched over a year. Finally the Supreme Court became involved and gave them not only their small request, but also the total abolition of segregated seating on public transportation.

of heating or cooling. However, since they were intended for relatively brief commutes, rather than long-distance travel, these problems were not major barriers to their use. Most children and their parents welcomed the simple availability of transportation on a daily basis.

Similarly, city buses underwent relatively little change, although some technological transfer from the intercity coach bus did occur, such as increased use of diesel engines for greater power and thus larger size. However, the greatest change in the city bus system would be social.

KEEP ON TRUCKING

The decades immediately after World War II were a boom time for the trucking industry. Like the bus lines, truckers had been hard-pressed to replace vital equipment during the lean times of the Depression; during the war they could gain replacement parts only if they could demonstrate a vital contribution to the war effort. But peace meant that new equipment became available, and in many cases it was better mechanically than its predecessors. Trucks in particular were early adopters of diesel engines because these larger and more powerful engines could haul heavier loads more efficiently than gasoline engines.

In addition, the interstate highway system proved a great boon to the development of long-haul trucking. Limited access highways made hauling more efficient because trucks no longer had to waste energy stopping, idling, and accelerating out of innumerable stop signs and stoplights. Instead, truckers could cruise along at a steady speed, stopping along the way only for necessities such as refueling or rest breaks.

However, the boon of the interstate was not without its drawbacks. The endless monotony of driving them could induce a sort of highway hypnosis that reduced a driver's alertness, which meant drivers were less able to react to sudden changes of conditions. In addition, the increasing numbers of trucks that came onto the interstate began to overstrain it. Planners had built interstate highways based upon projections from the number of trucks and cars that were traveling the existing state and U.S. highways, and had not anticipated the actual growth in the trucking industry. The pavement of the interstates began to wear out at an alarming rate, and the federal government had to begin allocating money for repairs and resurfacing even while significant parts of the interstate were still under construction. In an effort to stem the destruction, new regulations on loads were established based not upon the capacity of the trucks to carry them, but upon the ability of the highways to carry the trucks.

RAILROADS IN DECLINE

After the crowded trains of the war, the postwar years were a grim time for the railroads. People began taking longer road trips in their powerful new cars, and those who did not turned increasingly to the comfortable new coach buses. For longer distance, air travel was becoming increasingly common as technological change made airliners faster and more reliable. As a result, passenger train ridership dwindled steadily throughout the 1950s. Even sleek new designs such as the Zephyr could not bring enough romance back into rail service to make it commercially viable, and the 1970 bankruptcy of Penn Central was the final death knell of commercial passenger rail service.

Although freight service continued to be a mainstay of railroading, it too faced significant competition from the highway in the form of over-the-road

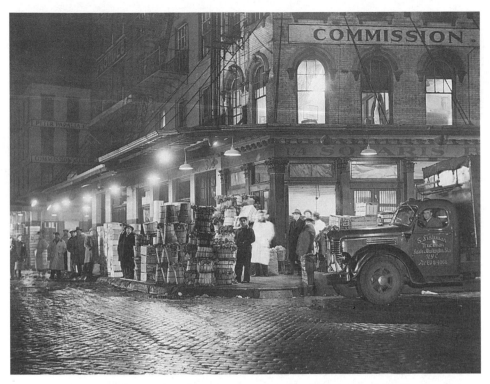

A truck beside a produce market on Washington Street in New York City in 1952. The interstate highway system sped the development of long-haul trucking, which became essential to the nation's trade in the postwar period.

trucking. Government regulation proved the greatest hampering agent, rather than technological issues. Strict regulation by the Interstate Commerce Commission, a legacy of an era when the railroads had held monopoly power over freight haulage and had used it with such impunity that overburdened consumers had demanded government control, made it difficult for the railroads to respond quickly to changing economic situations. In contrast, trucking companies were by and large free to set their own rates as economic situations changed.

RISE OF THE JET AIRLINER

The airlines were another major growth area for American transportation. The jet engine had originally been designed as a weapon in World War II, and it became the mainstay of the U.S. Air Force during the Korean War. However, it also promised greater speed and power to civilian aviation, and in a time when speed and power were synonymous with modern in transportation systems, it was only natural that commercial airlines would want to put jets into service, particularly on their longer flights.

The Interstate Highway System

Congress passed legislation to create an interstate highway system starting in 1925, but early development was slow due to lack of funding, the Great Depression, and World War II. The federal government at the behest of President Dwight Eisenhower renewed its attempts to develop the interstate highway system in the 1950s. Improved national defense was a key justification. The United States was at the height of the Cold War with the Soviet Union and fought in the Korean War in the early 1950s. Interstate highways would allow for more efficient troop movements, easier repair in the event of damage due to attack, and effective evacuation of urban areas in the event of a nuclear alert. Another key reason for an interstate highway system was the growing U.S. population and the growth of the suburbs in the post–World War II period. America's outdated roads were an increasing problem for suburbanites who faced lengthy commutes to their jobs in the cities and for companies that needed to transport goods long distances.

The 1952 and 1954 Federal Aid Highway Acts provided approximately $200 million in federal funds for interstate highway construction. The largest and most well-known of the highway acts, however, was the 1956 National Interstate and Defense Highways Act. The act called for the construction of over 40,000 miles of interstate highways, with the federal government responsible for approximately 90 percent of costs expected to exceed $30 billion. States would be responsible for the balance, as well as future maintenance costs. The act also called for the establishment of uniform design standards, including fully divided highways, minimum distances allowed between interchanges, lane widths, and when the use of overpasses or underpasses was required. A numbering system and marker designs were chosen the following year. Construction of the resulting interstate highway system was one of the largest public works projects in U.S. history. The system was designated the Dwight D. Eisenhower System of Interstate and Defense Highways in 1990 in honor of his commitment to the project.

The interstate highway system had many short and long term effects. Related industries such as construction and cement benefited financially and became more technologically advanced. Substantially lowered transportation costs and the ease of long distance transport fueled national business growth and productivity. Americans began taking long distance vacations to destinations such as amusement parks like Disney Land and national parks. Motels, rest areas, gas stations, restaurants, and campgrounds sprang up along the interstate routes to cater to travelers. The easing of commute times was a key factor in the continued expansion of suburban sprawl, at the same time increasing the decline of urban populations, tax bases, and quality of life. Many historians also feel that the success of the interstate highway system fueled Americans' dependence on automobiles and hindered the development of mass transit.

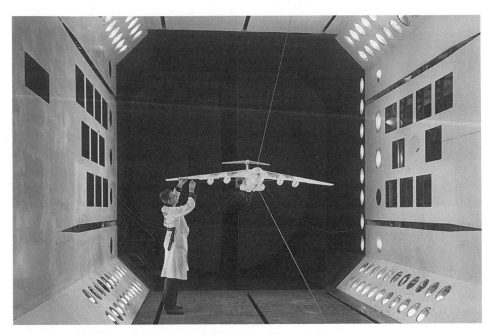

Testing a Lockheed jet aircraft model inside a NASA wind tunnel in November 1962. Technological advances that led to the development of passenger jets resulted in significant changes in air travel in the 1950s and 1960s.

The first commercial airliner was Britain's de Havilland Comet, a handsome aircraft with slightly swept wings suggestive of some of the new jet bombers. Able to fly higher and faster than any other airliner of its era, the Comet could offer passengers both a smoother ride than a propeller-driven airliner, and a shorter flight. However, the Comet had serious design flaws, including engines buried into its wing roots, making access for servicing difficult. The Comet was taken out of service in 1954, a mere two years after it was introduced. However, those two years had proved the commercial viability of a jet airliner, and U.S. aircraft builders such as Boeing and Douglas were developing their own models. Boeing's 707, the first of a long series of jet airliners, was introduced in 1955, and Pan American Airways quickly put it into service on their transatlantic flights. The 707's engines were enclosed in pods hanging below the wings, similar to those of American bombers, which made them much more accessible for maintenance.

To go with the technological innovations, airlines added in-flight services that made traveling by air an experience. Attractive and courteous stewardesses helped passengers to their seats and tended to their needs throughout the course of the flight. Complimentary meals and drinks were served on longer flights. Because flying was seen as an event, passengers generally dressed up for the trip.

Special Operations forces climbing down from a helicopter in the 1960s. Helicopters helped the military infiltrate more territory, resupply isolated troops, and evacuate the wounded.

COLD WAR MILITARY TRANSPORTATION

During the Cold War, the American military paid increasing attention to logistical issues of supporting a large military that might be called to fight abroad, perhaps in many places at once. The newly unified Department of Defense looked to technologies that offered the ability to deliver troops and materiel to widely dispersed fighting fronts as rapidly as possible. In addition to new and larger trucks and cargo planes, they developed new troop transports that would enable troops to regularly arrive at the battlefield ready to fight rather than wearied from extensive marches.

One of the most important developments of Cold War military transportation was the helicopter. Unlike the fixed-wing airplane, which required a lengthy airstrip to take off and land, a helicopter could put down on an area not much bigger than the aircraft itself. A helicopter could go right onto the battlefield to deliver men and supplies as needed. Because the helicopter could hover in midair, it could become a weapons platform for situations in which attack airplanes would be impractical.

Another important use for the helicopter that emerged in the Korean War was as an airborne ambulance. Helicopters could evacuate wounded soldiers to a hospital at the rear far more quickly than truck ambulances like those used in World War I and World War II. Many men who would have died in previous conflicts were saved, to fight again or to return to the United States for rehabilitation and entry into civilian life as disabled veterans.

CONCLUSION

In many ways the decades immediately following World War II were heroic ones for the United States. Technology allowed human beings to travel further and faster than ever before possible. Cars raced across interstate highways at extraordinary speeds. Social change smashed barriers that had limited some Americans' enjoyment of the transportation system. And the space program put human beings on another world.

But the 1960s were also a time of questioning the established wisdom about progress and the value of technology. The environmental movement pointed out the destruction caused by the unthinking use of finite natural resources to enable people to travel faster purely for the pleasure of going fast. For the first time, Americans began to look at the possibility of a world in which cheap oil could no longer be taken for granted. It was a theme that would become increasingly dominant in the 1970s.

LEIGH KIMMEL

Further Readings

Goddard, Stephen B. *Getting There: The Epic Struggle Between Road and Rail in the American Century*. New York: Basic Books, 1994.

Helms, Todd P. and Chip Flohe. *Roadside Memories: A Collection of Vintage Gas Station Photographs*. Atglen, PA: Schiffer Publishing, 1997.

Heppenheimer, T.A. *Turbulent Skies: The History of Commercial Aviation*. New York: John Wiley, 1995.

Jackle, John A. and Keith A. Sculle. *The Gas Station in America*. Baltimore, MD: Johns Hopkins, 1994.

Jackson, Carlton. *Hounds of the Road: A History of the Greyhound Bus Company*. Bowling Green, OH: Bowling Green University Press, 1984.

Lewis, Tom. *Divided Highways: Building the Interstate Highways, Transforming American Life*. New York: Viking, 1997.

Moon, Henry. *The Interstate Highway System*. Washington, D.C.: Association of American Geographers, 1994.

Nader, Ralph. *Unsafe at Any Speed: The Designed-In Dangers of the American Automobile*. New York: Grossman, 1965.

Schisgall, Oscar. *The Greyhound Story: From Hibbing to Everywhere*. Chicago, IL: J.G. Ferguson, 1985.

Volti, Rudi. *Cars and Culture: The Life Story of a Technology*. Westport, CT: Greenwood Press, 2004.

Williamson, Harold F. et al. *The American Petroleum Industry: 1899–1959, The Age of Energy*. Evanston, IL: Northwestern University Press, 1959.

Chapter 16

Public Health, Medicine, and Nutrition

*"Physical fitness . . . is the basis of dynamic
and creative intellectual activity."*
—President John F. Kennedy

BY THE MID-20TH century, Americans were enjoying one of the highest standards of health in the world. This was due in part to having avoided much of the destructiveness of World War II. While much of Europe and Asia was devastated, the United States had actually improved infrastructure such as roads and utilities as part of the war effort. And while many Europeans and Asians suffered from lack of food during the war, rationing of items such as sugar and meat, plus the availability of fruits and vegetables from home "victory gardens," meant that some Americans actually consumed healthier diets during the war than they do today. In addition, America had become a world leader in medical research and care by this time, and new social programs in the 1960s expanded access to medical care and created a cultural expectation (though not yet entirely realized) that medical care would be available according to need, not ability to pay.

So effective were medicine and public health at conquering infectious disease that attention in both fields was shifting to chronic diseases such as cancer and heart disease, which had become leading killers of Americans by mid-century. Both medicine and public health were slow to make this change in focus, but ultimately responded by creating the field of preventive

241

medicine, as well as the scientific study of health behaviors. Food supply was abundant in America in the 1950s and 1960s, and many Americans embraced the opportunity to experience culinary pleasures that had been denied during World War II. Prosperity plus increased foreign travel was also reflected in a broadening of interest in different types of food, including that seen as "foreign" or "gourmet." Ironically, the wide availability of foods that were relatively inexpensive laid the groundwork for a new type of health problem, one based on consuming too much, rather than too little. In addition, not everyone benefited from the postwar boom, and several federal government programs in the 1960s were inaugurated to alleviate hunger and malnutrition as part of the greater war on poverty.

PUBLIC HEALTH AT MID-CENTURY

By 1950, improvement in public health combined with medical care had brought many infectious diseases under control in the United States. This lengthened life expectancy, but had the paradoxical result of increasing morbidity and mortality due to chronic disease, because probability of death due to chronic disease generally increases with age. To put it another way, a baby who dies in infancy from dehydration due to diarrhea or a man who succumbs to tuberculosis at age 18 have had little or no opportunity to develop, let alone die from, heart disease or cancer. This produces the saying, well-known in public health, that anything that increases longevity will increase cancer mortality, meaning that as people live longer they are more likely to develop cancer simply because many cancers take years to grow.

Unfortunately, little was known about what caused most chronic diseases, or how to prevent or control them. Scientists have since discovered that many chronic diseases have complex causes, including a variety of genetic, behavioral, and environmental factors, and that the infectious disease approach of seeking a single cause is not helpful with many chronic diseases. While public health generally favored government intervention and emphasized programs that would improve the health of the entire community, the medical profession had always resisted government intervention in healthcare, and the medical model focused on the individual patient, rather than groups of people. A new medical specialty known as preventive medicine was developed in an attempt to bridge this gap. Specialists in this field were physicians who emphasized preventive care by conducting screening tests and giving health advice on a one-to-one basis with their patients.

Public health actually lost ground in the 1950s, as the communicable diseases that had been its early focus were largely conquered, and no one was certain how to apply a public health approach to prevent and control chronic diseases such as cancer, diabetes, and stroke. An emphasis on population health became more common in the 1960s with the Great Society reforms of President Lyndon Johnson, but often bypassed public health concerns while

The Framingham Study

As medical science and public health improved control of infectious diseases in the United States, chronic diseases became far more important as causes of death, and thus began to attract more research attention. One of the "new" diseases to attract such attention in the years after World War II was Coronary Heart Disease (CHD), a condition characterized by impaired blood flow in the arteries that supply blood to the heart. CHD often results in an acute myocardial infarction (AMI), more commonly known as a heart attack. In 1900 CHD occurred at a rate of 40 per 100,000 population and accounted for eight percent of all deaths in the United States.

By 1950 the CHD rate had risen to 356 per 100,000, accounting for 37 percent of all deaths. In an effort to understand the factors leading to this increase in disease and mortality, in 1948 the National Heart Institute (later called the National Heart, Lung, and Blood Institute, part of the National Institutes of Health) began a study that followed a cohort of over 5,000 adults over a period of years to discover what factors were associated with the development of CHD. Because the cohort was selected from the small town of Framingham, Massachusetts, it is known as the Framingham Study.

The original Framingham cohort consisted of about two-thirds of Framingham's adult (aged 30–62 years) population in 1948. All were free of heart disease at the beginning of the study. Every two years members of the original cohort were given a battery of medical tests and asked detailed questions about their behaviors, including diet, smoking, and exercise. Two additional cohorts have been enrolled.

In 1970 a cohort of over 5,000 offspring of members of the original cohort was enrolled, and from 2001 to 2005 a third generation cohort of over 4,000 members was formed of people who had at least one parent in the offspring cohort. In addition, the Omni cohort consisting of over 500 members of minority racial/ethnic groups (who were underrepresented in the original cohort) living in Framingham was enrolled in 1994, and an additional cohort of 405 members unrelated to the original Omni cohort were enrolled between 2003 and 2005.

Over 1,000 papers have been published using data from the Framingham Study. Among the major findings from this study are establishment of the relationship between levels of cholesterol and risk of heart disease, including the protective effect of high-density lipoprotein, as well as the negative effect of low-density lipoprotein; demonstration that obesity and lack of exercise are risk factors for heart disease; establishment of the health benefits to be gained by quitting smoking even after years of tobacco consumption; and discovery that high blood pressure was a health risk for women and older persons, just as it was for men and younger persons.

emphasizing access to medical and mental healthcare through the establishment of neighborhood clinics and community-based mental health services. On the positive side, the field of public health broadened in this era to include concerns such as hospital administration, international health, population control, and environmental health. Schools of public health increasingly trained future government employees and medical administrators, as well as public health professionals.

MEDICAL ADVANCES

The years following World War II saw great increases in the amount and quality of healthcare available to Americans. Research advances created whole classes of new antibiotics to cure previously dreaded diseases such as tuberculosis, as well as more common complaints such as strep throat. In fact, physicians became so enamored of antibiotics in this period that they were overused. For instance, antibiotics were often prescribed to treat viral illnesses against which they have no effect. Overuse of antibiotics has the unintended effect of fostering the creation of antibiotic-resistant strains of bacteria, a consequence that would become much clearer in the 1980s.

Safe and effective vaccinations for several common diseases were developed and disseminated across the population in the 1950s and 1960s. Devel-

A polio patient in Covington, Louisiana, used this artificial respirator known as an iron lung for nearly half a century from the late 1950s until his death in 2003. When closed and sealed at the patient's neck, these chambers used air pressure to force air into the lungs.

opment of the measles vaccine in 1964, the mumps vaccine in 1967, and the rubella (German measles) vaccine in 1970 meant that these diseases, which had formerly been considered rites of passage through childhood, became rare. This is significant not only because children did not contract those diseases, but also because in a minority of cases serious complications such as deafness and mental retardation resulted. Fewer cases of measles also meant fewer cases of deafness. Development of the Salk vaccine for polio in 1955, later superseded by the Sabin vaccine in 1961, led rapidly to the virtual elimination of this formerly dreaded disease in the United States.

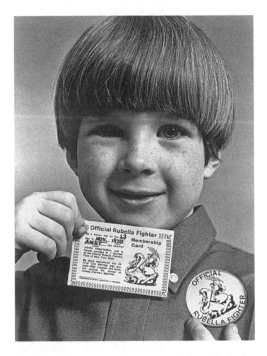

A vaccinated boy showing off his "Official Rubella Fighter Membership Card" and button during the "rubella umbrella" vaccination campaign.

HEALTHCARE INEQUALITIES

Despite scientific advances made in the field of medicine, many Americans did not have access to basic healthcare in the postwar years. One federal program that aimed to ameliorate this situation was the Hill-Burton Act of 1946, which provided federal funds for hospital construction, many of which were built in previously underserved rural areas. Several federal government programs designed to make healthcare more accessible to lower-income Americans were included as part of the Great Society reforms of President Lyndon Johnson, which aimed to eliminate or ameliorate poverty in the United States.

Expanding demand for healthcare meant increased demand for trained medical professionals. The federal government played a large role in expanding training in the medical professions in the 1960s, beginning with the 1963 Health Professionals Education Assistance Act, which provided construction grants to medical and other health professional schools in return for expanding their enrollment by at least 5 percent and maintaining that increase for at least 10 years. This act was amended in 1965 to provide matching grants for the construction of teaching facilities in medicine, dentistry, and other health professions, and provisions for training medical professionals was further expanded by the Health Manpower Act of 1968.

Jonas Salk, Alfred Sabin, and the Polio Vaccine

Polio is a viral disease that was a common childhood infection in the United States as recently as the 1950s. Although infection with the polio virus often results in a minor illness with flu-like symptoms such as fever, headache, muscle pains, and stiffness, some cases resulted in paralysis or death, making polio a much-feared disease. Polio epidemics occurred regularly in the United States before development of an effective vaccine. For instance, about 20,000 cases of the paralytic disease were reported in the United States in 1952, while in 1965 less than 100 cases were reported.

The first vaccine against polio was developed by Jonas Salk (1914–95) at the University of Pittsburgh. Tests on volunteers began in 1952. Salk and his family were among the first volunteers to receive the vaccine. In 1954 one of the first double-blind placebo controlled tests was conducted with the vaccine. Two million children received either the vaccine or a placebo, and neither the children nor the researchers knew which they had received. In 1955 the vaccine was declared safe and effective, and widespread immunization became the norm. The vaccine developed by Salk is called IPV for inactivated polio virus, because it used an inactivated form of the virus that was sufficient to cause immune response (and thus prevent infection) but not to cause illness.

Until recently IPV had been supplanted by an attenuated live-virus oral vaccine (OPV) developed by Albert Sabin and first licensed in the United States in 1961. The OPV was preferred because it could be consumed orally, while the Salk vaccine had to be injected. The OPV facilitated widespread vaccination that has eradicated polio from most of the world. However, OPV can revert to a virulent form of the virus, and suspected cases of polio caused by OPV have been reported. For this reason, OPV use was discontinued in the United States in 2000; the current CDC vaccination schedule for children recommends use of IPV.

A photo of a young polio victim taken to promote widespread polio vaccination, which began in April 1955.

ORGAN TRANSPLANTS

One frontier that symbolized the promise of modern medicine was the development of organ transplant technology. Early organ transplants received a great deal of publicity, far out of proportion to their therapeutic usefulness at the time. However, the pioneering surgeons of the 1950s and 1960s paved the way for what has become a fairly commonplace procedure (and one that is limited primarily by the availability of organs). In addition, organ transplantation was often touted as a bold new frontier for medicine, symbolizing the god-like power of physicians and surgeons in performing operations that must have seemed to many Americans like something from a science fiction novel, rather than medical practice.

The first successful organ transplant was performed by Joseph Murray in 1954. It was a kidney transplant between identical twins, which eliminated the need for immunosuppressive drugs to prevent the recipient's body from rejecting the foreign tissue. The first successful lung transplant was performed in June 1963 and the first successful liver transplant in 1967. The first human heart transplant was achieved in 1967 by Christiaan Barnaard in South Africa. However, as was true with many early transplant operations, the recipient lived only 18 days after the surgery. The first human heart transplant in the United States was performed in 1968. In this case the recipient lived about eight months. Organ transplants did not become a routinely life-extending procedure until 1970s and 1980s, when cyclosporine and other immunosuppressive drugs were developed that prevented the recipient's body from rejecting the foreign tissue.

HEALTHCARE COVERAGE

Expansion of health insurance coverage continued through the 1960s and 1970s, as medical care came to be perceived of as a human right for everyone rather than a privilege for those who could afford it. However, unlike many other industrialized countries, the United States never adopted a form of national health insurance for the general population. Instead most people in this period were covered by a private insurance plan obtained through their employer, with those over age 65 covered by the federal Medicare program. The poor received medical care through a combination of Medicaid (a health insurance program run jointly by the federal government and individual states), other federal and state programs, and private charity.

The Medicare and Medicaid programs were established as part of the Social Security Act of 1965. Medicare originally provided federal financing for medical care for the elderly (persons over age 65), and was expanded in the 1970s to include disabled persons and those with end-stage renal disease (ESRD). It is a federally-funded entitlement program that provides uniform benefits without regard to state of residence. Medicare greatly expanded the amount of medical services received by elderly persons, and made them the

Thalidomide and the FDA Drug Approval Process

One of the worst episodes of harm caused by a pharmaceutical product in the 20th century was associated with thalidomide, a drug developed in Germany and sold under various brand names 1957–61 as a sleep aid and antinausea drug. Because at the time thalidomide was believed to be completely harmless, it was widely prescribed to pregnant women to relieve morning sickness, a decision that proved to have horrifying consequences. Over 10,000 women who took thalidomide during pregnancy gave birth to children with severe birth defects, including phocomelia (misshapen limbs), missing limbs, cleft palate, and spinal cord defects.

Although thalidomide was sold in over 40 countries, it was never licensed for sale in the United States. The manufacturer's application for approval was rejected due to lack of information provided about the drug's mechanism of action. This meant that the epidemic of "thalidomide babies" born in Europe did not occur on the same scale in the United States because only a few American women took thalidomide during pregnancy, generally having received it from abroad or through trial samples that were distributed to U.S. physicians. Having dodged that bullet, many Americans interpreted the thalidomide tragedy as confirming the need for even stronger federal regulation of the development, testing, and sale of pharmaceutical products.

Senator Estes Kefauver began holding congressional hearings concerning the pharmaceutical industry in 1950. One of his concerns was the uncertain efficacy of many drugs introduced to the market. Although Kefauver originally met opposition to increasing federal oversight, the thalidomide tragedy gave him the support necessary to push through the 1962 Kefauver-Harris amendment. This amendment (cosponsored by U.S. Representative Oren Harris) to the Food, Drug and Cosmetics Act greatly expanded the oversight role of the Food and Drug Administration (FDA) in regulating pharmaceuticals. Most importantly it created the modern form of the FDA approval process, in which manufacturers of new drugs must provide evidence of a drug's efficacy for its proposed uses (something that had never been done for thalidomide).

The clinical trial process for new drugs was developed in order to meet the new standards of safety and efficacy demanded by the Kefauver-Harris amendment. Although this process increased the standard of evidence required to introduce new drugs to the American market, it was necessarily time-consuming and was challenged and somewhat modified in the 1980s, when organizations such as ACT-UP (AIDS Coalition To Unleash Power) demanded a more timely process to approve medications to fight HIV and AIDS. In response the FDA issued new rules to expedite the approval process for drugs developed to fight life-threatening diseases, and expanded access to drugs still in the approval process for patients lacking other treatment options.

After he was shot in 1963, John F. Kennedy was taken to Parkland Hospital's Emergency and Trauma entrance, shown above, which is about 10 minutes away from Dealey Plaza.

best-insured segment of the population. In 1980, 98 percent of Americans over age 65 had health insurance through the Medicare program, while just under 80 percent of those under age 65 had health insurance.

Medicaid provides health insurance coverage to low-income individuals and their families through a federal-state partnership in which the individual states set eligibility requirements, payment rates, and services covered, while financial responsibility is split between each state and the federal government. Medicaid provided a great expansion of medical care to the poor, but unlike Medicare, a person's eligibility for the program as well as the specific benefits provided vary from one state to another, and are regularly changed by state legislatures according to the political and fiscal climate.

Medical services offered by the Veterans Affairs (VA) adapted to the changing needs of veterans. For instance, the large number of aging World War II veterans led to the establishment of a VA nursing home program beginning in 1963, and a home healthcare program beginning in 1970. The VA also shifted in this period from a healthcare model based on long-term hospital care toward a model based on ambulatory or outpatient care. To illustrate the former model, a 1954 survey revealed that 65 percent of VA patients had been in the hospital over 90 days, a length of stay that would be considered extraordinary today.

MENTAL HEALTH

Social acceptance of psychological and psychiatric problems increased in the 1950s and 1960s, and it became more common for individuals to seek counseling for difficult situations (such as family conflict) that were not considered traditional medical problems. In the 1950s, the discovery of powerful new psychoactive drugs, which offered the first effective medical treatment for a number of psychiatric conditions, aided in public acceptance of psychiatric problems. The new drugs, some of which are still in use, include the antidepressants iproniazid (brand name Marsilid) and imipramine (Tofranil), the anti-manic drug Lithium, the neuroleptic chlorpromazine (Thorazine), and the stimulant methylphenidate (Ritalin). The professionalization of psychiatry was also aided by the publication in 1952 of the first edition of the *Diagnostic and Statistical Manual of Mental Disorders* (DSM). DSM represents an important effort to standardize the process of psychiatric diagnosis and place psychiatry on an intellectual standing equal to other branches of medicine. It was the first attempt to define and classify all the various categories of mental disorders then recognized.

The professional study of sexuality in the United States that began with Alfred Kinsey in the 1940s continued through the 1950s and 1960s. The most influential researchers were William Masters and Virginia Johnson, who worked at Washington University in St. Louis and conducted pioneering research into sexual function and sexual disorders. They developed a model of sexual response, with four stages, based on direct observation of hundreds of men and women going through a cycle from initial arousal, through orgasm and resolution. They were also among the first researchers to study sexual responsiveness in older men and women.

Masters and Johnson's greatest effect on mental health for the average American were their willingness to study sexual dysfunction scientifically, just like any other physical problem. They were also the first to develop a clinical program to treat sexual dysfunctions such as premature ejaculation and frigidity. Among their other accomplishments were the demonstration of the refractory period in men, the establishment (contradicting Freud) that there was no difference between a "vaginal orgasm" and a "clitoral orgasm" for women, and the finding that women were capable of multiple orgasm. Less positively viewed today is their program to "cure" homosexuality, although in their defense they were reflecting common beliefs at the time, and homosexuality was listed as a psychological disorder in the DSM until 1980.

NUTRITION

The experience of food shortages and rationing during World War II did not permanently alter American eating habits. In fact, the years immediately following the war were marked by increased indulgence in commodities not readily available during the war. Private ownership of automobiles became

Tobacco

Tobacco is native to the Americas, where it has been cultivated since approximately 4000 B.C.E. It proved a very popular export product as well. Within 100 years of European arrival in the Americas around 1500 C.E., tobacco was used throughout the world. However, the dominant mode of tobacco consumption today, cigarette smoking, became popular only in the early 20th century, facilitated by industrial methods of production and distribution. For instance, in 1900 the average annual tobacco consumption for Americans over age 15 was only 49 cigarettes compared to 111 cigars, 1.6 pounds of pipe tobacco, or 4.1 pounds of chewing tobacco. By 1960 the average annual cigarette consumption had risen to 3,888. Other forms of consumption declined as cigarettes became more popular, so the average consumption of chewing tobacco in 1960 was .5 pounds, and of pipe tobacco .6 pounds. Unfortunately, smoking cigarettes, at least in the quantity typical in the modern world, has been firmly established as a health hazard and has been the focus of one of the earliest public health campaigns aimed at altering individual behavior. After the 1964 publication of *Smoking and Health*, which was the first of many such reports issued by the U.S. Surgeon General, the Federal Cigarette Labeling and Advertising Act of 1965 was passed. It required the first warning label, which appeared in 1966 and said simply, "Caution: Cigarette Smoking May Be Hazardous to Your Health." The Public Health Cigarette Smoking Act of 1969 strengthened that warning and banned television and radio advertising of cigarettes.

The link between cigarette smoking and lung cancer was recognized as early as 1939, but did not gain public attention until the studies by Sir Richard Doll and Austin Bradford Hill in the 1950s. Their case-control study of 40,000 British physicians established not only that cigarette smoking was an important risk factor for lung cancer, but that a strong dose-response relationship existed between smoking and lung cancer, meaning that people who smoked more were at a higher risk of lung cancer. Other researchers have since established smoking as a risk factor for heart disease, stroke, emphysema, cataracts, and breast cancer.

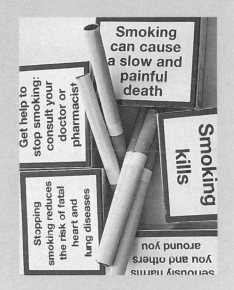

Cigarette warning labels, which began in 1966, have been amplified many times to note the increased risk of deadly diseases and danger to unborn children.

Julia Child's kitchen, which is now preserved at the Smithsonian National Museum of American History.

more common in the postwar prosperity also, which led to a rapid expansion in fast food chains. The first McDonald's opened in 1948, and by 1951 was selling over one million hamburgers a year. Jack in the Box was founded in 1951, Church's Chicken and Kentucky Fried Chicken in 1952, Shakey's Pizza in 1954, and Pizza Hut in 1958.

A number of new convenience foods appeared on the market in the 1950s. Frozen TV dinners were introduced in 1953 by the Swanson Company. The dinner was contained in a partitioned metal tray and could be heated in and consumed directly from the tray, presumably while watching television, which was becoming a common presence in American homes in the 1950s. Frozen orange juice first appeared on the market in the 1940s, after John M. Fox of the Minute Maid Company adapted a technique used to dehydrate blood plasma during World War II to preserve fruit juice. Jell-O, a flavored dessert gelatin mix invented in 1897, became increasingly popular in the 1950s as home electric refrigerators became common. Tang, an orange-flavored instant drink mix, first appeared on grocery shelves in 1959, but did not become popular until its association with the Gemini space missions in 1964 and 1965.

An alternative direction taken by some Americans was an interest in foreign foods and gourmet cooking and dining. American versions of foreign cuisine such as spaghetti and meatballs, teriyaki, sukiyaki, and egg foo yung enjoyed bursts of popularity in the 1950s. Celebrity cooks and critics such as Julia Child, who starred in the television program *The French Chef* (first aired in 1962), promoted the idea of cooking as an art form, fulfilling an interest fueled in part by Americans' increased affluence and increasing familiarity with European cultures. So while some Americans were going in the direction of spending less time in the kitchen, using more convenience foods or buying more meals from restaurants, others were taking up gourmet cooking as a hobby and a means to demonstrate their cultural sophistication.

Despite the general prosperity of the 1950s and 1960s, however, poverty remained a significant factor in the nutritional choices of many Americans during this period. Several federal programs attempted to close this gap. The Food Stamps Act of 1964 was the most extensive program. It had the dual purpose of aiding American farmers, and improving the level of nutrition affordable to the poor. Over half a million Americans received Food Stamp aid by 1965, a number which had increased to three million by 1969. Schoolchildren were aided by expansion of the National School Lunch Act (originally passed in 1946) to include the Summer Food Service Program in 1968 and the School Breakfast Program in 1975.

CONCLUSION

During the postwar period, the scourge of infectious disease was in large part replaced by the now familiar burden of cancer, heart disease, and other chronic conditions. Other changes included a further expansion of medical education, growth in government programs in both healthcare and nutrition, and the highly publicized development of organ transplantation. Interest in preventive medicine and health behavior awareness owes much to this time. Still, cures for cancer and heart disease have not come as quickly as the thrilling triumphs over infectious diseases in the 20th century once suggested. Even one of the great developments in medicine, antibiotics, has been shown to have drawbacks, as resistance has increased with overuse and diseases once thought nearly conquered, such as tuberculosis, have reemerged.

SARAH BOSLAUGH

Further Readings

Dawber, T.R. *The Framingham Study: The Epidemiology of Atherosclerotic Disease*. Cambridge, MA: Harvard University Press, 1980.

Gehlbach, Stephen H. *American Plagues: Lessons from Our Battles with Disease*. New York: McGraw-Hill, 2005.

Jones, James H. *Bad Blood: The Tuskegee Syphilis Experiment*. Rev. ed. New York: Free Press, 1993.

Kluger, Jeffrey. *Splendid Solution: Jonas Salk and the Conquest of Polio*. New York: G.P. Putnam's Sons, 2004.

Leavitt, Judith Walzer and Ronald L. Numbers, eds. *Sickness and Health in America: Readings in the History of Medicine and Public Health*. Madison, WI: University of Wisconsin Press, 1978.

Ludmerer, Kenneth M. *Time to Heal: American Medical Education from the Turn of the Century to the Era of Managed Care*. Oxford: Oxford University Press, 1999.

Nadakavukaren, Anne. *Our Global Environment: A Health Perspective*. 5th ed. Prospect Heights, IL: Waveland Press, 2000.

Novick, Lloyd F. and Glenn P. Mays, eds. *Public Health Administration: Principles for Population-Based Management*. Gaithersburg, MD: Aspen, 2001.

Oshinsky, Joseph. *Polio: An American Story*. New York: Oxford University Press, 2005.

Rosen, George. *A History of Public Health*. Expanded ed. Baltimore, MD: Johns Hopkins University Press, 1993.

Shilts, Randy. *And the Band Played On: Politics, People and the AIDS Epidemic*. Rev. ed. New York: St. Martin's, 2007.

Shorter, Edward. *The Health Century*. New York: Doubleday, 1987.

Smith, Andrew F., ed. *The Oxford Companion to American Food and Drink*. Oxford: Oxford University Press, 2007.

Starr, Paul. *The Social Transformation of American Medicine*. New York: Basic Books, 1984.

Stephen, T.D., and Rock, B. *Dark Remedy: The Impact of Thalidomide and its Revival as a Vital Medicine*. New York: Perseus, 2001.

Stone, Michael H. *Healing the Mind: A History of Psychiatry from Antiquity to the Present*. New York: W.W. Norton, 1997.

Warner, John Harley and Janet A. Tighe, eds., *Major Problems in the History of American Medicine and Public Health: Documents and Essays*. Boston, MA: Houghton Mifflin, 2001.

Watkins, Elizabeth Siegel. *On the Pill: A Social History of Oral Contraceptives, 1950–1970*. Baltimore, MD: Johns Hopkins University Press, 1998.

Index

Index note: page references in *italics* indicate figures or graphs; page references in **bold** indicate main discussion.

atomic bombs over Japan 54, 128
veterans 22
Wright, Frank Lloyd 38
Wurster, William 42

Y
Yasgar, Max 31
Yearbook of Agriculture 84

Z
Zager and Evans 152

PHOTO CREDITS: Library of Congress: 3, 6, 10, 14, 15, 16, 45, 46, 53, 55, 59, 65, 70, 73, 76, 81, 82, 83, 84, 87, 93, 101, 102, 103, 109, 111, 112, 113, 118, 119, 126, 129, 147, 148, 151, 159, 162, 164, 167, 171, 175, 180, 181, 183, 184, 186, 188, 189, 202, 213, 217, 220, 224, 227, 230, 233, 235. Loretta Carlisle Photography: vii, 21, 23, 25, 26, 29, 33, 37, 39, 40, 42, 44, 57, 68, 85, 88, 91, 98, 100, 105, 106, 107, 115, 131, 136, 137, 141, 143, 157, 158, 163, 169, 170, 185, 194, 199 (shelter), 209, 231, 232, 249. Wikipedia: 49, 60, 63, 99, 127, 128, 130, 132, 198, 205, 215, 221, 222, 229, 252. NASA: 1, 123, 135, 138, 237. NARA: 199, 204, 207, 209. Photos.com: 12, 24, 28, 31, 38, 43, 48, 61, 67, 97, 142, 145, 193, 206. iStockphoto: 30, 251. U.S. Air Force: 4, 197, 238, 200. CDC: 241, 244, 245, 246.

Produced by GOLSON MEDIA
President and Editor   J. Geoffrey Golson
Layout Editors   Oona Patrick, Mary Jo Scibetta
Managing Editor   Susan Moskowitz
Copyeditor   Ben Johnson
Proofreader   Mary Le Rouge
Indexer   J S Editorial